GOVERNANCE REFORMS: CHALLENGES AHEAD

GOVERNANCE REFORMS
Challenges Ahead

Edited by:
T.M. Joseph

KANISHKA PUBLISHERS, DISTRIBUTORS
NEW DELHI-110 002

KANISHKA PUBLISHERS, DISTRIBUTORS
4697/5-21 A, Ansari Road, Daryaganj
New Delhi-110 002
Phones : 2327 0497, 2328 8285
Fax : 011-2328 8285
E-mail: kanishka_publishing@yahoo.co.in

First Published 2009

ISBN 978-81-8457-109-7

PRINTED IN INDIA

Published by Madan Sachdeva for Kanishka Publishers, Distributors, 4697/5-21A, Ansari Road, Daryaganj, New Delhi-110 002, Typeset by Sunshine Graphics, Delhi, and Printed at Rajdhani Printers, Delhi.

Essays in honour of
Dr. Satyanarayana Sangita
who taught me
'Work is Worship'

Acknowledgements

This collection of 15 essays is mainly the result of the national seminar titled *Paradigm Shift in Governance: The Emerging Challenges and Strategies* organized by the Department of Political Science, Newman College, Thodupuzha, Kerala on 28th and 29th March 2007 with the financial support of University Grants Commission, New Delhi. The seminar evoked good response from different parts of the country. As many as 28 papers were presented in the two-day deliberations. But for the sake of thematic consistency, only 10 of such papers could be accommodated in this volume. The other five papers were invited from outside.

All the paper contributors were quick enough to submit their full length papers in time enabling the publication of this volume. I thank all authors for generously collaborating with this humble project.

The publication of this volume stands testimony to the promotion of academic activities in the college from the part of our Principal Rev. Fr. Paul Nedumpurath which is, again, vindicated by the accreditation of the College at 'A' grade by the NAAC last year. But for his constant and positive interventions, this work would not have been completed.

I remember with gratitude all my teachers especially Dr. S.N. Sangita, Dr. B.S. Bhargava, Dr. G. Gopakumar and Dr. K. Raman Pillai for having constantly promoted my academic interests. I also owe a lot to my academic friends: Dr. Jos Chathukulam, Dr. M.S. John, Dr. N. Sivanna, Dr. Veerasekharappa, Dr. H.S. Shylendra, Dr. T.V. Sekher, Dr. Sukhpal Singh, Dr. S. Rajendran, Dr. P.K. Viswanathan, Dr. V. Venkatakrishnan, Dr. Shaji Varkey, Dr. Raju Abraham, and Mr. R.H. Itagi for their support to my academic pursuits.

Last, but not the least, I thank Shri Vivek Chaturvedi, for Kanishka Publishers, Distributors Publisher of this book, for producing this book in quick time.

T. M. Joseph

Contents

List of Contributors

Dr. B.S. Bhargava Senior Fellow, Institute of Social Sciences, Southern Regional Centre, Bangalore.

Dr. B.S. Chandrasekhara Lecturer, Maharaja's College, University of Mysore, Mysore.

Dr. G.M. Dinesh Research Associate, Institute of Social Sciences, Bangalore.

Dr. K. Gireesan Senior Fellow, Centre for Rural Management, Kottayam, Kerala.

Dr. Jagannath P. Panda Research Faculty Member at the Institute of Defence Studies and Analyses (IDSA), New Delhi.

Dr. Jos Chathukulam Director, Centre for Rural Management, Kottayam, Kerala.

Dr. Jos C. Raphael Director, CECOD, Thrissur, Kerala.

Dr. T.M. Joseph (Editor) Reader and Head, Department of Political Science, Newman College, Thodupuzha, Kerala.

Dr. J. Mary John Development Consultant and Director, Adhwana Centre for Research and Documentation, Thiruvananthapuram.

Dr. Masood Ahmed Assistant Professor, Bansal MBA College, Kokta, Anand Nagar, Bhopal.

Dr. B. Mohanan Professor, Department of Politics and International Studies, Pondicherry University, Pondicherry.

Ms. Neeru Sharma Research Scholar, Jawaharlal Nehru University, New Delhi.

Dr. Pradip Narayan Researcher at Centre for Education and Communication, New Delhi.

Dr. S. Rajendran Professor and Head, Department of Economics, Periyar University, Salem, Tamil Nadu.

Ms. Rose Mary George Lecturer in Political Science at Providence Women's College, Kozhikode, Kerala.

Dr. S.N. Sangita Professor and Head, Centre for Political Institutions, Governance and Development, Institute for Social and Economic Change, Bangalore.

Dr. H.S. Shylendra Associate Professor at Institute of Rural Management, Anand, Gujarat.

Dr. Veerashekharappa Associate Professor at Post Graduate Department of Management Studies, Siddaganga Institute of Technology, Tumkur, Karnataka.

Dr. B. Venugopal Head, Department of Political Science, S.N. College, Kollam, Kerala.

Introduction

T.M. Joseph

The term 'good governance' continues to be a significant part of our political lexicon for the last one and a half decades. Though there is little unanimity with regard to the meaning of the term, the general understanding is that it refers to the way in which cities, provinces, or whole countries were being governed or should be governed. It could mean different things to different people in different contexts. For a banker financial accountability might form the crux of good governance, while for majority of ordinary citizens it could mean protection of their life and property, freedom from hunger or corruption free administration.

Basic Principles of Good Governance

The concept of good governance became prominent in the late 1980's simultaneously with the end of cold war. The idea is propelled and propagated by the Bretton Woods Institutions – the World Bank, the IMF and the WTO. The notion of good governance is a logical extension of the Structural Adjustment Programme (SAP), proposed by these institutions. Its aim is to complement SAP by political reforms to achieve greater accountability, transparency and efficiency in public service along with the protection of civil and human rights, and to ensure the rule of law through an independent judiciary (Oommen 2003:128).

It appeared when Structural Adjustment Programmes experienced serious implementation difficulties which were then diagnosed as failures of public management owing to unaccountable, patrimonial, and non-transparent governments. Consequently, World Bank (1992:3) defined governance "as the manner in which power is exercised in the management of a country's economic and social resources for development." Good governance, for the World Bank, appeared to be synonymous with sound economic management. In answering to widespread criticism of the international development community that top-down institutional structural reforms lead to institutional vacuum rather than a mobilisation of the societal self-help potentials, the Development Assistance Committee of the OECD formed a Working Group on Participatory Development and Good Governance. It linked good governance to participatory development, human rights and democratisation, and identified the rule of law, public sector management, controlling corruption and reducing excessive military expenditure as important dimensions of good governance (OECD 1995:14).

The new system of governance is making the state to loose its pre-eminence as an agent for development. The government has started receding to the background from many of its traditional areas of operation and the non-governmental organizations, community based groups and multinational development agencies have stepped in to fill that void. The thrust of the new approach appears to be one of maximising the growth potential by unleashing outward looking and market driven forces by making necessary adjustments in the structure of the economy and the manner of exercise of control over power and resources (Government of India 2002).

The Government of India, thus, acknowledges the universally accepted features of good governance like the legitimate exercise of political power along with creating administration which is transparent, equitable, participatory and accountable. But the thrust is made on contextualising them to the emerging needs of the country. 'Governance', to Government of India, 'relates to the management of all such processes that in any society, define the environment which permits and enables individuals to raise their capability levels, on the one hand, and to provide to realise their potential and enlarge the set of available choices, on the other' (Government of India 2002:177). Thus, the proclaimed goal of governance is to bring about human development. The processes of governance are managed by multiple institutions or agencies consisting of the state, market and the civil society; each playing a specific and a critical role in a harmonious manner.

In contextualising governance, the Government of India goes further and has identified specific operational strategies that are to be implemented for realising good governance for development. These strategies include: improved people's participation by way of effective decentralisation through local self governments and involving civil society and voluntary organisations to accelerate socio-economic development; ensuring right to information for transparency; reforming civil service to improve accountability and efficiency; administrative procedural reforms for a hassle free public-government interface; improving the fiscal health of government by improving the resource mobilisation through a transparent and equitable tax-administration and by correcting the subsidy and pricing system of various public services; reforming the judicial system for a speedy delivery of justice; improving the co-ordination between different public agencies and departments involved in development for a better synergy and efficiency; systematic and professional programme/project formulation, implementation and monitoring; empowering the marginal and the excluded to equip them to act as pressure groups to resist bad governance and exploitation by vested interests; and using information technology for a transparent and efficient administration (Government of India 2002).

An attempt is made in this book to look into the nature and extent of governance reforms in India. In the first chapter, Jagannath P. Panda deals with the conceptual clarity and significance of the linkages between the global and domestic governance process. It also seeks to establish a link between the governance reforms at the local level and with various systemic issues at the domestic level. In the process, he has attempted to compare the legitimization crisis at domestic levels of China and India. In the second chapter, Masood Ahmed makes an evaluation of poverty eradication measures in the country in terms of the exact number of people who benefit from it. The author ridicules the government argument that population explosion is the root cause for the failure in the poverty eradication drive. He pleads that the poverty eradication schemes will provide only temporary relief to the poor but calls for building assets in the backward regions to achieve sustainable development.

The third chapter is authored by Pradip Narayan who examines the impact of the neo-liberal governance paradigm, which is characterized by privatization, cost recovery strategies and downsizing of bureaucracy, on health sector reforms in India. Based on the experiences of Sub Saharan African countries, he calls for strengthening civil society organizations through increased participation, so that the health problems are politically solved by the local level institutions themselves. The fourth chapter is a structural reforms lead to institutional vacuum rather than a mobilisation of the societal self-help potentials, the Development Assistance Committee of the OECD formed a Working Group on Participatory Development and Good Governance. It linked good governance to participatory development, human rights and democratisation, and identified the rule of law, public sector management, controlling corruption and reducing excessive military expenditure as important dimensions of good governance (OECD 1995:14).

The new system of governance is making the state to loose its pre-eminence as an agent for development. The government has started receding to the background from many of its traditional areas of operation and the non-governmental organizations, community based groups and multinational development agencies have stepped in to fill that void. The thrust of the new approach appears to be one of maximising the growth potential by unleashing outward looking and market driven forces by making necessary adjustments in the structure of the economy and the manner of exercise of control over power and resources (Government of India 2002).

The Government of India, thus, acknowledges the universally accepted features of good governance like the legitimate exercise of political power along with creating administration which is transparent, equitable, participatory and accountable. But the thrust is made on contextualising them to the emerging needs of the country. 'Governance', to Government of India, 'relates to the management of all such processes that in any society, define the environment which permits and enables individuals to raise their capability levels, on the one hand, and to provide to realise their potential and enlarge the set of available choices, on the other' (Government of India 2002:177). Thus, the proclaimed goal of governance is to bring about human development. The processes of governance are managed by multiple institutions or agencies consisting of the state, market and the civil society; each playing a specific and a critical role in a harmonious manner.

In contextualising governance, the Government of India goes further and has identified specific operational strategies that are to be implemented for realising good governance for development. These strategies include: improved people's participation by way of effective decentralisation through local self governments and involving civil society and voluntary organisations to accelerate socio-economic development; ensuring right to information for transparency; reforming civil service to improve accountability and efficiency; administrative procedural reforms for a hassle free public-government interface; improving the fiscal health of government by improving the resource mobilisation through a transparent and equitable tax-administration and by correcting the subsidy and pricing system of various public services; reforming the judicial system for a speedy delivery of justice; improving the co-ordination between different public agencies and departments involved in development for a better synergy and efficiency; systematic and professional programme/project formulation, implementation and monitoring; empowering the marginal and the excluded to equip them to act as pressure groups to resist bad governance and exploitation by vested interests; and using information technology for a transparent and efficient administration (Government of India 2002).

An attempt is made in this book to look into the nature and extent of governance reforms in India. In the first chapter, Jagannath P. Panda deals with the conceptual clarity and significance of the linkages between the global and domestic governance process. It also seeks to establish a link between the governance reforms at the local level and with various systemic issues at the domestic level. In the process, he has attempted to compare the legitimization crisis at domestic levels of China and India. In the second chapter, Masood Ahmed makes an evaluation of poverty eradication measures in the country in terms of the exact number of people who benefit from it. The author ridicules the government argument that population explosion is the root cause for the failure in the poverty eradication drive. He pleads that the poverty eradication schemes will provide only temporary relief to the poor but calls for building assets in the backward regions to achieve sustainable development.

The third chapter is authored by Pradip Narayan who examines the impact of the neo-liberal governance paradigm, which is characterized by privatization, cost recovery strategies and downsizing of bureaucracy, on health sector reforms in India. Based on the experiences of Sub-Saharan African countries, he calls for strengthening civil society organizations through increased participation, so that the health problems are politically solved by the local level institutions themselves. The fourth chapter is a communitarian reform models may differ in their scope for contributing to poverty reduction and social inclusion, but no reform approach can be assumed to lead automatically to these goals. The paper contents that without paying attention to the poor and the disadvantaged groups of society in administrative reform, it is unlikely that any type of administrative reform will contribute to social inclusion and poverty reduction to the extend it could. G.M. Dinesh and B.S. Bhargava in their chapter entitled "Good Governance and E-Governance: The Case of Revenue Department in Karnataka" explain the success story of the Karnataka experiment of computerizing the land records in providing all sorts of information on land records to the common men in an efficient and cost-effective manner.

B. Venugopal, in his chapter on "Globalisation and Good Governance in a Democratic Society: The Indian Predicament", looks into the challenges thrown by globalization towards the good governance initiatives in India like ensuring social equality, redistribution and social justice. The chapter further examines the major ailments affecting the functioning of Indian Political System in relation to the interface between civil society and good governance. The last chapter in this book is by the editor (T.M. Joseph) himself, which is titled as "Good Governance through Electoral Reforms." He holds the view that the crisis of governance in India is very deep, as manifested in the form of large scale prevalence of poverty, unemployment, illiteracy, malnutrition, corruption, nepotism, communalism etc. and these can be addressed only by increasing the quality of elected representatives. The quality of elected representatives is, invariably, linked to the nature of electoral laws prevailing in the country. He argues that better governance can be achieved in India by reforming the electoral system.

REFERENCES

Abrahamsen, Rita (2000): *Disciplining Democracy: Development Discourse and Good Governance in Africa*, Zed Books, London.

Chandhoke, Neera (2003): 'Governance and the Pluralisation of the State: Implications for Democratic Citizenship,' *Economic and Political Weekly*, 38(28): 2957-68.

Government of India (2002): Tenth Five Year Plan (2002-07): Dimensions and Strategies, Vol. I., Planning Commission, New Delhi.

Jayal, Niraja Gopal and Sudha Pai (eds.) (2001) *Democratic Governance in India: Challenges of Poverty, Development, and Identity*. New Delhi: Sage Publications.

OECD (1995): *Participatory Development and Good Governance*, Development Co-operation Guidelines Series, Paris.

Oommen T.K. (2003): 'Civil Society and the Goal of Good Governance' in Rajesh Tandon and Ranjita Mohanty ed. *Does Civil Society Matter?* Sage, New Delhi, pp. 125n-144.

Shylendra, H.S. (2004): 'The Emerging Governance Paradigm and its Implications for Poverty Alleviation and Equity', Working Paper 182, Institute of Rural Management, Anand.

UNDP (1997), *Governance for Sustainable Development*, A UNDP Policy Document, New York.

World Bank (1992): *Governance and Development*, Washington DC.

World Bank (1994): *Governance: The World Banks's Experience*, World Bank, Washington D.C.

World Bank (1997): *World Development Report*, Washington DC.

1

Contesting Governance: Changing Face of Governance in Asia

JAGANNATH P. PANDA

Increasing globalization has led to more intense discussions of the concept "governance."[1] Today, as with any system of power within the nation-state, what is needed is good and effective governance-be it at the global, regional or domestic level-that is a system that offers a good balance between efficiency and legitimacy, adapted to this new universal context. But does this mean that the global meaning of governance is applicable to the domestic clouds and specifically at the grassroots level of a nation-state system? Further, a debate always lingers on the conceptual clarity of the concept "governance." What exactly is the meaning of "governance"? Is the concept of "global governance" different from the concept of "governance" itself? Is there a new face of governance emerging in a new capacity?

To the degree that one cannot discuss the subject of relevance and sustainability in the process of governance both at the global as well as domestic level without touching upon the contested meaning of "governance", this chapter deals with the conceptual clarity and significance of the linkages between the global and domestic governance process. Further, this chapter seeks to establish a link between the governance reforms at the global level and its linkages with various systemic issues at the domestic level. It further focuses on the most prominent issue that is the legitimization crisis in regional as well as domestic governance process. In this context, this chapter intends to refer two great civilizations and emerging powers of Asia: China and India.

Contesting Governance: Global vs. Domestic Phenomenon

As a preliminary step, a minimalist definition of governance can be the capacity of States, social actors, and economic operators to guarantee the systematic management between democracy, market and equity (UNDP, 1996).[2] Where as global governance refers to de jure mechanisms intended for the organization of international relations, as they concern the executive systems in charge of stating and applying international rules as well as public and private factors (Alliance for a responsible, plural and united world, 2000).[3] Looking at these meanings, governance can be termed as a slippery concept.

Further, looking from a broader international spectrum, the Commission on Global Governance (1995:2) argues that the concept of "governance" is a sum of the many ways that individuals and institutions, public and private, manage their common affairs.[4] Even for many celebrated scholars, since world politics is characterized by governance without government (Rosenau and Czempiel 1992),[5] the practice of governance encompasses a large choice of factors. In addition to the public (interstate) economic organizations such as the International Monetary Fund (IMF), World Bank and the World Trade Organization (WTO), States preserve a key decision-making role. Indeed, in the contemporary discourse of 'governance', many celebrated scholars have posited the prospect that networks of new social movements, publicly oriented Non-Governmental Organization (NGOs), and other non-State factors have the latent to create pressures for increased transparency and accountability.[6] At the same time, it is argued that a more legitimate democratic global as well as domestic politics would pursue and support such developments.[7]

Arguing from a domestic perspective of any nation-State, there are three divisions of governance that can be seen altogether. The first is a liberal idea based on voluntary interchange between factors. This vision is usually qualified as being "minimalist" as a result of the significance given to governance in terms of groups of rules and institutions running the voluntary interchange between citizens and political factors (Milani 2001b). A second vision of governance is that of the new institutional economic school, for which governance is the exercise of authority and control. According to this school, the purpose of governance is to regulate the exercise of authority by setting up incentives, schemes and commitment mechanisms (Milani

Chart–I
Levels of Governance

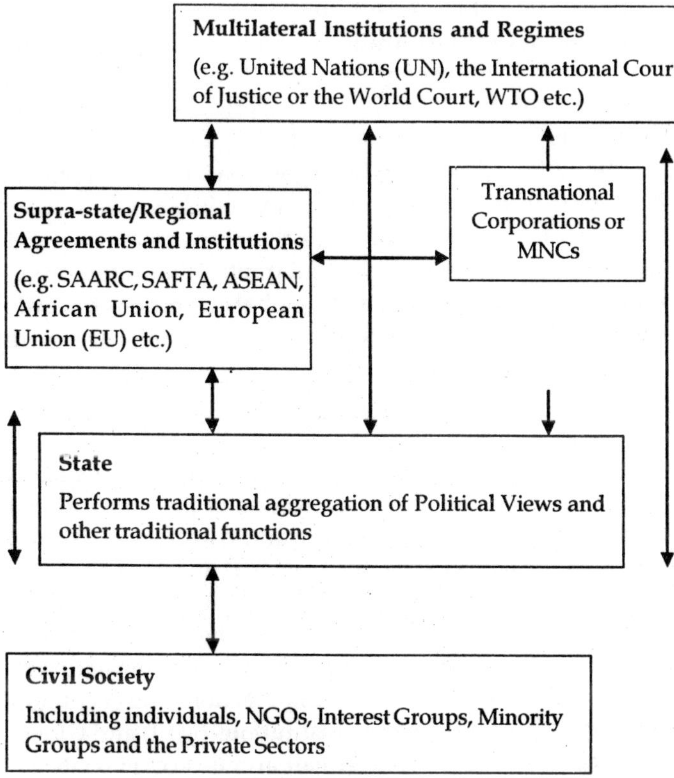

2001b). The third theory of governance is that of firm/corporate governance. Indeed, the most widespread usage of the term governance refers to corporate governance (Milani 2001b).[8] However, the state's legitimacy through governance can only be derived from a position of responsibility to and inclusion of its "stakeholders", i.e., citizens, in the decision-making process, thereby forcing it to engage in "joint governance" (Beausang 2002:14).[9] Next, the question remains, how can we derive linkages between national governance, global governance, and global civil society (refer Chart-I)?

Here, the role of business world (multi-national organizations) resemblance can be constructive in establishing a linkage, given that it is the business or corporate sector that has the most experience in organizing globalization. Because transnational corporations are the most sophisticated global factors, there is a lot to be learnt from their organization of the globalization of production, which can be adapted to the globalization of governance.[10] Nevertheless, global governance is mainly about harmonization between different levels of decision-making, i.e., the local, national, and global. The foremost challenge remains today for new global governance is to maintain a balance between coordination and autonomy of diverse levels. After all, the delicate point remains that while global governance should encourage local autonomy, it should guarantee that information feedback still flows from the local to the global institutions towards the endorsement of a common good. That is where the global is more than the sum of the locals/nationals.

New Challenges and the Changing Face of Governance

In the contemporary political economic discourse, governance is widely seen as an idea embodying a rejection of the conventional State-centric conception of world politics and world order. Added to this, instead of the nation-state, the principal unit of analysis for governance has always remained the global, regional or transnational system of authoritative rule-making and execution.[11] However, in recent times, there is a transformation in the nature of global governance as a result of the close interactions and encounter between the Multi-lateral Economic Institutions (MEI) and Global Social Movements (GSM).This transformation or makeover is labeled 'complex multilateralism' in credit of its movement away from an entirely State based structure.

It is seen that the relationship developing between MEIs and GSMs highlights a contest over governance between old and new forms of multilateralism. The 'old' or existing dominant form of multilateralism is a top down matter where State subjugated institutions are taken as given and minor adjustments in their process are suggested (Ruggie 1993).[12] The 'new' or promising multilateralism is an attempt to 'reconstitute civil societies and political authorities on a global level, building a technique of global governance from the bottom up' (Cox 1997: xxvii).[13] The new multilateralism offers a challenge to existing multilateralism not just because it entails institutional transformation, but because it represents an unusual set of interests. In fact, the new multilateralism slowly came into play with a coherent international economic policy framework to prevent economic collapse by avoiding balance of payment problems, promote economic development through international lending (World Bank), and facilitate international trade through tariff reduction (Vines and Gilbert 2004).[14]

Simultaneously, many factors have, however, significantly changed the social, economic, and political landscapes in which this new multilateral policy framework finds itself today; the end of a fixed exchange rate system; availability and rapid growth of international capital flows; debt and financial crises; scope and patterns of international trade; emergence of regional institutions; institutionalization of international human rights norms and transnationalization of social movements etc. Indeed, the scholars of international relations often argue that domestic governance is characterized by a hierarchy of institutions with the State at the top, while international politics is anarchic involving competition among juridically sovereign countries. Does this mean that the process of governance is State centric? It seems that if work on globalization emphasizes the obsolescence of the State, a focus on 'governance' can help to bring the State back in, though in a diminished capacity. Global governance's research agenda underscores the State's increasing marginal authority, sharing with other entities the regulation of economic and social matters. Though work on 'governance' often includes government,[15] it emphasizes the role of international regimes and networks in solving particular problems and the participation of non-state factors in these institutional arrangements.[16] State functions are described as affecting upwards-to new international institutions-downwards-in partnership with private sectors—and, presumably, to nowhere-the redistributive function of the State, for instance, is diverted formally to no specific State.[17] In this case, two different State models and effective governance process in Asia: China and India can be referred as relevant cases.

Governance in Asia and New Asian Drivers

Due to their geographical size and the mammoth pace of their development, both China and India comprise a "class of their own" amongst the group of anchor countries in the world. Both these powers' success story heavily depended on the process of governance in their personal capacity, calculus and ways. In fact, in the coming decades, the posture that the world adopts towards these "Asian drivers of global change" will be no less important than the state of transatlantic relations. Moreover, the debate of effective governance was given much less attention after the collapse of the Soviet Union. But now, the global attention moves towards China and India for their success story of effective governance.

Strategic communities often argue that the rise of China and India in the world economy and as important factors in global governance arenas amounts to a tectonic shifts.[18] Putting it in other words, it entails significant and profound impacts at every level. The rise of these two countries as relevant factors in global governance process is leading to the formation of a *de facto multipolar power constellation*.[19] But it is also clear that both the societies are certainly going to have to master a number of domestic or internal transition processes.

Question remains; could the domestic challenges that are anticipated in this connection in both the countries result in nationalistic, aggressive governance strategies? Further the challenges remain for both these countries are: how to promote policy dialogue at the government level and civil society organizations in the task of building institutions that encourage political pluralism, enhance democratic participation, and protect the right of freedom of expression and association? Added to this, how to encourage government to implement policies and to put into place mechanisms at the local and national levels to manage diversity and to build a social consensus in favour of development, human rights, and democratic pluralism where the 'majorities' do not decide alone the fate of the 'minorities'?

China's fast change is not only noticeable in the prosperous private sector enterprises and the radical renewal of its urban landscapes: it can also be seen in the transformation of its institutions. Over the past 25 years Chinese authorities have taken measures to adapt the role of government and public administration to an increasingly market-driven economy. Added to this, the administrative, productive and social service functions previously folded into a structure of closely linked organizations have been dispatched to different public and private organizations.

The most noticeable thing about China is that the State-owned enterprises have been separated from the public administration and new regulatory bodies have been set up which have been a key to the economic and social governance. The authorities have laid bases for modern tax, budget and civil service systems. Further, the most impressive thing about China is its current initiative towards a system based on the rule of law, and has embarked on an ambitious regulatory reform programme. Progress in governance was achieved in a relatively short period of time and has contributed in a crucial manner to sustain China's high growth rate. Such achievements are all the more commendable since the sheer size of China requires longer chains of command and multiplies the sources of potential problems. In order to continue in this direction, China needs to sustain reform efforts in four key directions: the role of the state; the tools of government; relations between levels of government and the institutional framework for market forces.

The rise of India and China as both economic and political powers is having, and will have, significant and far reaching impacts. Though India is not as prominent in world trade and finance as China, it has shown sustained growth for two decades and has good prospects for sustained growth over the next decades (Rodrik and Subramanian 2004: 3, Deatsche Bank Research 2005).[20] By 2020, it is likely to be the world's third largest economy. It is in this context believed that the rise of India and China as important factors for global governance and the world economy will transform today's "quasi-unilateral world order" into a de facto multipolar power constellation. It is also predicted that by 2025-2030 at the latest, the US, China, India, and possibly Europe will constitute four substantial poles of power in the architecture of global governance.

One of the compelling lessons that China and India offer to the rest of the poor countries is the profound importance for economic growth and poverty reduction of allowing private firms to compete in markets from which they were previously barred and of providing the complementary government services, such as infrastructure, that promote economic productivity. Moreover, the global governance debate that following the collapse for global of the Soviet Union took very little note at first of the rise of China and India. Though currently lot of attention is being paid to China, but in 15 years time India too will be an equally important player-and possibly even one with greater scope for global action, because it has a number of important comparative advantages over China (democracy, a balanced age pyramid).

It is an accepted fact that governance is a decision-making process that-though consultation, dialogue, exchange and mutual respect-seeks to ensure coexistence and, in some cases, coherence between different and sometimes divergent points of view. This may involve seeking some common ground and extending it to the point where joint action can be envisaged. Globalization, for its part, reveals a new sphere of common interests that transcends States, cultures and national histories. But the question always remain that what then are the specific challenges of global governance as opposed to the classical systems of national or domestic governance?

Chart–II

Framework for Analyzing Governance and Development

Determinants	*Governance Realm*	*Development Outcomes*
Historical Context	Civil Society	Political Freedom and Rights
Previous Regime	Political Society	Human Security and Welfare
Socio-Cultural Context	Government	Economic Growth
Economic System	Bureaucracy	Human Capital (Health and Education)
Int. Environment	Economic Society Judiciary	Trust and Social Capital

Source: ODI Briefing Paper, March 2006.

Experts argue that fundamentals of legitimacy must be based on institutions and procedures. Putting it in another way, the political system must represent the society, and allow it to see itself as a whole.[21] Since legitimacy depends on the nearness of the connection between the individual and the decision-making process, the first challenge of global governance is distance. The other legitimacy challenge refers to the so-called democratic deficit and the accountability deficit, which start while there are no means for individuals to confront international decision-making. The definite challenge of legitimacy in global governance is therefore to deal with the perceived too distant, non-accountable and non-directly challengeable decision-making at the global level.[22]

Being more specific, specially in the Asian context, there are two key governance challenges that can be seen as critical. The first challenge is to return investment and growth to Asia. The second is the need for political reform to permit conflict within societies-including ethnic conflicts-to be determined peacefully. However, the key always remain a priority in the recovery strategies of the Asian economies. From a macro perspective, the relationship between governance and development has risen up the international policy agenda. There is widespread agreement that governance matter-intrinsically and for improvements in economic and social outcomes (refer Chart-II). In fact, the Indian governance faces a very grave challenge in recent times. Increasingly—and positively since the arrival of the WTO the world is going to be governed by treaties and India needs to seriously take this task at the global level.[23] More than that, governance mechanisms are often created and entrenched through legal principles and regimes. Many existing legal mechanisms and principles have proven inadequate at domestic and international level in dealing with many of globalization's most pressing challenges. At the moment it seems that global governance emerges in a somewhat haphazard form in distinct issue and complex areas.

What is needed is a renewed normative vision of how governance should operate, institutions that reflect and foster this vision and a greater emphasis on the technical 'knowledge' in areas where it is most likely to mitigate against the downslide of globalization. Moreover, governing in multiple levels characterizes today's policy process at both the domestic and the international level. The concept of multilevel governance has been developed to account for the nested policy processes in the recent times, which bring together state and non-state factors from all levels of government. Yet, the concept of 'multiple governance' is no longer unique to the multilateral body like European Union. Likewise, international regimes increasingly resemble multilevel systems. Similar trends can be observed at the domestic level, where federal governments function like multilevel governance both centralizing and decentralizing trends. These tendencies need to be examined and explained further in academic and research parameters.

In its most determined and advance looking forms, governance seeks to generate a social fabric be it at the domestic or regional *vis-*

à-vis international level, albeit decentralized, ill woven and uneven, driven on an issue by issue basis, but cumulatively, amounting to more than the sum of its parts. It is not exclusively a moral fabric as much of the existing international system has and will continue to codify norms, because they are in the interests of States in various groupings and in particular, the powerful. It has a legal basis, in that international law codifies many of the norms that evolved between States.

REFERENCES

1. The term "governance" was first used in 12th century France, where it was a technical term designating the administration of baillages, or bailiwicks. It had always a close contact with the word "government," it comes from the Latin word for "rudder," conveying the idea of "steering". From France, it crossed the Channel and in England came to designate the method of organizing feudal power. The concept of "governance" disappeared in the 16th century, with the emergence of the nation-state, because the two notions "governance" and "government" are profoundly different. Gradually, governance removes the political dimension from government. The latter belongs to Westphallia nation states and their particular modes of government, legitimacy and representatives.
2. UNDP Human Development Report 1996, Oxford University Press, New York, 1996.
3. Alliance for a Responsible, Plural and United World, "Proposal for a global governance adapted to the challenges of the twenty-first century," http://www.alliance21.org/en/themes/global/pubs.htm.2000.
4. Commission on Global Governance, 1995. Our Global Neighbourhood: The Report of the Commission on Global Governance, Oxford: Oxford University Press.
5. Rosenau, James N. and Ernst-Otto Czempiel (eds.), 1992. Governance Without Government: Order and Change in World Politics, Cambridge: Cambridge University Press.
6. William D.Coleman and Sarah Wayland, "The Origin of Global Civil Society and Non-territorial Governance: Some Empirical Reflections," Global Governance, No. 3, Vol. 12, July-September 2006, p. 241.
7. *Ibid.*
8. Milani, Carlos R.S. "Une approche ethique des relations de pouvoirs," interview, in Courier de la Planete, number 58, year 2000/I, SOLAGRAI, Paris, 200, pp. 9-11.
9. Francesca Beausang, "Democratizing Global Governance: The

Challenges of the World Social Forum," Discussion Paper 59, Management of Social Transformations, United Nations Educational, Scientific and Cultural Organization, p. 9.

10. *Ibid.*

11. Andrew Jones, Dictionary of Globalization, Polity Press: Cambridge, 2006, p. 102.

12. Ruggie, John Gerald (ed.), 1993. Multilateralism Matters: The Theory and Praxis of an Institutional Form, New York: Columbia University Press.

13. Cox, Robert (ed.), 1997. The New Realism: Perspectives on Multilateralism and World Order, Basingstoke: Macmillan. United Nations University Press.

14. Vines, David and Christopher Gillbert 2004. "The IMF and International Financial Architecture: Solvency and Liquidity," in David Vines and Christopher Gillbert, eds., The IMF and its Critics. Cambridge: Cambridge University Press.

15. J.N. Rosenau, 'Governance, Order and Change in World Politics', in J.N. Rosenau and E-O. Czempiel (eds.), Governance Without Government: Order and Change in World Politics (Cambridge: Cambridge University Press, 1992), pp. 1-29.

16. O.R. Young, Governance in World Affairs (Ithaca and London: Cornell University Press, 1999).

17. S. Strange, The Retreat of the State: The Diffusion of Power in the World Economy, (Cambridge: Cambridge University Press, 1996).

18. "Unstable Multipolarity? China's and India's Challenges for Global Governance," Briefing Paper, German Development Institute, January 2006.

19. *Ibid.*

20. Rodrik, D. and Subramanian, A., 2004, 'Why India Can Grow at 7 per cent a Year or More: Projections and Reflections,' IMF Working Paper, 04/118, New York: International Monetary Fund.

21. Pascal Lamy, "Globalization and Global Governance," the Globalist, November 7, 2006, at http://theglobalist.com/StoryId.aspx?StoryId+5740 (accessed on July 3, 2007).

22. *Ibid.*

23. Dr. Rajeev Dhawan, "Indian Governance and Treaties: The Advent of the WTO," in Shiva Kant Jha, Final Act of WTO: Abuse of Treaty-Making Power, Centre for Study of Global Trade System and Development, New Delhi, p.vi.

2

Reforming the Rural Sector through Globalization of Indian Poverty and Agricultural Problems

MASOOD AHMED

Dimensions of Indian Poverty

Before liberalization India and poverty were synonymous to each other. In 1952 survey, the level of poverty was 45 per cent, which now stands at 26 per cent (According to the Planning Commission 260 million people (26% of population) still live below the poverty line in India) a decrease of 20 per cent, but the fact is in the last 10-14 years the poverty line moved down by 10 per cent, the promoter of reforms and liberalization are praising themselves. Now one can call this either a success of reforms or the wastage of economic resources for forty years before reforms and incompetence of successive governments during that period as the fact reveal 75 per cent of the total poverty ridden population belongs to rural areas which stills long for basic necessities.

	Poverty %		*Number of Poor (Millions)*		
Year	*Rural*	*Urban*	*Rural*	*Urban*	*Total*
1956-57	54.1		182		
1999-2000	27.1	23.6	193	67	260

Defining the Poverty

As per the Government's Ministry of Statistics and Programme Implementation: *"The official estimates of the poverty line are based on a norm of 2400 calories per capita per day for rural areas and 2100 per capita per day for urban areas."*

This definition in itself tells a different story in poverty measurement, if one compares it with the poverty measurement techniques adopted by the developed world. Now if a person is able to generate income, which enables him to buy nutritional quantity then, he will be considered above poverty line.

This concept of Poverty measurement frail on many ground, as it suggest only food is the necessity of life, secondly expenditure on food items only comes into purview ignoring all other expenditure necessary for living. If on observation one measures monthly cost of "Basket of Food" which is Rs. 62 in rural area and Rs. 71 in urban area in 70s with the passage of time and effect of inflation was Rs. 328 and Rs. 454 in the year 2000 and in present time is hovering around Rs. 540 in urban area. By this measurement anybody who earns more than Rs. 540 is living above poverty line, which is an absurd assumption in reality.

Poverty: The Problem of Few States

Another concern for us is the concentration of poverty in the few states. Today 83 per cent of poor people are residing in Uttar Pradesh, Bihar, Madhya Pradesh, West Bengal, Orissa, Andhra Pradesh, Rajasthan and Assam states. This may be the solution in disguise as efforts are to be done to provide resources to the targeted population. A scheme like National Rural Employment Guarantee Act (NREGA) is one such effort. This scheme focuses on providing employment in selected 200 districts (now 360 in 2007) for 100 days paying Rs. 60 for each day of work, which consist of manual labour. This scheme focuses on compulsory relief to the population living below poverty line and in time generating resources for the nation through development works like building irrigation canals, roads and other manual activity in the rural areas.

If the impact of poverty is to be measured then one can see that 84 per cent population of out-of-school children (6-11 years) and 72 per cent child workers belongs to the poverty concentrated eight states. (NSSO 55th Round) Poverty figures that open the debate on implementation of various schemes puts question mark on our future resources.

Globalize the Problem

Utilization of present resources demands two things. One measures to curb poverty figures to minimum by providing adequate opportunities that require social investment through various schemes, secondly to monitor demand and supply structure for essential commodities as per the poverty estimates that require maintaining prices of essential items at the level where 26 per cent population is able to survive.

Globalization and opening of market distort our effort to maintain that level. International Institutions demand to open up the agriculture sector to developed nations farmers (almost 2% of their total country population) and freedom over agricultural product price mechanism that will only lead to destruction of our agricultural sector and its dependent population (65% of India population; 650 million people) which ultimately results in increase in prevailing suicide rate of farmers.

Thus India is rightly asking the question that relate to all the developing countries, what is more important development of the developed ones or the survival of the developing ones? International Institutions (WTO, IMF, and WB etc.) are the new battle ground between the nations who are struggling with poverty and nations who are avoiding it.

Globalization has not only results in increasing the volume of international trade through means of liberalization and privatization but results in pressurizing the developing countries to adopt policies that goes against their interest and in favour of developed countries.

In present circumstances deadlock over various issues between the developing nations and developed ones are only due to their struggle to avoid poverty for their population.

Where is the Productivity?

Ability of agriculture sector remains in doubt due to various factors that include poor infrastructure, smallholdings, lack of education and training and too much dependence on nature. Since 1950-51 GDP at factor cost share of Agriculture sector is quadrupled in 50 years from Rs. 83154 Crs. which by the end of 1999-00 increased up to Rs. 314252 taking 1993-94 as the base year. In the same period Manufacturing and Construction, Financing and Business Services and Trade and Hotels Sectors increased its share to 15 times of their position in 1950.

GDP at Factor Cost by Industry of Origin

(Rs. Crores)

Year	*Agriculture, Forestry and Fishing, Mining and Quarrying*	*Manufacturing, Construction, Electricity, Gas and Water Supply*	*Trade, Hotels, Transport and Communication*	*Financing, Insurance, Real Estate and Business Services*
1950-51	83154	18670	16781	9380
1999-00	314252	279066	255807	145863
No. of Times increment	4	15	15	15

Source: www.indiabudget.nic.in.

Even if we observe advances given to agriculture and other priority sector there is a continuous increment in direct advances for agriculture alone it rises from Rs. 160 Crs. in 1969 to Rs. 22,079 Crs. in 2006 whereas amount outstanding on direct finance also rose from Rs. 40 Crs. to Rs. 112126 Crs. This is 5 times of the amount sanctioned for direct finance on agriculture sector alone.

Advances to Agriculture and other Priority Sector by Public Sector Banks

	June 1969	*March 2006*	*June 1969*	*March 2006*
Agriculture		23798	162	155219
* Direct Finance	160	22079	40	112126
* Indirect Finance	4	1719	122	43093
Advances to self-help GP		1067		4047
Total Priority Sector	260	35840	441	409748
Total Bank Credit			3017	1017656

Source: www.indiabudget.nic.in

Total outstanding advance to priority sector that was Rs. 441 Crs. in 1969 increased to Rs. 409748 Crs. in 2006, which is 40.2 per cent of the total outstanding amount from banking sector. This shows the weightage given to the poverty-ridden sector and need for contribution from the sector. If this sector remains a burden on our shoulder no developing country can progress, as resources allotted to the sector are not been properly utilized.

Government efforts to maintain relief measures like providing subsidies under the Non-Plan Expenditure which was Rs. 23593 Crs. in 1998-99 which goes on to Rs. 47520 Crs. in 2005-06. Major part of subsidy goes on maintaining adequate supply of essential items Food and Fertilizer are the most important one. At this juncture international turmoil in oil producing countries make it more difficult to curb inflation, Petroleum subsidy is needed to reduce pressure on rising transportation costs.

Government effort to reduce NPA and reduce interest payment on international advances seen through measures like writing off loans amounted to Rs. 1884 crores in the year 1999 and 2000 and payment to IMF in similar period upto Rs. 353 crores. India not able to hide subsidy figures that are necessary to help poor is one of the unfortunate countries that require them in the era of globalization and liberalization but struggling to convince other nations and WTO. Fault does not rest anywhere else but on adaptation of social policies that only create incompetence in the whole sector.

Growth rate of population and resources generation are never able to match each other. Other problems like illiteracy and social taboos only enhances the vote-bank democracy, a kind of politics where poor remain poor in order to serve the purpose for politician who are only interested in developing themselves.

The dream of social equality and self sufficiency in all aspect cherished under the long rule of congress, resulted in squeezing the resources from the able private bodies to public sector and over burdened agriculture sector. Inability to calculate the mistake and narrow future vision with democratic weakness like pampering the vote-bank generate incompetence and result in wastage of national resources that force us to change our approach and adopt what global institutions prescribe for us.

Accepting globalization and opening the markets for foreign investment resulted in many gains. Infrastructure development, availability of quality goods, entry of MNCs resulted in all round progress. India in the last 18 years emerges from the brink of economic disaster to become a leader in developing global economy.

The question that remains is on accountability of the resources in the period before liberalization. The loss of 42 years in social

Subsidies by Indian Government

(In Rs.Crores)

		1998-99	1999-00	2000-01	2001-02	2002-03	2003-04	2004-05	2005-06
A	Major Subsidies	20696	22678	25860	30447	40716	43535	44753	44480
	Food	9100	9434	12060	17499	24176	25181	25798	23077
	Indigenous (Urea) Fertilizer	7473	8670	9480	8044	7790	8521	10243	10653
	Imported Urea Fertilizer	333	74	1	47			494	1211
	Sale on Decontrolled Fertilizer with Concession to Farmers	3790	4500	4319	4504	3225	3326	5142	6596
	Petroleum Subsidy					5225	6351	2956	2683
	Grants to NAFED for MIS/PPS				353	300	156	120	260
B	Other Subsidies	2897	1809	978	763	2817	788	1204	3040
	Imp/Exp of Sugar, Edible Oil etc.	105	50	40	8				
	Interest Subsidies	1434	1371	111	210	750	170	564	2176
	Other Subsidies	1358	388	827	545	2067	618	640	864
	Total Subsidies	23593	24487	26838	31210	43533	44323	45957	47520

reforms can only be justified if one is able to eradicate social taboos like inequality in the prevailing system, illiteracy, caste and religious conflicts and democratic weakness (corrupt politics) which stand for its definition. Unfortunately social reforms are of limited success. It's true that after independence the resources we have are negligible and responsibility of poverty ridden huge population is enormous. At that time concept of socialism looks attractive and developing public sector for products where private capital is not available and thinking to develop core competency for self sufficiency through public sector is the right approach. The only wrong thing in the whole concept is the putting leash over private sector through License Raj, a system where every private establishment needs permission in the form of license for operation and mentality that every MNC is extension of East-India Company resulting in another economic colonization.

What Need to be Done?

Poverty never breeds in itself, it needs ground to grow, and conditions in the developing countries provide ample reasoning to commensurate the fact. Development needs a cycle of prosperity where break points are needed to push it further.

Cycle of Prosperity

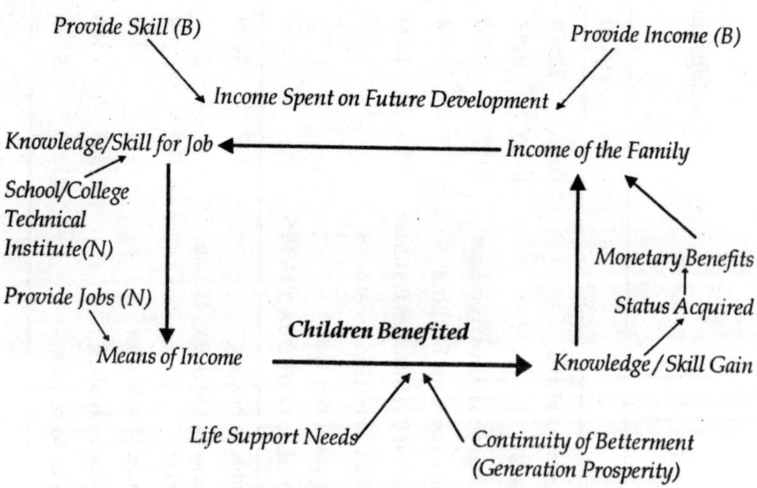

N => Necessaries Condition to be present for development.

B => Break Points: One which breaks the cycle and boosts the development of life.

Developed nations enjoy the cycle of prosperity due to timely interference that are available to them in the form of colonization, technological advancement, economic policies that are based on human wants and needs taking due care of human desire to earn a special place for himself (a form of greed that is good and result in competition for survival and development).

On the other hand, developing nations suffers due to cycle of depravity, where they languish in search for break points to change their destiny. Developing nations either have a weak democracy in terms of citizens not able to select leaders with vision to commensurate their destiny or dictatorships and situation of civil unrest. Conditions remain adverse due to lack of initiative and implementation of right policies. Cycle of depravity continues as generation is not able to prepare future resources in terms of human development that contribute in the development of the nation.

Cycle of Deprivation

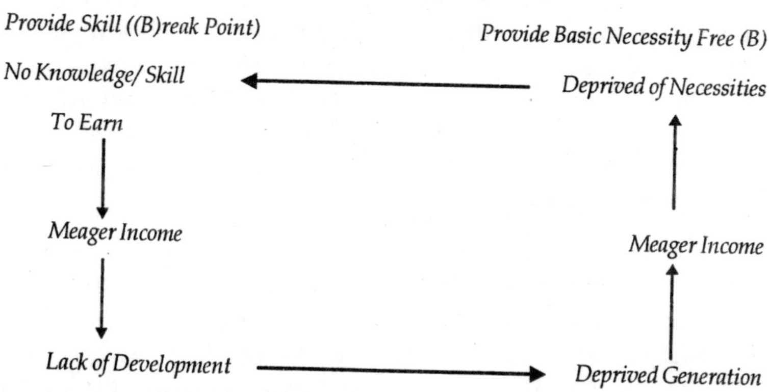

People remain poor because they are not able to cross the barrier; their resources are not enough to provide necessary skills which can increase their income. Human Development Indicators (HDI) portrays augmentation of living conditions. Increment in Income or purchasing power over the years only reflects measures to enhance HDI.

On the similar grounds poverty estimates and measurement techniques adopted by nations provide incomplete information. Estimates like 26 per cent population suffers from poverty in India describe the inability of 26 crore people to earn enough so that they can have 2400 calories in their belly. Other necessity for life is completely ignored like availability of decent meal, shelter, cloth, enough opportunity to earn and climb the ladder of HDI.

Efforts by Government of India in the forms of various schemes to augment growth of agro and rural industry can be taken as an attempt to push reforms as well as to keep social lines intact. Providing funds to unemployed youth under Prime Minister's Rozgar Yojana (PMRY) to set up their own business unit, scheme started in 1993 and as per official data it provided job to 38.13 lakhs persons since its inception. Other schemes like Rural Employment Generation Programme (REGP), National Rural Employment Gurantee Act (NREGA), Khadi and Village Commission (KVIC) and other schemes applied time to time meet with success which can only be seen on chapter.

The number of poor in 1956 was 182 million that is around 50 per cent of total population living below poverty line at that time. In the present scenario, its 26 per cent population living below poverty line while 260 million people under it. The situation is paradoxical as number of poor people is increased by 42 per cent while in percentage terms with total population it reduced to by almost 50 per cent. Thus number game is only to hide incompetence that exists in the present system.

The huge amount of money and resources attached to poverty removal programme need to be evaluated with the exact population that benefit from it. Criteria that provide aggregates certainly fail to establish the necessity of such schemes. Government argument that increase in population always put extra pressure on limited resources and ever increasing population of poor put them on back foot looks ridicules as since our independence if we calculate the money spent on uplifting poor in both urban as well as rural, I am sure that the amount is enough to remove poverty of every other person.

The need of the hour is to provide means to create cycle of prosperity in the poverty ridden regions. Schemes like NREGA will only provide relief in short term, in the longer term we need means to sustain the momentum and not only generate revenue but built asset in the regions that suffers most.

REFERENCES

Ahluwalia, Montek S. (1978), Rural Poverty and Agricultural Performance in India', *Journal of Development Studies*, 14 April, pp. 298-323.

Bhalla A. (1995), *Unseen Development in the Third World: A Study of China and India*, Basingstoke, Hampshire, England: Macmillan.

Chadha, G.K. and P.P. Sahu, 'Post Reform Set Backs in Rural Employment-Issues that Need Further Scrutiny', Economic and Political Weekly, Vol. 37, No. 21 pp. 1998-2026.

Chandra, Rames (2001), Regional and Sectoral Distribution in Economic Growth: Indian Agriculture Policy at Crossroads.

Chelliah, R.J. and R. Sudarshan (eds.) (1999), Income Poverty and Beyond: Human Development in India, Social Science Press, New Delhi.

Dandekar V.M. and N. Rath (1971), *Poverty in India*, Indian School of Political Economy, Pune.

Datta, K.L. and Savita Sharma (2000), *Facets of Indian Poverty*, Concepts Publishing House, New Delhi.

Deaton, A. and Jean Dreze, 'Poverty and Inequality in India: A re-examination', Economic and Political Weekly, Vol. 37, No. 36 pp. 3729-48.

Dreze, Jean (1990), 'Poverty in India and IRDP Delusion'. Economic and Political Weekly, 25(39), pp. 95-104

Dreze J. and Sen .A. (1989), *Hunger and Public Action*, Oxford University Press, New Delhi.

Guhan, S. (1994), 'Social Security Options for Developing Countries', *International Labour Review*, 133(1).

IFAD, Rural Poverty Report (2001), *The Challenge of Ending Rural Poverty*. Oxford University Press.

Kapila, Uma (ed.) (2002), *Indian Economy Since Independence*, Academic Foundation, New Delhi.

Kohli, Atul (1987), *State and Poverty in India*, Cambridge University Press, Cambridge.

3

Health[1] Sector Reforms: Where Lies the Problem-Reform Content or Reform Process? Learnings from Sub-Saharan Africa

PRADIP NARAYAN

Provision of health care to all is not only a *mean* to achieve poverty reduction but also an *end* in itself. Human Development Index, conceptualized as a comprehensive measure of development by United Nations Development Programme, has life expectancy as one of its three components.[2] There also is an *economic case* for better provision of health care as adequate health facility produces a skilled and healthy manpower to the process of economic growth. *Ethically* as well, the health care is a basic need that a state should make available to its entire people. Further, in an era that is conscious of human rights, it is the fundamental *right* of everyone including poor to have an affordable access to quality health care services. Due to the above reasons, the health sector continues to receive attention from the international organizations even in the present era of state-minimalism and market fundamentalism.

For a poor country it is an enormous task to provide access to high quality and affordable health care to all its population. The Washington Institutions[3] identify fund-constraint[4] as the main problem. Merely, opening the sector to private participation was not considered a viable alternative as the market does not make positive discrimination in favour of the poor. Therefore, the reforms are designed to raise the efficiency of the public sector. As is generally said, reforms breed reforms[5] (Therkildsen, 2000 p. 64), the latest series of public sector reforms are inspired by the New Public Management (NPM) paradigm—which seek to transform the state into a market-like institution. The standard neoliberal prescriptions in the form of contracting-out, user charges and downsizing are offered as technical solutions.

In India, the health sector reforms form part of the broader reform measures adopted under the Structural Adjustment Programme (SAP). Instead of increasing the outlay on the health sector the government is exploring alternative means of financing through methods like taking loans from the World Bank and other international agencies, and through the levy of user charges. (Nandraj, 1997). Since 1995, the World Bank has initiated the State Health Systems Project in the states of Punjab, Karnataka, West Bengal, Punjab, Orissa and Maharashtra (World Bank, 2002). In all these projects, the system of user fees was prescribed as a mode to mobilize additional resources. However, fearing public resentments, the user charge was not introduced in primary health care centres in Andhra Pradesh. (Baru,1999). In Punjab, the introduction of user charges[6] in about 150 public health care institutions has allegedly caused severe hardships to the poor, forcing various advocacy non-governmental organizations to demand the abolition of the user-charge system. (Nagar, 2002). Thus the reforms are either non-starters or they face an enormous pressure from various interest groups during their implementation. The service delivery of health care to the poor thus involves a number of stakeholders viz. policy-makers, bureaucracy, professional bodies, private health care providers and community. There are winners and losers in the deliberation. The dynamics of power relations among the stakeholders is influenced by the social, economic and political environment of the place. Is such reform measures can solve the problems of health sectors in poor countries? This chapter examines the deficiency in the conceptualization of problems in health sector as economic problems. Analyzing the social impact of cost-recovery strategies on the marginalized people in the countries in Sub-Saharan Africa, where the reforms are in place for almost two decades, this essay places the health sector reforms in a political perspective, and emphasizes, in the case of India, the need for viewing the problems in the health sector as political issues to avoid the further exclusion of marginalized sections viz. women, poor, dalits and adivasis.

Inadequacy Due to Fund-Constraint

Poverty and ill-health are intertwined in a two-way causal relationship (Wagstaff, 2002). If alleviation of poverty becomes the condition for good and adequate provision of health services, then this results in confusion over the means-goal relationship. Of course, if poverty is alleviated, then there will be little problem in health-care provisions. But poverty reduction in itself is a broader goal requiring various actions, one of them being efficient delivery of health services. Therefore, it will be ineffectual to consider poverty as a problem. Rather, poverty is an issue that has to be kept in mind while framing health policies. In other words, the policy makers shall have to be aware that it will be difficult for the poor to pay for the health services. The high cost may act as a deterrent for poor people to receive health-care before the illness aggravates. Moreover, even if they pay for the service, it will be at the cost of some other essential expenditure viz. food, cloth, shelter or drinking water.

Similarly, at the macro-level as well, a country with high GDP will have a better and efficient health accessible to its entire people. Pritchett and Summers (1996) through cross-country analysis, argue that a positive association exists between "health" and "wealth" and substantiate that countries with higher incomes enjoy better health.[7] However, this does not mean that policies have to be focused on economic growth alone. There are countries like Sri Lanka, China, Vietnam, Costa Rica and the state of Kerala in India that have improved health indicators at very low levels of wealth. Lower Wealth "will unfortunately remain with us in many parts of the globe." (Wuyts, 1992 p. 18). Therefore, the low GDP per capita of a country is no reason for the state not to pursue intervention to improve health standards. The above countries adopted pro-poor distributive strategies to tackle socio-economic problems. The achievement of Kerala[8] is a result of a relatively fair distribution of wealth and resources and a sustained investment of 15 per cent of its budget on health sector. (Thankappan, 2001).

The good health that the affluent enjoy and the ill health that afflicts the poor have to do more with the standard of living of the people than with the curative aspects. Access to safe drinking water, healthy nutrition, housing and sanitation are the determining factors of the health standards of the people. The poor not only are deprived of these basic needs, but also are also not able to receive adequate medical response in the event of illness and disease. Health care for them is inaccessible and/or unaffordable. Even when accessible and affordable, this health care may be qualitatively substandard.

The adverse impact of diseases is felt more in the poorer countries than in the richer countries. Despite medical advancement, the diseases like malaria cause disproportionately larger number of deaths in poor countries. Using the above arguments, health is, thus, viewed merely as an economic problem[9] (Stillwaggon, 1998 p. 8), putting the onus on the state, the market and the multilateral organizations to provide an affordable health care to the people. Such an analysis has led to universal prescriptions with focus on effective use of existing resources and mobilization of additional resources, ignoring the process aspects of the reforms.

Health Sector Reforms in Sub-Saharan Africa

Most of the countries in Sub-Saharan Africa are not only poor but also face a severe debt crisis making it impossible for the States to frame and implement pro-poor health programmes. Adding to that, the countries like Ethiopia, Eritrea, Sudan, Chad, Angola and Somalia have all been thrown into turmoil and conflicts in recent years, which destroyed public services among others, and therefore, "the vast majority of population has little or no access to any kind of public health care." (Allen, 1992 p. 244). Inability of the governments to finance the health sector, forced them to recourse to foreign loans[10] and aid that forced these debt-ridden countries to surrender their sovereignty in policy making to donors and multilateral institutions. A large proportion of national budgets of these countries are now allocated to service the external debts. Most often, the servicing of loans is at the expense of social expenditure. Even where the ratio of social spending to total budget expenditure is maintained or even increased,[11] it is largely possible only through further foreign aid and loans. (SAPRIN, 2001).

Another alternative to them is to open the health sector to market forces regulated by the "invisible hand" of the market. However, allowing private sector to operate freely would make the services costly and unaffordable to the poor. It does not mean that these countries do not have private health sector. A very large private sector, in the form of large and small companies, individual providers, NGOs, shopkeepers, midwives and nurses, exist in low-income countries providing accessible (with flexible opening hours) services, which are at times cheaper as well. (Mills *et. al.*, p. 326). Nevertheless, the state remains the primary provider of health services to the poor and it is the presence of this public sector, which keeps the prices of even the private health services low in the market. Thus on the one hand, poverty deprives the poor from accessing the private health-care. On the other hand, a cash-starved state is not able to provide health services at an affordable cost.

Prior to the introduction of the reforms, the public health sector in these countries provided a highly subsidized health care. Its non-competitive and monopolistic nature caused an abnormal increase in the cost of maintaining the bureaucracy and deterioration in the quality of services. The presence of ghost workers and non-linkage of pay with performance caused a further burden in the public exchequer. Moreover, due to rise in corruption, poor eventually had to pay for services in the form of bribes. Despite a good spending in the health sector, the services did not match the intended health outcomes. To address these problems and to utilize the existing resources effectively, the governments in low-income countries, through the projects of World Bank and international NGOs, implemented public sector reforms inspired by NPM. The liberalizing themes started appearing in the health sector through these donor-funded public sector reforms in Tanzania and Uganda. (Therkildson, 2000: p. 663).

The Health Sector Reforms included Result oriented Management, Performance budgeting and pay-performance linkage so that the public health machinery is not only efficient but also accountable to the concerns of people. The slimming of bureaucracy was attempted to accomplish significant reduction in staffing and thus release resources for improved pay and services. A sustainable financial support to the health sector necessitated the application of cost recovery strategy. The most common approach was the introduction of user-charges. Less common, though introduced in a few countries, is health insurance, prepayments, and earmarked health taxes. The cost recovery strategies enhance the coverage of services where the people are prepared to pay to secure access. (Colclough, 1997: p. 18). They also provide a limited autonomy to the health sector and reduce the dependency of state on foreign donors. Nearly 75 per cent of the World Bank projects in Sub-Saharan Africa included the establishment or expansion of user fees. (Sexton, 2001).

However, despite the high cost of reforms, these reforms did not translate into service delivery improvements. (Wood and Clarke, 2001 p. 72). There has not been much reduction in corruption or increase in quality, though; the cost of maintaining the bureaucracy has come down. (Clarke and Wood, 2001 p. 73). Instead, there have been a number of negative effects of these reforms. Firstly, with the retrenchment of personnel and freezing of fresh recruitments from the public sector, especially when it being the largest and main employer, there was a rise in unemployment. The income of many households fell making the health services more unaffordable to them. Secondly, the costs of the reforms were borne more by the socially and economically backward sections than the other sections. The pay and the conditions of health care workers, especially nurses, deteriorated. The vast majority of nurses were women, and women, historically, have been paid less than men for similar work. Therefore reforms caused an adverse impact on women, as women comprise the major part of workforce in health sector (Corkery, 2000 p. 267). In Nigeria, Kenya and Ghana, introduction of user charges reduced people's use of medical services and led to reduction in hospital births and an increase in maternal deaths (Sexton, 2001). Further, the inferior social status of women in Uganda forced them to forgo medical care (SAPRIN, 2001). In Ghana and Zimbabwe, though there were facilities of waivers, not all poor people were aware of the facility, so only a small number actually benefited from exemptions (SAPRIN, 2001; Sexton, 2001). The adverse impact of the "reforms" on the marginalized sections of society suggests that they their voices are not being heard and if heard are ignored. The reforms produce winners and losers. The group that is able to exert the maximum pressure on the reform process gains the most. Therefore, for reforms to benefit the poor, there is an urgent need to curtail those forces that use reforms as a technical tool to achieve their economic gains.

Health Sector Reforms: A Political Arm-Twisting

The diverse body of stakeholders in the health sector includes community, doctors, health workers, private hospitals, medical shops, taxpayers, bureaucrats, and various groups favouring or opposing specific components of the reforms. They have diverse objectives and preferences. Community wants accessible and high quality health services. Government doctors and health workers want higher pay. Private hospitals compete for patients. Local drug firms demand subsidies. Multinationals want unregulated market. Taxpayers want low costs. Are all these stakeholders involved in the formulation and implementation of health policies? If they are, then why the fruits of the reforms are not equally distributed?

Firstly, one has to analyze the politics of setting priorities. The health sector faces diverse problems from poor quality to financing to inaccessibility. The reforms are very comprehensive to include all programmes for the betterment of all the sections, but the sequencing of reforms are done in a manner that the initial benefits go to the affluent section of people with the promise that, at a later stage, the reforms will benefit the poor. Therefore, there is privatization but no reduction in cost of health services. User charges are introduced but there is no enhancement in quality of health care. Better remuneration for health officials, but no reduction in corruption. Extensions of health care in urban areas, but rural areas remain unattended.

Secondly, the health sector reforms have to be seen in the perspective of overall economic reforms. Andreano (1997) feels, in respect of Tanzania,[12] that the health reform agenda characterized by decentralization of Ministry of Health, contracting-out in health sector, reduction in government regulations and introduction of user charges are the result of the influence of liberalizing themes emanated from Structural Adjustment Programmes (SAP) (Thomason, 2001). The implementation of SAP has actually resulted in path-dependency problem for the state. Once initiated, it becomes difficult for the state to go back to the pre-reform stages. SAP has also weakened the State by diminishing its role in not only the regulation of economy but also in policymaking. The state has been forced to relinquish its command over purses to national and foreign capital. It is mainly the political-administrative elites-not various interest groups that influence the policy content. (Therkildsen, 2000 p. 63). There is little public debate and support for the policies and implementation.

Thirdly, the health programmes are adopted by the state, as if the reforms are to be implemented in a *tabula rasa*. None of the component of reforms gets implemented without opposition from the group that has to vacate its space. The group may be the health professionals who oppose reduction in budget allocation for wages and salaries, or the politicians who resist decentralization of health services or the bureaucrats who oppose the pressure of increase in transparency or the health workers who go on strike against downsizing. Against them are the increasing influence of the national and foreign capital, which fights for increasing privatization and contracts to fill their bellies. This process of bargaining is overseen by the national political elites who have their own political agenda. The politically driven reforms are implemented in the background of a dynamic equilibrium reached in the power struggle between these factors. This results in a wide gap between the policy and its implementation. Incidentally, this gap manifests itself in the form of rich-poor divide, urban bias and exclusion of powerless sections of society.

Finally, there is a presumption that the health reforms adopted by the state correspond to the interests of the majority of population. This may not be true. The policies normally reflect the interests of particular sections of the dominant class. In other words, the pro-poor health policies will not be adopted unless they conform to the underlying forces. It would be naïve to believe that governments will implement effective reforms when the state is captured by the rich, powerful and dominant elites. Thus there is a question mark in respect of 'will', 'power' and 'ability' of the government to frame and implement pro-poor health reforms.

Visible Hand of a Free State

It may be utopia to believe that the state can be freed from the capture of the dominant elites because the state itself strives to continue its hegemony over the common people through the rational tools of planning, knowledge and statistics. The activities, functions and power of the state correspond to the equilibrium reached between the struggles of the different interest groups. Therefore, one way of building a pro-poor state is to strengthen the groups that represent the interests of the poor and marginalized sections of society. This necessitates mobilization of people at the grassroot level and strengthening the demand side. The communities should be empowered to demand the low-cost high-quality health services from the state. The health service users associations, community associations and local governments have to be institutionalized in the policy-making process. Decentralization itself is a political process that involves shift of power from the national level to the community level. A real decentralization is possible only through political mobilization at the grassroot level.

Another way to counter the state-capture is through campaign for public access to information regarding flow of funds in health sector. A transparent health sector will not only be less corrupt but also more efficient. There would be a continuous effort by machinery to produce positive health outcomes relative to the funds spent. This will also empower community and the users to monitor the health programmes. The community thus will not only ensure that the local health centres receive the allocated funds and but also see that funds are transformed into positive health outcomes.[13]

In this chapter, using the case of Sub-Saharan African countries, I have shown that the health sector problems are generally as a problem of fund-constraint, for which, in the neoliberal paradigm, the standard solutions are privatization, cost-recovery strategies and downsizing of bureaucracy. Hence, the contents of reforms for most of the countries are identical. What is ignored is that these reform measures are to be adopted and implemented in a political environment that is unique to each region. There is a need for an increased attention to the processes and players involved in the formulation and implementation of reform measures rather than to the contents of the reform.

Health is a political issue. The health sector problems are politically negotiated and settled among the interest groups. In order to make the reform process a political, the health problems are treated as economic or medical problems, and a rational and scientific reform process is enunciated to tackle these problems. Therefore, reforms become subverted and ineffectual. It is time that the attention is paid to community participation and empowerment so that the health problems are politically solved by the local level institutions. The strengthening of civil society and local village institutions is one of the best means to enforce accountability and to enhance performance of the health service sector.

NOTES

1. The article is heavily drawn from my essay, "Problems of Health Sector in Poor Countries" submitted to the School of Oriental and African Studies, London. I have also incorporated certain comments made by my tutor, Dr. Subir Sinha.
2. The other two components being per capita income and literacy.

3. The US Treasury, the International Monetary Fund (IMF) and the World Bank (WB) are collectively called as Washington Institutions.
4. The prescriptions of Washington Consensus (WC) like privatization and liberalization were not initially considered feasible for the health sector. In fact WC prescribes directing public expenditure towards the health sector. (Williamson, 2000 p. 252).
5. Reforms once initiated never stops. Newer reforms are implemented to remove the adverse impacts of existing reforms. Further reforms spread from one sector to other sectors.
6. The poor people are exempted from the user charges. They are given "yellow cards". Few poor people are aware of this waiver. Therefore, they end up paying user charges as well as bribe. Insaf International and PUCL are demanding the abolition of user charge system. (Nagar, 2002).
7. Empirically there is positive association between wealth and health, but their research does not prove causation relationship between the two.
8. Many economists feel that the Kerala model is not sustainable. However, this does not reduce the importance of Kerala's achievement in the health provisions due to the sustained investments. Another view is that such a thing was possible due to the presence of political environment favourable to pro-poor health investments. Hence may not be replicated in other regions.
9. The increasing recognition of health as economic problem is evident from the shift of leadership in the health sector reforms from WHO and UNICEF to WB and IMF at the global level.
10. For example, Tanzania's debt stood at US$7.4 billion (130% of its GDP) at the end of 1996 (Therkildsen, 2000 p. 61).
11. Following the reforms, Uganda saw an increase in social spending for health and education. (SAPRIN, 2001).
12. This is generally true for many developing countries including India. Based on World Bank's projects, user charges have been introduced in the Indian States of Punjab and Andhra Pradesh.
13. In the case of Uganda, there was a dramatic improvement in the flow of funds to the education sector, when the community were given the access to information in respect of functionings of primary schools. (Republic of Uganda, 2000). Right to Information movement in Rajasthan is another successful example.

REFERENCES

Allen T. (1992), 'Upheaval, Affliction and Health: A Ugandan Case Study' in H. Bernstein *et. al.*, (eds.), *Rural Livelihoods: Crises and Responses*, Oxford: Oxford University Press.

Andreano R. (1997), Health Sector Reform: Background Paper for International Health Policy Programme Conference, 6-9 October 1997 "Health Sector Reform – The Experience of the Last 10 Years and Prospects for the Future, Tanzania.

Baru (1999), 'The Seven-year Hitch: A Detailed Report on the Seven-year Health Reform Project in Andhra Pradesh' *Humanscape, May 1999.*

Colclough C. (1997), 'Education, Health, and the Market: An Introduction', in C. Colclough ed. *Marketising Education and Health in Developing Countries*, Clarendon Press, Oxford, pp. 1-34.

Corkery J. (2000), "Public Service Reforms and their Impact on Health Sector Personnel in Uganda", ILO papers, http://www.ilo.org/public/english/dialogue/sector/papers/health/pubserv6.pdf

Harrison G.(2001), "Post-Conditionality Politics and Administrative Reform: Reflections on the Cases of Uganda and Tanzania", *Development and Change*, Vol. 32, pp. 657-679.

Lubben M. Mayhew S.H., Collins C., and Green A., (2002), "Reproductive Health and Health Sector Reform in Developing Countries: Establishing a Framework for Dialogue" in *Bulletin of the World Health Organization*, 80(4) pp. 325-330.

Mills A. Brugha R. Hanson K. and McPake B. (2002), "What can be done about the Private Health Sector in Low-income Countries" in *Bulletin of the World Health Organization*, 80(4) pp. 325-330.

Nagar S. (2002), "Yellow Cards for the Poor", Indiatogether website, available at http://www.indiatogether.org/health/reports/insaaf01.htm#contact last accessed on July 10, 2003.

Nandraj S. (1997), "Unhealthy Prescriptions: The Need for Health Sector Reforms in India", Informing and Reforming (The Newsletter of the International Clearing House of Health System Reform Initiatives), No. 2: 7-11.

O. Therkildsen (2000), "Public Sector Reform in a Poor, Aid-Dependent Country, Tanzania", *Public Administration and Development*, Vol. 20, No. 1, pp. 61-71

Pritchett L. and Summers L. (1996) 'Wealthier is Healthier', *Journal of Human Resources* 31(4), pp. 841-866.

Republic of Uganda. 2000. "Tracking the Flow of and Accountability of UPE Funds." Report by International Development Consultants Ltd. Ministry of Education and Sports, Kampala. February.

SAPRIN Report (2001), "Impact of Public Expenditure Reforms on Health Care, Education and Other Public Services" http://www.solidaritet shuset.org/ rorg/ Tema/sap/saprap-1.htm

Sen. G. (1992), 'Social Needs and Public Accountability: The Case of Kerala', in M. Wuyts *et. al.*, eds., *Development Policy and Public Action*, Oxford: Oxford University Press.

Sexton S. (2001),"Trading Health Care Away? GATS, Public Services and Privatization" http://www.thecornerhouse.org.uk/briefing/ 23gats.html.

Stillwaggon E. (1998), 'The Plague of Poverty' in *Stunted Lives, Stagnant Economy. Poverty, Disease and Under Development*. Rutgers, London.

Thankappan K.R. (2001),"Some Health Implications of Globalization in Kerala, India" in *Bulletin of the World Health Organization*, 79(9) pp. 892-893.

Thomason J.A. (1998), Health sector reform in developing countries: a reality check, available at http://www.acithn.uq.edu.au/Conf97/papers97/ #Abstract, last accessed July 10, 2003.

Wagstaff A. (2002), "Poverty and Health Sector Inequalities." *Bulletin of the World Health Organization*, 2002. 80(2): pp. 97-105.

Williamson J. (2000), "What Should the World Bank Think About the Washington Consensus?" *World Bank Research Observer*. Washington, DC: The International Bank for Reconstruction and Development, Vol. 15, No. 2 (August 2000), pp. 251-264.

Wood. D. and Clarke. J. (2001), 'Civil Service Reform in Tanzania', in W. Court and M. Minogue (eds.), *The Internationalization of Public Management: Reinventing the Third World State*. Cheltenham: Edward Elgar.

World Bank (2002), "India Country Assistance Strategy Progress Report" available at http://lnweb18.worldbank.org/SAR/sa.nsf/Attachments/ tes/$File/prrpt.pdf last accessed on July 10, 2003.

Wuyts. M.(1992), 'Deprivation and Public Need', in M. Wuyts *et. al.*, eds., *Development Policy and Public Action*, Oxford: Oxford University Press.

4

Social Capital, Governance and Sustainable Development: Role of State and Society

S.N. SANGITA

Social capital (co-operation for collective action on the basis of association, networks, norms, trust and reciprocity) is a pre-requisite for long-term improvement of natural capital (sustainable use of community forestry resources). Collective action can increase the provision of public goods such as irrigation, crop insurance and sanitation. It also improves the management of Common Prosperity Resources (CPRs) such as grazing lands, ground water basins, fisheries and forests (Anderson and Locker 2002: 102). In recent years, social capital has been enlarged in participatory and deliberative institutions in sectors like watershed, irrigation, micro-finance, forest, health, education and such other activities throughout the world.

Community institutions/groups in the nature of participatory, joint, decentralised, indigenous, and co-management accounting 4,08,000 – 4,78,000 involving 8.2 – 14.3 million members have been formed mostly in developing countries in the last decade of the 20th century (Pretty and Ward, 2001). Many such initiatives have been taken in India in recent years by both government and civil society organisations. The Central Government has initiated a major programme known as Joint Forest Management (JFM) in 1990 to regenerate degraded forests and support livelihood systems of forest people with the joint responsibility of government and the people to share the benefits equally. Nearly 36,130 Village Forest Committees (VFCs) came into existence in all the states covering plantation area of 10.25 million hectares of forests during 1990-2000, (Bahuguna, 2000; Murali, *et.al.*, 2000; SPWD, 1998).

At the same time, civil society organisations like Village Communities, Youth Clubs, and Village Elders are also protecting vast tracks of local forests in different parts of the country. Most of these groups have come into existence in the last 20-30 years in a big number on the basis of self-initiative in response to the livelihood, biomass and other needs of the people (some of them in existence for the last 70-80 years without government recognition). Nearly 9,775 Community Forest Managements (CFMs) were protecting 3,34,205 hectares of forest in states like Orissa, West Bengal, Gujarat, Himachal Pradesh, Karnataka, Tamil Nadu and Haryana (Ravindranath, *et.al.*, 2000; Poffenberger, *et. al.*, 1996). Along with this, van panchayats (forest councils) in Uttar Pradesh (UP) hills or Village Forest Panchayats (VFPs) in Uttar Kannada (UK) (Karnataka) are managing village forests on the basis of Government Acts/or Statutes (Indian Forest Act, 1927).

Keeping this in view, the study examines the role of social capital in the management of Community Forest Resources (CFRs) in three regimes (Andhra Pradesh (AP), Karnataka and Orissa) with a view to understand the role of the state and society. The main issues raised in this chapter are: How village communities are being motivated to cooperate for collective action of CFR management? What strategies are being adopted for inculcating the habit of cooperation among villagers for collective action? What types of governance institutions (policies, laws, regulations, rules, norms and networks) have been adopted for management of CFRs? What are the drivers for creating social capital? Whether the social capital can be created with the state and civil society intervention within a short span of time? What are the advantages and disadvantages of such capital on collective actions? These are the issues that have been examined with empirical evidence from three case studies representing JFM, CFM and VFP located in Andhra Pradesh (AP), Karnataka and Orissa. This chapter has been structured into seven sections.

The second section deals with data sources and conceptual framework. Motivation for collective action is discussed in the third section. Fourth section focuses on socialisation of village communities for collective action. In the fifth section, laws, rules and networks for promoting collective action is covered. The sixth section covers with the drivers responsible for formation of social capital and finally, this chapter concludes with the pathways for promoting social capital.

II

Data Sources and Methodology

Three types of cases representing JFM, CFM and VFP were selected, because of wide variations in their approaches, strategies and institutional mechanisms for collective action. Binjageri and Sulia (Magarabandh) to represent CFM clusters were selected from Nayagarh District, Orissa. The Binjageri represents a successful case of regenerating forest cover on barren land and brought lush green natural forest with the support of the local people from 22 villages since 1970. Sulia in the same district represents the effective protection and management of the existing forest cover of 3500 acres covering 17 villages since 1990. Rampachodavaram and Sudhikonda forest ranges—in East Godavari district, Andhra Pradesh, Haliyal, Gopshitta, in Uttar Kannada district, Karnataka were selected to represent JFM which was implemented with the World Bank and DFID assistance respectively during 1995-2000. Kumta forest range in Uttar Kannada (UK) district, Karnataka was selected as a special case to study the eight decades old village forest panchayat. Three villages from each cluster/forest range on the basis of performance (high, moderate and low) were selected. Information regarding socio-economic profile, membership, perceptions and involvement were ascertained from 15 respondents from each village through an interview schedule. Forest officials, NGOs, VFC members and academicians were interviewed; secondary data was collected from the government departments and NGOs.

Social Capital: Conceptual Framework

Social capital has been defined by scholars in a variety of ways (Arris and De Renzio, 1997). Woolcock and Narayan, (2000: 226) define social capital in terms of norms and networks that enable people to act collectively for mutual benefit. Putnam (1995) defines social capital as a social organisation such as networks, norms and trust that enable participants to coordinate and cooperate more effectively to pursue shared interests. Fukuyama (1995) describes social capital as "a capability that arises from the prevalence of trust in a society or certain parts of it. Trust, according to him, can be embodied in the smallest social group like family, as well as the largest of all groups like the nation, and in all the other groups in between. Inglehart interprets social capital as "a culture of trust and tolerance" (1997: 188). Social capital also can be classified into trust, reciprocity and exchange, common rules, norms and sanctions and connectedness, networks and groups (Pretty and Ward, 2001: 209).

In order to develop a general, coherent theory of social relations, Coleman uses the term in conjunction with the concepts of physical and human capital, drawing explicit distinctions among them. Physical capital according to him refers to investment in tools, machinery and other tangible productive equipments, while human capital refers to those, which are less tangible investments in the skill and knowledge of the individuals. Social capital is even less palpable because it stems from changes in the relations among individuals that facilitate action (cited in Jackman and Miller, 1998: 48).

Social Capital and its Implications

Many scholars have highlighted the implications of social capital on polity, economy and society. Social capital is a necessary condition of social integration, economic efficiency and democratic or political stability (Arrow, 1972: 357; Coleman, 1988: 306; Ostrom, 1990; Putnam, 1993, 1995 and 2001; Fukayama, 1995). Banfield (1958), Putnam (1993) and Fukayama (1995) point out that interpersonal trust facilitates cooperation with the strangers, which is a pre-requisite for industrial development. Putnam asserts that social capital improves the efficiency of society and government by facilitating coordinated actions. Social networks (civic associations) and the culture of interpersonal trust in North Italy were mainly responsible for high quality democracy and development (Inglehart, 1999: 89). Similarly, in his study *Bowling Alone* in U.S.A., Putnam finds the decline of social capital since 1960, which negatively impacted democratic participation. Social capital is highly correlated with good educational and health outcomes and good government (Hellivel and Putnam, 1995).

Fukuyama's study (1995) highlighted the role of trust in economic performance. Political and economic development depends on values involving trust, ethical codes, and orientations to work and risk-taking (Harrisons, 1997). Inglehart points out that inter personal trust and membership in voluntary associations are "strongly associated" with stable democracy and economic development. Inter personal trust is very low in non-democratic societies (Inglehart, 1999). Inter personal trust, according to Almond and Verba, is responsible for less democracy in Italy and West Germany compared to Britain and U.S.A. Krishna (1999) finds correlation between high levels of social capital and high development of performance of local government in Rajasthan villages.

Similarly, there is a correlation between trust and development. Trust may make a society healthy, wealthy and wise. When people trust each other, they are more likely to accommodate each others' preferences—and make for a more pleasant society with a better quality of life. Trust lubricates cooperation (Putnam, 1993: 171). It reduces the transaction cost between people and so liberates resources. This saves money and time. It can also create a social obligation to reciprocate the trust. Trust prompts people to take active roles in their community to behave morally and to compromise. People who trust others are not so quite ready to dismiss ideas they disagree with. When they cannot get what they want, they are willing to listen to the other side. Communities with civic activism and ethical behaviour, where people give others their due, are more prosperous (Uslaner, 1999: 122).

Trust sometimes matters a lot. Generalised trust in others encourages people to join voluntary associations (Putnam 1995; Brehm and Rahn 1997; Uslaner 1996). It also makes them more likely to engage in a variety of other collective actions such as voting, working on community problems, donating to charity, volunteering time, and willing to serve on a jury (Uslaner, 1999: 128). Trust no doubt takes time to build but can be easily broken when society is pervaded by distrust. Reciprocity and exchange also increases trust (Coleman, 1990; Putnam, 1993). It, in turn, contributes to the development of long-term obligations among people. Economic (labour, grain, market and so on), social and cultural exchanges are very helpful to promote mutual confidence and trust and thereby development. Communities endowed with a diverse stock of social network and civic associations are in a stronger position to resolve conflicts and confront poverty and vulnerability. For example, weak, hostile, or indifferent governments have a profoundly different effect on community life and development projects than do governments that respect civil liberties, uphold the rule of law, honour contracts and resist corruption (Woolcock and Narayan, 2000).

All forms of social capital are not good for the society. A society may be well organised with strong institutions and has embedded reciprocal mechanism and not based on trust but on fear and power, such as feudal, hierarchical, racist and unjust societies (cited in Pretty and Ward, 2001). Formal rules and norms can also harm and exploit some groups. Exploitation of women, children, and Scheduled Castes (SCs) under the religious social order can be mentioned in this regard. Some associations can also act as obstacles to the emergence of sustainable livelihoods. They may encourage conformity, perpetuate adversity and inequality and allow certain individuals to get others to act in ways that suit only themselves (Olson, 1965; Taylor, 1982 cited in Pretty and Ward, 2001).

III

Motivation for Forest Development and Protection

Villager's Perception and Local Initiative in CFM

People take initiatives to protect the forest provided the perceived benefits are higher than the costs., The acceptance of JFM is very high when people understand the significance and benefits from it. If people are convinced through the perception (education and empowerment), observation (observing good experiments) and through experiences (enjoying the benefits) that the benefits are higher, the interest in collective action is very high. When people's dependency on the forest for their livelihood is high, and the perceived scarcity and threat from such resources are also very high, people take initiative to protect the forests. Similarly, people who are nearer to the forests may evince more interest rather than persons who also depend upon forest but live far away.

In the CFM villages (Binjageri and Magarabandh), the initiative had come from the local people due to threat perception and depletion of resources. According to people's perception, the flora and fauna of Binjageri hill were virtually undisturbed till 1940. It was a thick forest with wild animals and a number of streams used to flow from it. It was subject to rapid deforestation since the Independence. By the late sixties, Binjageri was completely denuded. Streams dried up and fields were silted. The surrounding villages faced scarcity of fuel wood, water for irrigation and threat of loss of soil fertility due to increased soil erosion. 1978 was the turning point when the dead body of the poor man was thrown over the riverbed and eaten away by the jackals, when his brother failed to arrange wood for funeral. The entire village was shocked and realised the importance of the forests (Shashikant *et. al.*, 1991; Human and Patnaik, 2000).

Efforts for environmental awareness and conservation have already begun in this and surrounding villages by Dr. Narayan Hazari from Kesharpur Village, a Reader in Utkal University. He started writing letters to villagers of Kesharpur expressing his concern for Binjageri hill and urging them to regenerate it. He used to organise Bhagpat (reciting religious scriptures like Ramayana and Mahabaratha for village people assembled in the evening) in villages around Binjageri during summer to educate about the environment. This gradually had some impact on some of the perceptive villagers.

As a result of these efforts, people of Kesharpur took a decision to protect a patch of Binjageri in 1976. These efforts have been further strengthened with the involvement of forest officials, local MLA and local college National Social Service (NSS) volunteers. The environmental awareness campaign (already initiated in early seventies in other villages) through padayatras, slogans and meetings motivated the other villages around Binjageri hill to protect the forest. This movement has eventually culminated as a federation known as *Brikshya of Jeevan Bandhu Parishad* (BOJBP) (Friends of Trees and Living Beings) with the representatives form 22 villages around Binjagiri in 1982 under the leadership of Joginath Sahu and Vishwanatha (a school teacher) and Udayanath Khatai (a marginal farmer).

Similar is the case with the villages in the Magarabandh cluster. It was in 1990, that Sulia was being continuously and thoroughly degraded. People started taking out the rootstocks. The FD officials remained mute spectators to the process of denudation. It was at the juncture that the initiative for the protection of the forest came from the village elders and later joined by the youth Raghunath Pradhan, a respected social leader and a group of young people from adjoining villages joined hands and traversed from village to village, held meetings and convinced the villagers of the need to protect forests. Representatives of the villages met 8-10 times during 1990 and what finally emerged was a Regional Forest Protection Committee of 23 villages. This committee is known as Sulia Paribesh Parishad charged with the responsibility of protecting the Sulia Reserve Forest from pillar No. 180 to 201. It is now registered under the Society Registration Act of 1860.

Emotionalism and Democratic Culture in VFP

In village forest panchayat in Halkar, Uttar Kannada district, the motivation for promotion of forestry is more due to emotional attachment with the forest and democratic culture. Eighty-year old village forest is a pride for many villagers. They have a strong incentive to maintain the oldest democratic institution and village forest, while similar institutions had collapsed elsewhere. Their pride with these institutions has been further strengthened with the visits of outsiders (scholars, practitioners, NGOs and other villagers) to study the village forest. Secondly, the threat perception for the villages' forest from the outsiders and FD is also a strong cementing force for the villagers' solidarity. On many occasions, villagers stood strongly whenever there was a threat from the outsiders. Villagers won the case in the High Court against the Karnataka Government in 1986 when the village forest was merged with FD in 1979 under the New Karnataka Forest Act, 1963. Very recently, they even prevented the local MLA from encroaching the forest land adjacent to Kumta town for construction of houses in connivance with the officials. All villagers irrespective of party affiliation protested and demonstrated against MLA action. There were occasions when the villagers took a delegation to higher-level officials to protest against harassment from the local forest officials regarding the cutting of matured trees. Instances were also noticed when the villagers persuaded the revenue officials to hold elections and general body meetings, whenever there was some indifference or delay on their part.

Economic Incentives in JFM

Unlike CFM, the main initiative for promoting village forestry in JFM villages has come from the FD which had very little time to motivate the people to develop the forest. The target set for the administrators to form VFCs under JFM was too high and the time given for them was too short. In order to adhere to the targets, the administrators used economic incentives to form VFCs. In their preliminary interactions with the villagers, wide publicity was given about immediate individual and community benefits (such as gas stoves and wages for individual households and television sets, roads and so on for community) to motivate the people. In fact, many villagers conceived this programme in terms of wages, gas stoves, biogas plants, smokeless *chullas*, agricultural implements, community halls, schools, roads which were provided under JFM funds. Even lands with old plantation were given to harvest to get immediate income for villagers. (Saxena, *et. al.*, 1997: 37). FD gave Rs. 11.7 lakhs to 20 out of 308 VFCs in UK towards its share from harvest till 1999. Even it distributed Rs. 14,000 each to 7 VFCs in Haliyal division towards their share under NTFPs sales (Murali *et. al.*, 2000). This demotivated the people in some places to own the plantations after the decline of government funds.

IV

Socialisation for Collective Action (Forest Development and Protection)

Empowerment through Mobilisation and Education in CFM

Mobilisation of people through padayatras and cultural shows etc. were the main strategies adopted in CFM villages of Binjageri and Magarabandh to bring awareness and promote green cultures among the villagers to protect the forests, wild life and plant trees. Firstly, padayatras, public meetings and protest movements were quite popular strategies adopted to motivate the villagers. This is evident from the increase of the villages covered with padayatras and meetings to around 100 in 1984 as against 34 and 4 villages in 1984 and 1970 respectively. Secondly, activities like painting and essay competition, debates, dramas and other cultural events were also organised to attract the students and youth towards the environmental issues. In an exhibition organised in 1996, posters and balloons with messages on them – about the need for clean air, clean water, economic use of fuel, protection of wild life and evils of dowry and untouchability were displayed. Thirdly, dramas, plays and songs were organised to spread the message of forest conservation. Services of poets, novelists, artists and social workers were availed to spread the message of environmental awareness. A number of leaflets, posters and booklets in Oriya language with catchy slogans and moral message from religious texts were used.

Fourthly, interest in forest was created among the children by enacting plays, composing and singing green songs and organisation of green clubs, essay writings, debates and quiz competitions. This is partly responsible for children's involvement in green activities such as campaigning, raising nurseries, planting trees and also brings awareness in their families and communities of environmental issues. Fifthly, Gandhian techniques like personal appeals, padayatras and fasting were adopted to promote solidarity among the forest groups. People who committed offences (cutting and stealing) were not penalised with harsh punishments like fines and so on. Instead, they were asked to submit an apology or asked to perform community service (planting and protecting trees). Sixthly, green culture has become the main philosophy for people in Binjageri. No festival or religious ceremony takes place without the planting of trees to mark the occasion. Many social and religious ceremonies such as marriages and funerals are marked by tree planting. Saplings are being used as gifts and prizes. In their greetings, local people quote, chant or sing slogans about trees. Solidarity has been maintained among the villagers to protect the forest.

Training, Exposure Trips and Interaction with Public Personalities in JFM

Training, Exposure Trips and Interaction with public personalities are the main instruments for cultivating habits of cooperation in JFM villages. Firstly Sensitisation of village communities through training, workshops and exposure trips has helped to develop positive attitudes and values among the people for collective action. Information on forest laws, policies, regulations, community rights, resource management, bookkeeping, and thrift and conflict resolution was provided during the training. Nearly 381 orientation courses, 145 interaction seminars and 401 workshops were conducted in Adilabad district in Andhra Pradesh during 1994-99 (Rangachari and Mukerji, 2000: 140). During 1992-98, nearly 11,795 persons from FD, VFC and local NGOs were trained in Uttara Karnataka district, Karnataka under WGFP. Of these, FD officials constituted around 51 per cent as against 49 per cent belonging to VFC and

NGOs. Field level officers like Range Forest Officers and Foresters gained maximum benefit and they accounted for 31 and 39 per cent respectively (Ravindranath, *et. al.*, 2000).

Many NGOs also conducted training programmes, seminars and workshops with the support of OXFAM and other agencies. MYRADA, the largest and the popular NGO in Karnataka conducted 224 training programmes for VFC members, NGOs and FD officials during 1993-96 (Saxena, *et. al.)* 1997. In Haliyal taluk, Indian Development Society (IDS) conducted 152 training programmes for 3,907 participants representing FD, VFC and village communities at the cluster and the village levels in 1996. Secondly, exposure trips were also arranged for VFC members to visit the successful management systems and interact with the public officials and important personalities. For instance, under JFM, 3,000 out of 863 VFC members in Adilabad district in Andhra Pradesh visited other districts during 1994-99, where VFCs were successful. VFC members and presidents were encouraged to interact with the top public officials including the Chief Minister.

V

Institutions (Law, Rules and Regulations) and Networks

Laws, rules and regulations provide incentives for people to cooperate towards collective action. Laws relating to rights are critical for collective cooperation. For instance, rights relating to alienation (sale and lease of forest land and withdrawal of forest products), exclusion (demarcation of forest boundary, membership, withdrawal and transfer of membership in VFC), management (regulate internal use patterns and transform the resource by improvements such as planting, thinning and harvesting) and withdrawal of resource units (permission for using, harvesting and restriction) are very vital for forest management. People have more incentives to form the groups, if they are given all the above rights under law. Similarly, conflict resolutions including penalisation can be clearly dealt with the transparent law.

Clearly established rights enhance the confidence of the communities to protect and manage forest lands. Clear tenure security rights enhance the authority of community management groups to carry out protection activities, especially when under pressure from neighbouring villages and private interest groups. When the outsiders question the authority of community groups for action against illegal felling of trees and smuggling of wood, the group can challenge the offenders if they are vested with the authority under law. In such a situation, they can approach the FD, police or courts for penal action against such offenders (Poffenberger and Chhatrapati Singh, 1996: 74). People's confidence in collective actions cannot be sustained if the FD alters the agreements reached with the people or bring about changes at the instance of the government without any proper mechanisms to account for the people for such changes (denial of agreed share of VFC's harvest to the people by the FD). Rights derived by law are more durable and sustainable than the executive orders and informal networks and arrangements.

In VFC in Halkar, all the above four rights have been given to the people to mange forest resources on the basis of Indian Forest Act, 1927 where rights are clearly established. Alienation and exclusion rights are very clear and transparent. Demarcation of boundary, membership on the basis of cattle and land, proportional representation to all the communities in the governing council and regular elections in the presence of Tasildhars are clearly mentioned in the Act. This provides complete autonomy to take decisions relating to regeneration, silvicultural, harvesting and other management practices for the last eighty years. The effective enforcement of these laws also enhanced the confidence of the people in the institution. These rights were well protected from external agencies like neighbouring villages and government. Halkar VFC filed a case in the Karnataka High Court when government took away its rights over the forest land by merging with the reserved forest under 1963 Karnataka Forest Act after the reorganisation of the State. Villager's confidence was further reinforced in the village forest after winning the case in their favour. Even this law helped them to prevent the encroachment of this land for construction of houses.

While in CFM villages, the rights over these forests were established by the people themselves when they started protecting the small patches of forest lands. Lands close to the villages were demarcated and developed regulations for protecting these forests and harvesting forest products with the consent of the people. Effective mechanisms were evolved on the basis of their traditional institutions. They negotiated with the neighbouring villages and reached agreements for realising their rights. For instance, many VFCs operating in south West Bengal negotiated with the neighbouring communities to clarify the rights and territorial responsibilities when they began to initiate protection activities. In many cases, these communities had the strongest incentives to avoid conflicts with their neighbours over forest rights and access (Poffenberger and Singh, 1996: 73). In Eastern India, many villages on their own or with the assistance of local government initiated negotiations with the neighbouring villages and reached agreements on forest management rights. In some cases, they formed federations for a group of villages and various institutions including conflict resolving mechanisms were developed. Even they were assisted by government and other external agencies in evolving appropriate rules. For instance, in Binjageri and Magarabandh, some forest officials were effective in creating opportunities for neighbouring villages to reach resource use agreements among themselves and ratify their decisions. Even FD recognised some of these rights and permitted transport of poles and other articles made out of bamboos at the check-post.

In JFM, there is ambiguity in devolving rights and many states had failed to provide long-term tenurial rights to the communities. Although VFCs were established under Societies Registration Act, the FD has unilateral powers to dissolve the VFCs. Besides, there was no mechanism to ensure that FD fulfils its commitments under JFM agreement. For instance, according to the original agreement, a certain per cent of the compounded fine on the smuggled wood (illegal cutting and transport) collected by the VFC goes to the VFC members. However, the FD has not implemented this. Similarly, the denial of rights over the collection of Non Timber Forest Products (NTFPs) and their percentage to the VFC members also created some misunderstanding. Thus the ambiguity in formulating rules created distrust in some villages under JFM.

Networking

Networks played a very important role in promoting social capital among village communities. Both horizontal and vertical networks among CSOs facilitated free flow of information for strengthening their solidarity. Firstly, horizontal networks of NGOs facilitated the frequent interaction at the taluk, district and state levels to share information, coordinate their efforts, share experiences and articulate their problems. Secondly, networks also provided information to strengthen the solidarity of the movement. Information related to rights and responsibilities of forest people, policies and laws and successful cases were communicated to the forest groups through publications by state level NGOs and networks. Even some of the NGOs were bringing newsletters and other publications to empower the people with information. Thirdly, networks also brought solidarity by organising awareness camps, annual conferences and training programmes, which have been, discussed elsewhere. Fourthly, the state level NGO networks in these three states were receiving assistance from external organisations like OXFAM, Ford Foundation, SPWD and so on to strengthen the NGO network at grassroots for organising conferences, awareness camps, training programmes, exposure trips, preparing monographs, conducting studies, printing of newsletters and so on (Sangita, 2004).

VI

Drivers for Promoting Social Capital

Non-Governmental and Peoples' Organisations

NGOs played a very significant role in motivating the people and promoting trust between the FD and villagers. NGO's familiarity and their good work in the villages helped them to gain the confidence and trust of the people. They secured villagers' confidence by tackling core problems like poverty, exploitation and other types of deprivation. The social capital thus accumulated over the years has been availed for motivating the villagers for collective action. For instance, Shakti, an NGO operating in tribal villages for the last 10 years in Rampachodavaram, AP addressed the core problems like land alienation, exploitation, poverty and so on. It helped in restoring their lands from the non-tribals and also in ensuring right prices for their NTFP. They presented tribal cases before the officials, courts and newspapers and got justice. Subsequently, Shakti organised thrift groups for improving the economic status of tribal women in a number of villages. On many occasions, they mobilised the people against illegal felling of trees, smuggling of wood and so on. Besides, Shakti recruited many tribal people as volunteers on a fixed honorarium to work for the tribal development. Some of their members subsequently became the Presidents and members of the VFCs. The social capital thus accumulated by Shakti over a period of 10 years was availed by the FD to start VFCs in many tribal villages including our sample villages.

Similar is the case with many organisations associated with VFCs in AP. For instance, a freedom fighter, who was working in the tribal block, was instrumental in the formation of many VFCs in the Nexallite infected areas in AP. It was not possible for the FDs to start VFCs in the area without the cooperation of the NGOs. In fact, the NGOs' involvement in forest protection activities increased in recent years. For instance, one-sixth of the VFCs in Rajahmundry circle, Andhra Pradesh, were supported by the NGOs (Sangita, 2003). Similarly, 30-40 per cent of the VFCs in Uttara Kannada, Karnataka, were supported by the NGOs (Sangita, 2003). They were instrumental in establishing network with VFC Presidents, NGOs and forest officials and organised many training programmes, workshops and awareness camps.

Women Self-Help Groups (SHGs)

Women Self-Help Groups (SHGs) and Micro Finance Organisations (MFO) can play a very significant role in promoting VFCs. Apart from physical capital (productive income generating assets), SHGs can also create human-capital (education and training to develop skills, design, develop and manage the community or individual enterprises) and social capital (habits of cooperation, group solidarity and social cohesion). Studies found that in villages where SHG members met weekly as a condition for borrowing, communication among participants greatly increased the chances of successful collective action.

Van Bastelaer (1999) argues that social capital was created when MFOs like the Grameen Bank in Bangladesh and its replicators required all members to show uniform behaviour every week, such as reciting the list of decisions that accompany group membership. This routinisation created a corporate culture, or cultural habit. Such cultural habits, in combination with strengthened allegiances among borrowers and their families, reduced incentives to behave in ways detrimental to the common good (Anderson *et. al.*, 2002: 99). As Ostrom and others noted, it took effort and energy to create social capital. Group based micro-finance could lower the costs of monitoring and enforcing existing rules and norms, and also the costs of crafting new rules (Ostrom, 1990, 1992). Regular meetings, frequent interaction, and common credit goals can facilitate the communication, knowledge about fellow factors, common understanding about the incentive structure and the required trust among the members to collective action (Ostrom, 1994; 532, cited in Anderson *et. al.*, 2002: 99). The presence of Self-Help Groups (SHGs) in many of our sample villages were mainly responsible for starting of VFCs.

Leadership

Enlightened Leadership

In CFM village, the leadership was mainly responsible for motivating the people to protect and conserve forests. For instance, in Binjageri, the leaders like Joginadha Sahoo, a respected middle school teacher, Narayan Hazari, an important faculty member in Utkal University, Bhubaneshwar, played a key role in motivating the people to protect the forest. In fact, the vision, commitment, simplicity, honesty and sincerity of these leaders were all mainly responsible for attracting thousands of people in hundreds of villages.

The survival of the Halkar VFP forest panchayat for the past eighty decades can be attributed to the enlightened and selfless leadership. The advocate, the retired inspector, the retired teacher and enlightened village elders are continuing the traditions that were established by their grand fathers and fathers. On the other hand, the poor leadership was responsible for the collapse of a similar system in Kallabbe, which is 20 kms. away from Halkar. The President and the members of the VFP in Kallabbe started violating the rules by encouraging illegal cuttings for their personal benefit. Similarly, the factional leaders in some villages were mainly responsible for the decline of VFCs. We came across many such instances outside our sample villages, which were known for murder, violence and ultimate destruction of forest.

Administrative Leadership

Administrative leadership is also an important motivating factor for the village communities in forming joint forest management. Many forest officials in Uttara Kannada in Karnataka and Sudhikonda in Andhra Pradesh were responsible for creating interest among the villagers towards joint forest management. They were instrumental in building rapport with the villagers. Some of the FD officials spent long hours with the villagers while forming VFCs. They also maintained cordial relations with villagers by attending to their personal needs and family functions like marriages. In order to involve the people in the programme, some officials were very generous and innovative in their approach. However, this rapport could not be sustained by the officers who succeeded them that ultimately led to distrust.

Social Capital in Villages

In many villages the existing traditional organisations (like village councils, village school(s), temples, village land, village ponds and so on), are instrumental for strengthening the functioning of VFCs. For instance, in Orissa, the informal village councils have been managing village schools, temples, village land and village ponds, grain banks as common resources. In fact, many primary, upper primary and middle schools were established by the villagers through their contributions in the form of money and labour, which was allowed by the Orissa Government. Even in the heterogeneous villages, the presence of village development and festival committees were responsible for the success of VFCs.

However, certain type of community organisations played negative roles. For instance, the number of caste associations without any interaction among themselves through community organisations for festivals and development, youth organisations and political parties can be mentioned in this regard. In some villages, the non interaction among various caste associations, particularly SCs has affected the functioning of VFCs. Similarly, the village factions and political parties in some villages were responsible for the destruction of forests occasionally.

The cooperation based on patron-client relationship was also acting negatively. For instance, in some villages the forest officials and village elite were cooperating merely for their mutual interest rather than the mutual trust. The forester needed the cooperation of the villagers informing VFCs to fulfill the target. On the other hand, the villagers needed wood from the forests for their agricultural implements. The second type of patron-client relationship was repression and fear. We noticed such type of relationship between the FD officials and VFC members in some villages. The tribal people were cooperating with the foresters to form joint forest management essentially for the power, which they were using against the innocent forest tribals by implicating them in petty or false offences like cutting of a small timber and so on. But, the presence of naxallites is responsible for the collapse of patron-client relationship affecting the interests of the poor.

VII

Pathways for Accumulating Social Capital

The social capital has been accumulating mainly on two pathways, viz., state initiative and civil society initiative. The state initiative is mainly in the form of laws, rules, regulation, policies and their effective enforcement, networks and credible leadership etc. Firstly, the state laws provided the necessary conditions for village communities to promote collective action. In VFP, the statutory powers given to the people over the land, trees and tree products and their management were responsible for people's trust in the governance institutions. Boundary rules (membership on the basis of land and cattle, proportional representation in executive committee and regular elections) had been clearly stated in the Village Forest Act. The restoration of these rights by the Karnataka High Court when they were taken away by the State Government further enhanced the people's trust in the laws. The absence of statutory powers and ineffective enforcement of promises and agreements was partly responsible for lack of trust between officials and villagers in JFM.

Secondly, the state can create social capital by partnership with village communities by joint planning, management and production. In JFM, village communities were given rights over the trees, tree products and control over the management. The state also provided expertise and finances for collective action. The frequent interaction and training of officials and villagers have resulted in building up trust between the FD officials and the villagers.

Thirdly, the credible and responsive administrators were responsible for creation of social capital. The committed officers and their personal rapport with villagers were mainly responsible for starting VFCs in JFM areas in Karnataka and Andhra Pradesh. Such evidence came from forest protection experiments in East India, in Arabari, West Bengal. FD officials were instrumental in facilitating the formation of Forest Protection Committees (FPCs) without special budgets and projects (Poffenberger and Mc Gean, 1996: 29). Both higher and lower level officials worked remarkably well and the forest growth was rapid and at the same time, the intensity of tensions and conflicts got minimised. The number of FPCs doubled each year increasing from less than 50 to nearly 2000 and covering 3.2 lakh hectares during the fifteen year period 1986-90 (Poffenberger and Mc Gean, 1996: 31). Similarly, the interaction of higher-level officials with the village communities in CFM villages boosted their motivation levels to protect the forests. Even the silent support given by many forest officials in the form of financial assistance for plantation, and training as well as permission to transport of bamboo articles and poles can be mentioned in this regard. The social capital created by the state is very significant particularly to protect the rights of village communities; it can spread to a wider area in a country like India within a short span of time. It can provide expertise and resources and protect the disadvantaged who depend on forests for their livelihoods. However it is very expensive and also causes wastage of resources.

The social capital can also be accumulated by the civil society. This comes mainly from two sources-endogenous and exogenous. People themselves started cooperating with each other to protect the small patches of the forest on the basis of their personal experience through the observations of their own forest and the loss they incurred in terms of fodder, fuel wood, NTFP, siltations of fields, low water tables and so on. People's interests to organise also originated when they observed the benefits derived by the neighbouring village forest protection. For instance, the initiative was started in Kesharpur and spread to other villages in due course of time through spread-effects. The individual motivation would be boosted-up with the dynamic leadership for the movement emerged within or outside the village. For instance, the role of teachers, youth clubs and elderly village leaders provided the necessary leadership to get the momentum to the forest movement. Even the leaders from outside the village were also instrumental in strengthening the movement.

Fourthly, the external agencies also provided necessary inputs for strengthening the CFM movements in Orissa. For instance,

OXFAM provided assistance to BOJBP in organising various training programmes, workshops, awareness camps and so on. Their assistance to RCDC helped disseminate information mainly through newspapers to forest communities about various laws, rights and other issues relevant to forest people. They conducted many studies and shared information with the CFMs. Their documentation also helped the forest groups to strengthen their organisational abilities and implementation practices. The visits by outsiders had strengthened further the people's movements. Fifthly, involvement of Government Officers with activities such as seminars, workshops, training programmes and plantations gave legitimacy to the CFM efforts in the absence of legal recognition.

Social capital generated through this process is cost effective, although it takes 3-5 years. This is based on local knowledge and local skills. It is much more credible since the institutions are designed by the local people through democratic processes. The institutions and the rules they designed have much more acceptance by the people. The major limitations of this social capital are in regard to sustainability. In the absence of legal recognition it is very difficult to maintain the forest in the context of bigger markets and parties (political parties, interest groups etc.) that are interacting much more intensively with the village communities. It has not designed proper institutional mechanisms to resolve the conflicts particularly inter or intra village conflicts and conflicts between FD and CFMs. It has no legal status to approach police stations, courts and the FD to prevent illegal felling and cutting by the outsiders. The present conflict resolution mechanisms are mainly leader oriented. They are able to resolve conflicts through satyagrahas, fastings, prostrating and so on. The younger generation may not be quite familiar with such techniques. In the absence of these mechanisms, the markets may encourage the individual villagers in connivance with the forest contractors and officials to cut the valuable trees for urban markets. Similarly, the party politics and village factions also come in the way of resolving these conflicts. In fact, we have come across instances where village politics and intra-village conflicts destroyed forests within a short span of time in some of the villages. On few occasions, many people were killed over the forest conflicts in Orissa villages. Such conflicts can be resolved via legal recognition by the state to some extent.

The social capital from the external agency is based on networks or partnerships among the civil society actors. External NGOs play a very significant role in promoting social capital among the villagers individually or in collaboration with the other bigger NGOs or the government. Firstly, NGOs like MYRADA and IDS, on their own encourage the villagers to take-up plantations on village lands. Secondly, NGOs also act as catalysts to bridge the trust between FD and village communities in the initial stages of VFC formation. The social capital which many NGOs built in the villages over the years through varied programmes (such as SHGs, employment, training, empowerment, health and rural development) was availed for the forest programme. Besides, they play a key role in changing the attitudes of the people for collective action through workshops, training programmes and awareness camps. Thirdly, they have established networks at the taluk, division, and district levels to interact and share their experiences and strengthen their articulation capacity. Even they have encouraged villagers to interact with the outside world to have better information. Fourthly, they have brought out literature relating to forest laws and rights, in the form of manuals to guide the village communities. Fifthly, they play advocacy role and act as a pressure group to influence the policies. External NGOs like OXFAM, Ford Foundation have also strengthened the NGO networking by providing financial and technical assistance to strengthen the NGO network and institution building.

The social capital accumulated through NGOs is very vital for forest movement in protecting the forest. They are not very costly. First of all it is very easy to reach vast sections of society through the NGOs' network, which has been built over the years. Secondly, the NGOs' social capital is very vital when there is mistrust between the FD and village communities. Thirdly, this capital can be created at a lesser cost since many people are willing to organise. The main limitation of this social capital is its non-availability uniformly throughout India. It is mainly concentrated in urban areas. In fact, many of these organisations have been working in the villages having their offices located in the urban areas. Fourthly, many NGOs have come to avail the benefits from the government and the funding organisations. Such NGOs may destroy the social capital, which has been built over the years.

Pattern of Cooperation in CFM, JFM and VFP Governance Regimes

Activity	*CFM*	*JFM*	*VFP*
Initiation/ Motivation	Local, perceived benefits, experience	National & international	Ownership rights
Socialisation	Empowerment: religious & cultural discourse & Gandhian techniques	Training, exposure trips & interaction with public personalities	Participatory culture & inclusive democracy
Laws: Ownership rights	No legal rights, negotiated rights within & outside the village	Ambiguity in rights of ownership	Constitutional rights
Sanctions & conflict resolution	No legal rights, Gandhian techniques	Not yet evolved	Complete
Networking	Vertical & horizontal among CSOs	Vertical among Government	No
Efficiency	Cost effective	Costly	Less cost
Equity	Low	High	Moderate
Sustainability	Not legal	Not economic	Sustainable

REFERENCES

Ajay Kumar, (2000), "A Decade of JFM in India: Looking Back for Better Foresight", *Indian Forester,* May: 579-594, Dehradun.

Amit Mitra, Mariette Correa, (1997), '*Oxfam Support Project, Uttara Kannada: An Evaluation of the First Phase of Work in Support of the KFD/DFID Western Ghats Forestry Project*', Oxfam (India) Trust, February, New Delhi.

Arnold, J.E.M., and W.C. Stewart (1991), "Common Property Resource Management in India", *Tropical Forestry Papers,* No. 24, Oxford Forestry Institute, University of Oxford, Oxford.

Bhat P.R. *et. al.,* (2000), "Joint Forest Planning and Management in Uttara Kannada: A Micro and Macro Level Assessment", in Ravindranath N.H., K.S. Murali and K.C. Malhotra (eds.), Joint Forest Management and Community Forestry in India—An Ecological and Institutional Assessment, Oxford and IBH, New Delhi, 59-98.

Binay Kumar Pattnaik and Sumana Dutta, (1997), "JFM in South-West Bengal—A Study in Participatory Development", *Economic and Political Weekly*, 32 (50), 13 December: 3225-32.

Carroll, T. (1992), *"Intermediary NGOs: The Supporting Link in Grassroots Development"*, Kumarian Press, West Hartford, CT.

Chambers, Robert, N.C. Saxena and Tushaan Shah, (1989), *"To the Hands of the Poor: Water and Trees"*, Oxford and IBH Publishing Co., New Delhi.

Chatterjee Mitali (1996), "Gender Roles in Joint Forest Management", in S.B. Roy, (eds.), Experiences from Participatory Forest Management, Inter India, New Delhi.

Chopra, Kanchan,Gopal K. Kadekodi and M.N. Murthy, (1990), *"Participatory Development: An Approach to the Management of Common Property Resources,"* Sage Publications, New Delhi.

Fernandes, Walter, G. Menon and P. Viegas, (1988), "Forests, Environment and Tribal Economy: Deforestation, Improvement and Marginalisation in Orissa," *Indian Social Institute*, New Delhi.

Gadgil, M. (1987), "Depleting Renewable Resources: A Case Study from Karnataka Western Ghats", *Indian Journal of Agricultural Economics*, July-September, Bombay.

Gaonkar D.S. and B. Shivanna Gowda, (2000), "Joint Forest Management in Uttar Kannada District, Karnataka", *Indian Forester*, May: 554-568.

Gibson C. Clark, Margeret A Mc. Kean and Elinor Ostrom (eds.), People and Forests—Communities, Institutions and Governance, The MIT Press, London.

Gopal Naik, (1997), "Joint Forest Management: Factors Influencing Household Participation", *Economic and Political Weekly*, 32 (48), 29th November: 3084-89.

Government of Andhra Pradesh, (1997), 'Joint Forest Management in Andhra Pradesh (Focus on NGO Participation)', September, Hyderabad.

Government of India, (1976), *"Report of the National Commission on Agriculture (Part IX: Forestry)"*, Ministry of Agriculture and Irrigation, New Delhi.

Government of Karnataka, (1996), "Western Ghats Forestry Project—Effectiveness of an All Women VFC: Satageri", October, Bangalore.

Government of Karnataka, (1996), "Western Ghats Forestry Project—An All Women VFC: Banasageri When Men Migrate Women Manage", November, Bangalore.

Government of Orissa, (1992), "Note for the State Level Meeting of Forest Officers (11th February, 1992)", Social Forestry Project, Social Forestry Directorate, Bhubaneshwar, (mimeo).

Guha, Ramachandra (1994), "Forestry Debate and Draft Forest Act", *Economic and Political Weekly*, August 20.

Gupta, A.K., (1996), "Socio-ecology of Stress: Why Do Common Property Resource Management Projects Fail?" in Proceedings of the Conference on Common Property Resource Management, ed. National Research Council, National Academy Press, Washington, D.C.

Jodha, N.S., (1989), "Management of Common Property Resources in Selected Areas of India", in *Local Institutions and Resource Management*, eds., Anis Dani and J. Gabriel Campbell, ICIMOD, Kathmandu.

Jules Pretty and Hugh Ward, (2001), "Social Capital and the Environment," *World Development*, Vol. 29 (2): 209-227.

Kameshwara Rao K. *et. al.*, (2000), "Community Forest Management and Joint Forest Management in Eastern Ghats, Andhra Pradesh" in Ravindranath N.H., K.S. Murali and K.C. Malhotra (eds.), Joint Forest Management and Community Forestry in India—An Ecological and Institutional Assessment, Oxford and IBH, New Delhi, 99-120.

Kameswari, V.L., (2002), "Gendered Communication and Access to Social Space Issues in Forest Management," *Economic and Political Weekly*, February 23: 797-800.

Kant, Shashi, Neera M. Singh and Kundan, K. Singh, (1991), "Community Based Forest Management Systems (Case Studies from Orissa), ISO/SWED Forests, Indian Institute of Forest Management and Swedish International Development Authority, New Delhi.

Kiser, Larry and Elinor Ostrom, (1982), "The Three World of Action: A Male Theoretical Synthesis of Institutional Approaches," in Elionor Ostrom (ed.), *Strategies for Political Enquiry*, Sage Publications, Beverly Hills, CA.

Mallik, Madhushree and S.N. Sangita, (1992), "Local Organisations, Common Property Land Resources and Rural Poor", *Wasteland News*, Vol. VIII (3), February-April, New Delhi.

Mukherji, S.D., (2000), "A Case Study of Joint Forest Management in Andhra Pradesh", *Indian Forester*, May: 452-462.

Nandiani Sundar, *et. al.*, (1996), "Defending the Dalki Forest: Joint Forest Management in Lapanga", *Economic and Political Weekly*, Vol. 31 (45 and 46), November 9-16: 3021-29.

Ostrom, Elinor, (1992), *Crafting Institutions for Self Governing Irrigation Systems*, Institute for Contemporary Studies, San Francisco.

Poffenberger, Mark *et. al.*, (1989), "Forest Regeneration through Community Protection: The West Bengal Experience."

Poffenberger, Mask, (1990), "Joint Management of Forest Land: Experiences from South Asia", Ford Foundation, New Delhi.

Potter David (1998), "NGOs and Forest Management in Karnataka," in Roger Jeffery (eds.), The Social Construction of Indian Forests, Manohar, Delhi.

Regional Centre for Development Cooperation, (1999), "Community Forestry for Village Development" (Community Forest Management in Mayurbhanj and Bolangir Districts of Orissa and Its Contribution to Village Development, World Wide Fund for Nature (India), New Delhi.

Regional Centre for Development Cooperation, (1999), 'Community Forest Management in Mayurbhanj and Bolangir Districts of Orissa and its Contribution to Village Development', May, Bhubaneshwar.

Sangita, S.N., *et. al.*, (1992), "Politics, Administration and Social Forestry on Common Lands: Experiences from India", *Indian Journal of Administrative Science*, Vol. III, (1 and 2), January-December: 107-23.

Sarin, Madhu (1993), "From Conflict to Collaboration: Local Institutions in Joint Forest Management" (Joint Forest Management, Working Paper No.14), Society for Promotion of Waterlands Development and the Ford Foundation, New Delhi.

Saxena N.C., Madhu Sarin, R.V. Singh, Tushar Shah (1997), 'Western Ghats Forestry Project: Independent Study of Implementation Experience in Kanara Circle', May, Bangalore.

Sexena, N.C., (1987), *Commons, Trees and the Poor in the Uttar Pradesh Hills,* ODI Social Forestry Network Paper 5f, London.

Sexena, N.C., (1988), *Participatory Planning for Wastelands Development,* FAO, Bangkok.

Shah, Tushar, (1989), "Collective Action on Village Commons: Community Fodder Farms in Kheda District, Gujarat", Institute for Rural Management, Anand, Gujarat, (mimeo).

Shashi Kant, Neera M. Singh and Kundan K. Singh (1991), 'Community Based Forest Management Systems' (Case Studies from Orissa), *Indian Institute of Forest Management,* Bhopal.

Singh, Katar (1994), "Managing Common Pool Resources: Principles and Case Studies", Oxford University Press, New Delhi.

Sivaramakrishnan, K. (1998). "Comanaged Forests in West Bengal: Historical Perspectives on Community and Control", *Journal of Sustainable Forestry,* Vol. 7, No. 3/4.

Sundar Nandini, *et. al.*, (2001), "Branching Out—Joint Forest Management in India", Oxford, New Delhi.

Tang, Shui Yan, (1992), *Institutions and Collective Action, Self Governance in Irrigation,* Institute for Contemporary Studies, San Francisco.

Wade, Robert, (1988), *Village Republics: Economic Conditions for Collective Action in South India, Cambridge University Press, Cambridge.*

World Bank (1993), "India—Policy and Issues in Forest Sector", Washington, D.C.

Yadama, Gautam N. and Margie DeWeese-Boyd (1998), "Co-Management of Forests in the Tribal Regions of Andhra Pradesh, India: A Study in the Making and Unmaking of Social Capital."

5

Social Capital: Its Quantity and Quality in the Margins of Kerala

J. MARY JOHN AND B. MOHANAN

To the accepted list of factors of production, social capital has been added by some researchers due to its importance in building up value and sustainability to the socio-economic development processes (Coleman 1988). Many have attempted to define social capital since Robert Putnam's path-breaking study on the impact of decentralization processes in Italy and the publication of his book 'Making Democracy Work' (1993). According to Putnam, social capital refers to features of social organization such as trust, norms, and networks that can improve the efficiency of society by facilitating coordinated actions (*Ibid.*, 167). Authors like Ismail Serageldin and Christian Grootaert (2000) found much value in social capital as a contributing factor in sustainable development process.

Following Putnamian thinking, the World Bank defines social capital as "The norms and social relations embedded in the social structure of societies that enable people to coordinate action to achieve desired goals." The Bank adds, "social capital refers to the institutions, relationships and norms that shape the quality and quantity of a society's social interactions. Social capital is not just the sum of the institutions which underpin a society—it is the glue that holds them together." For the Bank, social capital is "a set of horizontal associations between people, consisting of social networks and associated norms that have an effect on community productivity and well-being. Social networks can increase productivity by reducing the costs of doing business. Social capital facilitates coordination and cooperation."

This article examines the quality and quantity of social capital produced in and through Civil Society Organisations (CSOs) at the grassroots in Kerala. Quality refers to the internal dynamics of processes taking place in the CSOs such as decision-making, conflict resolution, leadership, dimensions of trust, mutual relationships among members etc., while quantity refers to the number of CSOs, the number of people associated with them, the number of meetings conducted, frequency of meetings, duration of time taken for such meetings in the CSOs, etc.

Civil Society Organisations

Civil society organisations operate outside the laws of *politics* (which centres on power and is governed by the ways and means of grabbing power) and *family* (which is personal and private and is governed by rules of purely emotional order) and *market* (which is profit-oriented and governed by the rules of economics). Thus, civil society has a unique collective space to operate where it has to keep independence from the influence of politics, personal affinities and market forces. The shrinking space of strong civil society is the result of tempting forces of politics, personal interests and market forces. Thus, civil society organisations are the natural space to measure social capital.

The civil society takes varied forms in India. It really reflects a rich diversity in its forms and external appearance. But, they share a common vision, orientation and direction by its definition. Rajesh Tanden (2001) maps the contemporary organizational forms of civil society. His map includes traditional associations formed around a tribe, ethnicity or caste. These associations, among other functions, mediate inter-family relations and develop elaborate systems, norms and procedures for managing natural resources. The second category in the map is religious associations, which take up charity and social service to the poor and needy. These religiously inspired civil society organisations intervene in sectors like education, health care, drinking water, aforestation, social welfare, etc. The third in the mapped categories is social movements. These movements are further classified into

(*i*) movements focusing on the needs and interests of a particular group of people like tribals (indigenous people), dalits (untouchables) and women;

(ii) movements protesting against a set of practices, institutions, policies and programmes like liquor policy, dowry, etc.;

(iii) movements protesting against displacements due to development; and

(iv) movements focusing on protection, preservation and regeneration of environment, anti-corruption campaigns against government officials, civil liberties and human rights campaigns, campaigns for right to information and right to livelihoods, etc.

The next broad category in the mapping refers to membership associations. This is further classified into four sub-groups. They are:

(a) Representational associations including trade unions, peasant organisations, business associations and traders' associations, consumers' associations, etc.;

(b) Professional organisations existing largely among lawyers, teachers, doctors, nurses, engineers, managers, journalists, etc.;

(c) Socio-cultural organisations referring to youth clubs, sports and arts clubs, which meet the social and cultural needs of their members.

The fifth and last large category is Intermediary Associations (IAs), which are again categorized into six groups. They are:

(a) Service delivery organisations like schools, hospitals, Village Development Organisations (VDOs) that take up programmes for drinking water, sanitation, micro-credit, etc. Orphanages, homes for the destitute, homes for the elderly, etc. also come under this sub-category;

(b) Mobilizational organisations facilitating awareness and empowerment among the weaker sections;

(c) Support providers to other community based organisations or other intermediary organisations like research and information sharing, capacity building and networking activities;

(d) Philanthropic organisations providing resources to other civil society organisations;

(e) Advocacy for a particular cause like environment, gender, human rights, child labour, Panchayati Raj Institutions, etc.;

(*f*) Networks are associations of other intermediaries and act as networks to build up a collective voice and strength around a cause. That the caste and religious associations form part of the civil society is a key issue still alive among the scholars of civil society.

Kerala's recent achievements in health and education are attributed to the power of public action even in conditions of stagnation in the productive sectors of economy. To many, Kerala's successes in literacy movement and people's planning are the results of collective thinking and action for a common cause at the grassroots level. It was found that a general civil culture of the people has contributed land, building and similar immovable assets for schools, hospitals, Panchayat offices, etc.

Doubts are now raised if the much-acclaimed public action has ceased to be the locomotive of Kerala's development. Moreover, the rural-urban divide forces us to examine if the strength of civil society and the consequent generation of social capital are evenly or unevenly distributed in the mainstream and marginal territories of Kerala.

In this background of understanding of the concept of social capital and civil society, a field study was carried out in 16 Grama Sabha (GS) constituencies in four Grama Panchayats (GP) in four Districts, which lie at the borders of the State of Kerala. Four GS constituencies were selected from each GP. Kadinamkulam GP of Trivandrum District represent the coastal villages and the erstwhile Travancore State; Ayyampuzha GP of Ernakulam District represents central eastern border and the erstwhile Cochin State; Chaliyar GP of Malappuram District represents north eastern border and the only Muslim dominated district in the State while Meppadi GP of Wayanad District represents the northern border and the erstwhile Malabar province. Fifty respondents from each GS constituency were selected according to the systematic random sampling method. Fourteen elected representatives were added to the list of respondents to catch their views. Thus the 814 respondents were selected from the voters list prepared for the 2000 local body elections in Kerala. Out of them, for this study, those respondents who were somehow associated with any of the Civil Society Organisations (CSOs) were contacted.

A list of various categories of Civil Society Organisations (CSOs), functioning across Kerala was prepared in advance and a census of those CSOs, within the sample Grama Sabha constituencies was made first, because there was no such list available to measure the quantity, which is very important for the study. Relevant data regarding their functioning were collected from the present office bearers of such organisations or the knowledgeable members.

Here, social capital is studied in terms of membership in and or relationship (association) with Civil Society Organisations (CSOs) and the involvement of members in the internal dynamics and activities of such organisations. The purpose is to capture the major features of such social organisations such as:

(i) trust built up among the members and in the village,
(ii) networks of such CSOs,
(iii) shared norms, created and abided by, with these organisations,
(iv) sustainable and productive relationship built up among the members and in the village, in and through the organisations, and
(v) the civic consciousness of the members.

Citizens' association with local CSOs is possible in more than one way. They can associate with local organisations as members, beneficiaries, leaders, volunteers, staff, etc. This associate opportunity forges relationships leading to social capital formation. The personal interviews among the respondents revealed that 30 per cent had some kind of association/involvement (membership status, beneficiary status, leadership status, volunteer status, staff status, etc.) in the local CSOs (Table 5.1). Majority of the respondents did not have any association with any of the surveyed organisations.

Profile of Study Areas

The profiles of the selected Panchayats were compiled depending mostly on the Village Development Reports (VDRs) prepared by the Village Panchayats with people's participation. The profiles are constructed with information about the area, population, main crops, religious and caste composition. An attempt has also been made to identify indicators of public action in these Panchayats. The Village Development Report of Meppadi GP shows that the local people

Table-5.1
Distribution of Respondents According to Association with/Involvement in Civil Society Organisations (CSOs)

Name of Panchayats	*CSO Dummy Variable*		*Total*
	No Association/ Involvement in Any of the CSOs	*Has Association/ Involvement in at Least One CSO*	
Meppadi	175 (85.8)	29 (14.2)	204 (100)
Chaliyar	153 (76.1)	48 (23.9)	201 (100)
Ayyampuzha	105 (51.5)	99 (0.5)	204 (100)
Kadinamkulam	137 (66.8)	68 (33.2)	205 (100)
Total	570 (70.0)	244 (30.0)	814 (100)

Figures in parentheses indicate percentages.

organized the first public upsurge in this locality in 1950 against the 'Kankanis' who exploited the tea plantation labourers. In the agitation, well known reformers of Kerala like 'Vishnubharathiyan', K.A. Keraleeyan, C.K. Govindan Nair and K. Kelappan participated. Evidences show that the Panchayat has a very recent history of social mobilization for common cause. 'Gramodharana Samiti' (Group for the Reformation of the Village) and several cultural centres in Thrikaippetta were involved in reformative activities. 'Gramodharana Samiti' built the Thrikaippatta-Muttil Road in 1954. Kakkavayal-Muttil Road also was constructed by the people's initiatives. It is recorded that there had been instances of popular agitations against the feudal landlordism. The march of the agricultural labourers for just wages is considered important by the local people and quoted as instances of public action and collective struggle.

Historical roots of public action in Chaliyar GP reveal indicators of public action. In 1912, the British started rubber cultivation on a major scale in the Panchayat area. Many people from Tamil Nadu and from the Palakkad district migrated to this place at this time. Subsequently, several groups of people were brought from Malappuram area to Chaliyar to work in the rubber plantations. The owner at this time was a Britisher, who resided at Malappuram town. The workers were left to the supervision of a manager called 'Maesthiri', who exploited the labourers. 'Maesthiri', appointed by the landowner, was a middleman between the landowner and the labourers. The labourers after their work had to give the manager the wages and the manager in turn would provide the daily household provisions to the families of labourers at Malappuram, from the provision store owned and managed by the manager himself. Accounts were settled yearly. When the settlements were made at the end of the year, the labourers invariably found that they had to pay balance money to the manager. This continuous exploitation infuriated the labourers and they decided to protest against the manager and the landowner who conspired against the labourers. This was the beginning of the first people's movement in the area.

Muslim Labour Union under the Muslim League was the first labour organization formed in this locality. A trade union was registered on 19 December 1952. They conducted the first rally and public meeting in the area on 20 December 1952.

The labourers, though immigrants, got involved in the social life of the local population in addition to their interventions in the labour issues and problems. They stood firmly with the tenants ('kudiyanmar') against the middlemen ('idakkudiyanmar'). Moreover, there was a natural relationship between the plantation labourers and agricultural labourers and small farmers. The former purchased the produces of the latter. The economic relationship gradually paved the way for a solid background for collective action for common purposes. There was no problem for the people, who came from different places and cultures to live together for decades and in socio-religious harmony.

This must be read with the instances of voluntary public contributions mobilized in a considerable manner for various purposes of common interest. It is reported that three acres of land was contributed to the Eranhimangad High School. One acre of land was bought and given for the Primary Health Centre by the people. In addition, five cents of land for the construction of a pond, 30 cents of land for constructing a nursery building, 10 cents of land for the Homeo Hospital were made available free of cost by the people. These are considered by the local people as shining examples of their cooperation and harmonious life that existed among the people of different religions and castes.

Ayyampuzha Panchayat has a recent history of public action. The Panchayat has a more recent history of labour insurgencies mainly in 1966, 1972 and 1975 motivated by the need to ensure rights of the labourers in the Plantation Corporation. These strikes have generated a lot of political and social mobilization in the area. Leaders of Communist Party of India (Marxist) (CPI-M) like A.K. Gopalan and E.M. Sankaran Namboothirippad visited this area in connection with the labour agitations.

The Panchayat of Kadinamkulam has villages, where intensive social service activities, aimed at empowerment of the poor and at improving the quality of life of the people were promoted during the 1960s by Trivandrum Social Service Society, a Voluntary Organisation, owned by the Catholic Diocese of Trivandrum. Fishermen families from other parts of the district were brought to create new villages of fisher folk and a new culture of development and empowerment. A culture of social and political mobilization has been active since then in the area.

It can be noted that all the Panchayats, selected for the study, are located at the margins of the State of Kerala. Meppadi Grama Panchayat and Chaliyar Grama Panchayat are on the northeastern borders, Ayyampuzha Grama Panchayat is at the brink of the eastern border and Kadinamkulam Grama Panchayat is on the southwestern border of the State.

A study on the margins is relevant in Kerala context as the geographical coverage of the borders at the east and west is very large. It will be wrong to make a general statement only by looking at the mainstream landscape, as it very often happens. When it is almost universally believed that Kerala has a dense presence of social capital emerging from its history of public action, this article makes an inquiry as to whether the same is really sure of the marginal villages.

Socio-economic Profile of Respondents

The respondents' socio-economic status was very low. The respondents of the study belong to the rural background, since this is a study of citizens in the remote border villages, that is, villages on the margins of Kerala. Their social and economic situation is lower than the Kerala standard, especially in education, employment, income and possession of household facilities. The economic status of the respondents has, apparently, direct relationship with their low level of education, irregular and low profile occupation, very low income and the area of land owned by them. At the margins of Kerala, communities of people, whether they are agricultural wage labourers, small farmers, small artisans, or fish workers, live in poverty, struggling to make both ends meet. It is against these questions that we are studying social capital in the selected villages and institutions existing in these villages.

The study revealed that 30 per cent of the local people had association with a variety of CSOs at the grassroots level.* Association with more CSOs indicates a more vibrant civil society. Among those who were associates in any of the CSOs, vast majority (88.1%) had their involvement in only one organization, 10.2 per cent had it in 2 organisations, 0.4 per cent had it in three organisations, 0.8 per cent had it in four organisations and 0.4 per cent had it in five organisations.

Self Help Groups (SHGs) are the most popular type of CSOs, in which largest single group of the respondents (14.3%) were involved.

Further enquiries were made to those, who had some kind of association with one or many of the CSOs in their localities, because they were in a better position to inform about the functioning and dynamics of the CSOs.

As conceptualized earlier, social capital refers to membership in/association with civil society organisations, trust built up in and through the CSOs, the density of networks of CSOs, shared norms, sustainable and productive relationships and civic consciousness.

Membership in/Association with Civil Society Organisations

Only 30 per cent of the respondents had membership in/association with any of the local Civil Society Organisations (CSOs) in the sample

Panchayats. Among those who were members/associates in any of the CSOs, vast majority (88.1%) had membership in only one organization. SHGs were found to be the most preferred type of local institutions in which majority took membership. SHGs had a short life span. Though many of them were affiliated or connected mutually or to higher tiers, these had a very feeble and short life span.

Trust

Majority of those who were members/associates in the village level CSOs (53.3%) reported that they trusted their leaders very much. However, only 38.5 per cent reported that the leaders of their CSOs very often resolved the conflicts in the CSOs. The majority was not able to resolve the conflicts. Majority (50.8%) shared that their organisations very rarely took up collective activities for common purpose. Only 24.7 per cent of those who responded said that mutual trust among the members/associates of their organisations had been to a great extent instrumental for taking up and promoting collective activities in their operational areas. Majority did not feel so. Only 20.6 per cent of those who responded felt that the collective activities were to a great extent successful due to the mutual trust built up among the members. The majority again did not think it this way. Only 19.3 per cent held that their participation was satisfactory. For others, their participation in their organizational activities was lukewarm. At the same time, majority (77%) said that their organisations very rarely took initiatives for activities for supporting the poor and needy in their villages. Like wise, majority (77.9%) said that they very rarely participated in voluntary action conducted by their CSOs in the village to support the poor. Only 39.8 per cent said that their organization always took decisions by majority. The majority did not feel so. 34.8 per cent reported that their organisations very rarely took unanimous decisions. The above indicators and evidences clearly show that the trust created by rural remote CSOs was low.

Networks

The density, interactions and dynamics of the CSOs were assessed in terms of total number of CSOs in the study areas, longevity of the CSOs, number of members in the CSOs, frequency of General Body and Executive Body meetings of these organisations, time spent for General Body and Executive Committee meetings and the status of affiliation, networking and federation of the CSOs. The number of organisations alone does not matter much.

Total number of CSOs surveyed in the 16 Grama Sabha constituencies was 215, distributed among the four Village Panchayats. This means that only 13 or 14 CSOs were found functioning in each Grama Sabha constituency, on an average. Majority of the local CSOs (57.3%) had a very short life history of less than three years. Majority among them is less than one year or just one year old. Only 7.4 per cent of the organisations had a longer history of more than 15 years.

It is to be noted that majority (61.9%) of the CSOs in the study areas had a membership of below 20 persons. Local CSOs in which the largest section of people had membership/ association were Self Help Groups (SHGs). This has to be read with the understanding that these organisations of 20 members were initiated as a convenient mechanism to avail of the benefits of government and non-government schemes. There were only 10.7 per cent of CSOs, which had more than 100 members in their admission roll.

The General Body of majority of the local CSOs (74.4%) met once a week. Whereas more frequency indicates denser and livelier interactions, in our study more frequent interactions took place in SHGs only, which had, in practice, a very small scope of functioning in the rural context of Kerala.

The Executive Committee (EC) meetings of majority of the CSOs (149- 69.3%) were held once a week. This may appear to be another indicator of dense activities. However, the CSOs which convene and conduct EC meetings most frequently are SHGs which have a comparatively short life span.

Only 29.3 per cent CSOs took two hours for conducting their EC meetings. It is to be noted that 50.2 per cent of the CSOs took less than two hours for their general body meetings and that only 17.3 per cent took more than two hours. Majority (82.4%) of the CSOs took just an hour or less for their EC meetings. Shorter duration of meetings points to the lack of interest of members, lack of meaningful subjects for discussion, lack of unity among members, lack of vision for the organization or lack of trust among them. In any case, it is an indicator for low quality of social capital.

Status of Affiliation, Networking and Federation

It was noted that the vast majority of the local CSOs (91.1%) was affiliated/networked/federated to like-minded organisations or Panchayati Raj Institutions. These are, again, SHGs affiliated in connection with some welfare schemes. Very often, this networking is not voluntary but directed by the Gram Panchayats or Block Offices which were managing the development funds through SHGs. The quality of this networking may not be of sustainable nature due to its vested interest.

Shared Norms

It was found that the local CSOs very rarely made norms other than those prescribed in the byelaws. However, it was noted that, once made, the largest section always abided by such norms (26.6%). The data also showed that the majority did not answer to this question, may be, due to their lack of active involvement in the CSOs.

Sustainable and Productive Relationships

Majority (54.7%) reported that CSOs helped the associates to a great extent in building up sustainable and productive relationship among the members/associates. However, only 26.2 per cent said that the membership in CSOs and the relationships fostered in the CSOs helped them in enhancing their economic status to some extent. Similarly, only 33.2 per cent reported that the membership in CSOs and the relationships fostered in the CSOs helped them to a great extent in enhancing their awareness level in civic rights and duties. Only 33.6 per cent held that the membership in CSOs helped them in enhancing their skills in communication and leadership to a great extent. Further, the membership in/association with CSOs helped only 33.2 per cent of the associates to deepen their relationship with the members, which helped them to a greater extent to work together in other sectors and circumstances. 45.5 per cent held that the mutual trust built up in and through the organization led them to life-long relationships to a greater extent. For 49.6 per cent of the associates, mutual trust and understanding fostered in the organization among the members/associates would deepen the process of democratization within the CSOs. The majority (52.9%) felt that the relationship and mutual trust existing among the family members of the associates/members of CSOs was good. Majority of the total respondents (50.8%) said that they always took part in the special functions like marriages and funerals in the families of other members of CSOs. 41.8 per cent of the total respondents who had membership in/association with any of the CSOs held that the participation of their CSOs in the development of the village was good. The results show that the CSOs sometimes promoted and sometimes did not promote the mutual relationship among the members of the CSOs.

Civic Consciousness

82.4 per cent of the surveyed local organisations did not discuss political issues in their meetings. This may be due to the prevalent view among the rural communities that discussing politics would lead to unhealthy partisan politics in the CSOs' dynamics. At the same time, 57 per cent of CSOs took up local issues for discussion and action. 84.4 per cent said that their CSOs conducted periodical elections to elect their office bearers. For 68 per cent of respondents, the elections in their organisations were competitive and serious. However, 57.4 per cent of the associates of CSOs did not read newspapers daily.

The findings taken together revealed that the stock of social capital was not explicitly or strongly present in the selected villages. Though there are certain indications of social capital emerging as a mild presence, there is no evidence to show that there is substantial stock of social capital so as to influence the process of sustainable development in democratic ambience.

Dominant Factors of Social Capital

In order to confirm the importance of the underlying factors or forces among a number of interdependent variables or components of social capital in the study areas, the tool of factor analysis was used. A factor is understood here as an underlying dimension of several related variables. Though quantitative data regarding quantity and density of networks of CSOs were collected, they were not included in the factor analysis.

It was found, as seen in Table 5.2, that the combination of trust and civic consciousness, as the first and therefore the most dominant combination contributing to the quality of social capital. The second factor is sustainable and productive relationships. The third factor is found to be shared norms.

Table-5.2
Rotated Component Matrix [(a)] for Social Capital (Total)

Variables of Social Capital	*Components* 1	2	3
Trust	.891	-.103	.032
Norms	.047	.026	.999
Sustainable and Productive Relationships	.081	.971	.025
Civic Consciousness	.784	.330	.044

Extraction Method: Principal Component Analysis.
Rotation Method: Varimax with Kaiser and Normalization.

(a) Rotation converged in 4 iterations.

Correlation Between Social Capital and Selected Variables

Correlation analysis was used to understand the extent to which social capital and selected demographic and socio-economic variables such as age, education in school years, family ownership of land, monthly income level of the family and economic status (index) were related in the study areas.

Table 5.3 gives the results of correlation analysis. The column labeled *Pearson's r* is looking at each variable, one at a time, and stating how strongly it is related to social capital. The column labeled as *Partial correlation coefficient* is reporting the results of a multiple correlation analysis. It again looks at the influence of each independent variable, but this time the effects of the other independent variables have been removed. Accordingly, economic status (–.161) has the strongest inverse influence on social capital, meaning that when economic status increases, social capital decreases. But, when the effect of economic status on social capital is considered after removing the effects of other independent variables, the result varied to a certain extent, noting that it has a very low inverse (–.104) influence on social capital. In the partial correlation analysis, age (–.191) has emerged as having the strongest inverse relation to social capital. When the age of the respondents increased, their contribution towards social capital formation decreased. Education in school years (–.149) has the next strongest inverse influence on social capital. It is also noted that all the selected variables together account for only 7.6 per cent of social capital in the study areas.

Table–5.3
Coefficients of Correlation Between Social Capital and Selected Socio-economic Variables

Selected Socio-economic Variables	*Correlations*		
	Pearson's r	*Partial Correlation Coefficient*	
Age	-.135	-.191	
Education in school years	-.121	-.149	
Family ownership of land in cents	-.101	.009	
Monthly income level of the family	-.032	.128	R = .276
Economic status (index)	-.161	-.104	R Square = .076

Association Between Social Capital and Selected Variables

The study looks into the association between social capital and the selected socio-economic and demographic variables. Analysis using Likelihood Ratio Chi-Square is done to examine the association between social capital and variables such as religion, caste, age group, sex, education, occupation and membership in political parties. The Association between social capital and other variables such as land ownership, monthly income and economic status is examined by analysis using Linear-by-Linear Association Chi-Square.

Table 5.4 below provides the Chi-Square statistics for social capital and selected socio-economic variables. As per the table, relation between social capital and religion, caste, age group is found to be significant. Sex, education in school years, occupation, membership in political parties, land ownership, monthly income and economic status indicate no significant relation with the social capital.

Inferences from the Statistical Analysis

It was noted, as per the factor analysis, that in the study area, mutual trust and civic consciousness taken together formed the first and most important factor of social capital. This finding points to the need for trust building and enhancement of civic consciousness among the citizens of a particular locality in order to generate

Table-5.4
Association Between Social Capital and Selected Socio-economic Variables

Selected Variables	*Likelihood Ratio/ Linear by Linear Association*	*df*	*Asym.Sig. (2 sided)*
Religion	21.678 [a]	8	0.006
Caste	106.101 [a]	12	0.000
Age Group	4.779 [b]	1	0.029
Sex	4.572 [a]	4	0.334
Education in School Years	37.412 [a]	36	0.404
Occupation	14.593 [a]	16	0.555
Political Party Membership	5.757 [a]	4	0.218
Land Ownership	0.112 [b]	1	0.738
Monthly Income	0.051 [b]	1	0.821
Economic Status	3.856 [b]	1	0.40

(a) Likelihood Ratio; *(b)* Linear by Linear Association.

sustainable and meaningful type of social capital. Putnamian thesis is once again confirmed that social capital takes roots from a civic culture and tradition. Trust and civic culture together is behind a strong presence of social capital. Civic culture is again related to people's involvement in public action, participation in social organisations, habit of news paper reading , club-going, etc.

This fact leads us to link the finding with Maslow's hierarchy of needs. Only in an economically comfortable society, civic action will flourish except in abnormal situations of extremism, revolution and terrorism. The question whether social capital originates from economic progress and it leads to economic progress remains still unresolved. But, certainly, according to this inquiry, social capital originates from civic-ness and trust. Such social capital is feeble in the remote villages of Kerala.

It is also noted that there is a significant correlation between social capital and age. The partial correlation coefficient for social capital and age (-.191) indicates a weak inverse relationship between the variables. After age, education in school years (-.149) has an inverse relationship with social capital. It has to be noted that younger generation has longer school years and civic-ness goes along with education and not with economic progress. Young people also have more time to spend on common and public action. The power of youth and their associations emerge again as the source of qualitative change and progress. History has proved this fact in many instances where the revolutionaries or world leaders in their youthfulness moved 'mountains' of incivility, and that always either in civic tradition or organizational context.

As per the Chi-Square statistics for social capital and selected socio-economic variables, association between social capital and religion, caste, age group is found to be significant. Sex, education in school years, occupation, membership in political parties, land ownership, monthly income and economic status indicate no significant association with the social capital. This discovery does not create surprise, since, in Indian context caste and religion are the two very strong pillars which create values and cleavages among the members. They create manifold spaces and opportunities for their followers and members to relate and network for common good.

Concluding Observations

As mentioned earlier in view of this analysis, mostly younger adults are more interested in associating with local civil society organisations. However, the CSOs in the study areas are not active and vibrant enough to reflect this youthfulness. The youth may have gone to the CSOs not out of enthusiasm to involve in collective activities for common good, nor out of their civic consciousness, but because they had no other avenue to spend time or out of their eagerness to avail financial benefits from welfare schemes. Majority of the rural youth are unemployed or underemployed in Kerala and are affected by the problems emerging from unemployment. They may have gone to the organisations with this frustration and negative attitude and so they could not positively contribute much to the common good through the CSOs. Though there are youth clubs and arts and sports clubs even in rural areas, they are not able to create any impact on the rural life. A positive conscious citizenry can make the CSOs active, vibrant, and useful instruments for creating solid social capital. The vicious circle is very much visible in the study areas.

It was also seen that less educated or illiterate people associated more with local institutions. SHGs are found to be the most preferred CSOs in these remote rural pockets. The real focus of the functioning of the SHGs is related to economic benefits, though there are lofty ideals for the formation of SHGs. Moreover, SHGs are promoted very often in connection with some economic programmes sponsored by the Governments or in connection with some economic benefits designed by the Non-Governmental Organisations (NGOs). In any case, the motive is economic benefit for the poorest of the poor, the illiterate and least educated, who are generally associated more than the rich with local CSOs in the remote villages of Kerala. This explains the low quality of social capital in the marginal villages of Kerala.

Finally, the civic-ness and the consequent social capital are not uniformly high in Kerala. It varies in mainstream and marginal locations as it happens in the case of socio-economic development. The study again warns us against conceiving social and economic development as one reality but prompts us to look at them distinctly, as it happened in Kerala model of development.

REFERENCES

Coleman, S. James (1990): *Foundations of Social Theory*, Cambridge, Harward University Press.

Coleman, S. James (2000): 'Social Capital in the Creation of Human Capital', in Partha Dasgupta and Ismail Seregeldin (eds.) *Social Capital: A Multifaceted Perspective*, The World Bank, Washington D.C., pp. 13-39. The article first appeared in *The American Journal of Sociology*, 94: Supplement, 1988, pp. S95-S120.

Putnam, D. Robert (1993): *Making Democracy Work: Civic Traditions in Modern Italy*, Princeton University Press, Princeton, New Jersey.

Putnam, D. Robert (2000): *Bowling Alone: The Collapse and Revival of American Community*, Simon and Schuster, New York.

Tandon, Rajesh (2001): 'Civil society in India: An Exercise in Mapping', *Innovations in Civil Society*, Vol. 1, No. 1, July, pp. 2-10.

Tandon, Rajesh (2002): 'Participation, Civil Society and Governance', *Key Note Paper Presented at the National Assembly of Caritas India at New Delhi on October 8.*

6

Total Sanitation Campaign and *Nirmal Gram Puraskar:* An Overview of Four Indian States

K. GIREESAN AND JOS CHATHUKULAM

Background

Mahatma Gandhi included the issue of sanitation as a major component of his constructive programme formulated for attaining independence. Promotion of sanitation was very close to his heart and he advocated that 'Cleanliness is next to godliness'. Gandhiji spoke and wrote extensively on topics related to sanitation, hygiene and environment. Through his articles, essays and letters, Gandhiji offered detailed comments on cleanliness and good habits, and its relationship with good health. He squarely blamed the unclean and unhygienic conditions for the emergence of communicable diseases in the country. Many times, he appealed to educated Indians to become missionaries in hygiene and sanitation. Perhaps he is the greatest leader of any country who realised the significance of sanitation and hygiene in the overall development of a nation. The comments of that great visionary, "If we do not keep our backyards clean, our swaraj will have a foul stench", remains poignantly relevant even now.

However, the sanitation coverage in rural areas of India remained very low in the early 80's. It is estimated that about three crore persons in rural areas suffer from sanitation-related diseases. An annual loss of 18 crore man-days and Rs. 1200 crores to the economy is estimated to sanitation related diseases alone.[1] According to a baseline survey on water and sanitation in 1997, only 20 per cent households reported having private latrines and most people defecate in open space in most of the states.[2] Census reports 2001 indicates that the overall sanitation coverage in India is 37 per cent and the sanitation coverage in the rural areas is further less, i.e., 22 per cent only. While analysing the sanitation coverage in South Asia, India (22%) lags far behind most of the neighbouring countries like Srilanka (80%), Bhutan (70%), Bangladesh (44%), Maldives (41%) and Myanmar (39%).[3]

Government of India launched the first-ever structured programme for promoting rural sanitation in 1986 – Central Rural Sanitation Programme (CRSP). In 1999, CRSP was restructured from allocation mode to a demand driven and community based programme as Total Sanitation Campaign (TSC). From 2003, an award (Nirmal Gram Puraskar) has been instituted by the Ministry of Rural Development, Government of India to recognise the role of PRIs and motivate them in the sanitation movement across the country.

Total Sanitation Campaign

TSC is the most comprehensive programme on rural sanitation ever launched in the country, which involves the Central Government, State Government, Civil Society Organisations and Community as Partners. Introduction of TSC has resulted in generating a major shift in the approach and strategies adopted in the implementation of conventional sanitation programmes. The campaign provided space for each district to submit its proposal, keeping in view the specific sanitation situation prevailing in its area of jurisdiction. In addition, TSC provided ample scope for meeting the local-specific needs and demands during the operationalisation of the campaign. Its thrust on 'demand driven approach' and emphasis on Information, Education and Communication (IEC) activities to increase awareness among the population regarding health and hygiene, good sanitation practices, etc. with beneficiary participation has been a paradigm shift from the 'allocation based' sanitation programmes. Various components of TSC include Individual Household Latrine (IHHL), School Sanitation and Hygiene Education (SSHE), Anganawadi Sanitation, Community Sanitary Complex (CSC) and Alternate delivery mechanisms like Rural Sanitary Marts/Production Centres (RSM/PC).

TSC is implemented in a decentralised mode and the role and involvement of Panchayati Raj Institutions (PRI) is very prominent. PRIs have a major say in all the phases during the operationalisation of the programme like planning, implementation and monitoring, with major thrust on awareness building and social mobilisation of all segments of the society. In addition, this has also provided lot of scope for people-centred and community-led initiatives, local interventions, and adoption of a technology according to customer preferences. In general, TSC resulted in a holistic and integrated approach to sanitation programmes.

Civil Society Organisations like Non-Governmental Organisations (NGO) and Community Based Organisations (CBO) also play an important role in awareness generation, advocacy and educative campaigns to spread the message of 'Total sanitation' in the rural areas. However, the involvement of civil society organisations depends upon their acceptability, approach, credibility, professionalism, willingness and many other aspects.

Nirmal Gram Puraskar

Recognising the role of PRIs and towards motivating them for promoting rural sanitation, an incentive scheme called Nirmal Gram Puraskar (NGP) was initiated on 2 October, 2003. The concept of NGP is to reward those GPs, blocks and districts that have achieved full sanitation coverage. It is an award instituted by the Department of Drinking Water Supply (DDWS) in the Ministry of Rural Development (MoRD), Government of India (GOI) under TSC for bringing dignity and quality in life.

The cash incentive based on population criteria at the time of inception of NGP is given below.

Table-6.1
NGP—Incentive Pattern

	GP		*Block*		*District*	
Population Crite·'a	*Upto 5,000*	*5,001 and Above*	*Up to 50,000*	*50,001 and Above*	*Upto 10 Lakhs*	*Above 10 Lakhs*
Cash incentive (Rs. in lakhs)	2.0	4.0	10.0	20.0	30.0	50.0

Source: Website of Department of Drinking Water Supply, MoRD, GOI.

The Union Ministry of Rural Development has changed the criteria for awarding NGP to GPs at the conference of State Ministers for drinking water and sanitation. This was borne out of the arguments that the states where the GPs have less population were receiving more money when compared to the States with larger population in each GP. The slab in respect of the GP was revised based on classification of population and amount of award money as given in Table 6.2.

Table-6.2
NGP—Revised Incentive Pattern*

	GP				
Population Criteria	*Less than 1,000*	*1,000 to 1999*	*2,000 to 4999*	*5,000 to 9999*	*10,000 and above*
Cash incentive (Rs. in lakhs)	0.5	1.0	2.0	4.0	5.0

Source: Website of DDWS, MoRD, GOI.

*Note:** The criteria for Block and District remained the same as in Table 6.1.

The cash incentive for PRIs can be utilised for improving and maintaining the sanitation facilities in their respective areas, with more focus on solid and liquid waste management and maintenance of the sanitation standards. It is expected that such incentives will give a positive boost to the sanitation drive across the country and will play a major role in making India *open defecation free* by 2012.

Four aspects are considered for scrutiny while selecting the PRIs for NGP. They are:

- *(a)* All households should have access to toilets with full use. There is no practice of open defecation and no place for open defecation in the respective PRI;
- *(b)* All schools should have sanitation facilities, which are also put to use. All co-educational schools must have separate toilets for boys and girls;
- *(c)* All Anganawadis should have access to sanitation facilities; and
- *(d)* General cleanliness is prevailing in the village.

For the first award, applications from 481 PRIs from 10 states were received. Out of which, 360 applications were forwarded to District Level Monitoring (DLM) agencies for verification of the claims. Based on the reports, 38 GPs were selected for the award by NGP Committee headed by the Secretary, DDWS, MoRD, GOI. The first award ceremony of NGP was held on February 24, 2005, in which the President of India gave away the awards to the Presidents/Pradhans of PRIs.

A close look at the trend of NGP applications awarded since its inception will bring out some interesting features.

Table–6.3
NGP – Number of Awardees Year-wise

	No. of GPs Awarded in		
State	*Year 2005*	*Year 2006*	*Year 2007*
Andhra Pradesh	–	10	143
Arunachal Pradesh	–	–	2
Assam	–	1	3
Bihar	–	4	40
Chhattisgarh	–	12	90
Gujarat	1	4	576
Haryana	–	–	60
Himachal Pradesh	–	–	22
Jharkhand	–	–	12
Karnataka	–	–	121
Kerala	1	6	220
Madhya Pradesh	–	1	190
Maharashtra	13	380	1974
Mizoram	–	–	3
Orissa	–	8	33
Rajasthan	–	–	23
Sikkim	–	–	27
Tamil Nadu	12	119	296
Tripura	1	36	46
Uttar Pradesh	–	40	488
Uttaranchal/Uttarakhand	–	13	109
West Bengal	10	126	468
Total	**38**	**760**	**4946**

Source: Website of DDWS, MoRD, GOI.

NGP can be used as a 'proxy variable' to ascertain the progress of TSC implementation in different States, though no direct relation could be yet established. It is observed that the achievement in terms of NGP awardees in each State match with the corresponding progress it has made during TSC. From Table 6.3, we can see that the States like Gujarat, Kerala, Maharashtra, Tamil Nadu, Uttar Pradesh and West Bengal have made significant achievement over the period. And the States like Andhra Pradesh, Haryana, Karnataka and Tripura have achieved moderate progress. However, the States like Bihar, Chhattisgrah, Jharkhand, Madhya Pradesh, Orissa and Rajasthan could not make the desired progress. We can see that Kerala and Uttar Pradesh had a giant leap in terms of number of NGP awardees over the period, whereas a steady progression could be seen in the case of Tamil Nadu and West Bengal. In this context, one may see a correlation between the progress made by each State in the field of TSC and the number of NGP awardees in each passing year.

Even among the States with high achievement, distribution of progress in the districts has not been even, which depends upon several factors. Table 6.3 also indicates the need for classification of the States based on their performance into categories like Low, Medium and High with necessary policy level interventions and strategies for each category separately. It is seen that among the North-Eastern States, only Tripura could perform relatively better. A separate approach and strategy is needed in those states to improve the sanitation situation.

There is an increasing urge for submitting the applications for NGP by the PRIs by each year. It is also observed that the number of awardees in each state has been on the rise in the subsequent years. This shows that initiation of NGP acts like a real incentive to the PRIs, thereby giving a positive boost to the sanitation drive across the country.

Objective

The broad objective of this chapter is to highlight the growing importance and significance of Nirmal Gram Puraskar during the Total Sanitation Campaign and to portray the reflections gathered during the field visits through four states—West Bengal, Uttar Pradesh, Tamil Nadu and Kerala. Efforts were made to study the significant aspects of the scheme execution in different States and to analyse them from a close range. The reflections have been gathered during the discussions with the elected members of PRIs, field level officials involved with the scheme execution, representatives of CBOs functioning in the area and a cross-section of the society. They were gathered from the extensive field visits made by the DLM team through these States for the verification of claims by the PRIs for the award during the last three years.

Methodology

Methodology adopted during the NGP evaluation by our team has been indicated in this section and the same has been incorporated for the analysis of this chapter as well. For verification of claim submitted by PRIs, a detailed questionnaire was provided by the DDWS, MoRD, GOI to the verification agencies. It aims at assessing the overall sanitation and hygiene situation in the area by commenting on the sanitation situation in the sample households as per the population of PRIs and its use by the population, method of disposal of child faeces, sanitation conditions prevalent in the schools and *anganawadis* in the village area, hygiene education provided to students and children, verification of open defecation menace in the traditional places, general cleanliness in the village, method of waste disposal, and awareness among the sample population regarding hygiene and clean environment.

A strategic approach to the evaluation exercise was adopted by our team. Understanding the significance and considering the seriousness of the exercise, senior members from our organisation were assigned with the task. This helped in many ways, as the team member has to interact with a wide range of persons like members of the three-tier PRIs, senior district/block officials, political party leaders, media persons and even illiterate villagers. In addition, this gave a clear message to the hosts as to the seriousness of the evaluation exercise undertaken. In areas where the language of communication was the major issue, necessary support was obtained from the CBOs/NGOs and post-graduate students from Universities and Colleges. But no sub-contracting of the assignment was done.

The evaluation exercise was carried out keeping its motivational aspect in view. During the field visits, every effort was made to make a small address to the children, students and the villagers highlighting the significance of TSC and NGP. In all the areas, 'Bastis' (Colonies) of marginalised sections like SC/STs were invariably visited to confirm the veracity of the claim.

During the presentations, NGP has been presented as the 'most prestigious award' presented by the President of India to a GP. During the interactions with the community and elected members, it is mentioned that the award is presented to the 'whole village' and the President of GP would be representing the village to receive the same.

During the interactions with the elected members and officials of the PRIs, the style of communication and body language of an evaluator was never assumed by the team members. Instead, they were asked to present their claim for the award by narrating the activities carried out by them. In this regard, our view is that it is better for an evaluator to assume the features, vigour and enthusiasm of a TSC activist, in addition to a pro-active body language. Each evaluator should internalise the philosophy, processes and the dynamics of TSC and the politico-administrative environmental settings. After the field visits, the team members used to conduct a debriefing session at the Panchayat also. Appreciation of the significant efforts taken up, suggestions for overcoming the shortfalls during the execution and long term perspective for addressing the issues of sustainability are conveyed through the session. Number of TSC district officials and UNICEF consultants accompanied the team members during the field visits commented that they gained lot of insights by exchange of experiences and information with our team members.[4]

In some places, press conferences were organised, which provided occasions to sensitise the media about NGP. During such occasions, media persons posed several questions to the evaluation team as well, which helped to fine tune the exercise in many ways. In brief, NGP evaluation was used by the team as an exercise for strengthening the TSC activities taken up in different states. In some parts, the evaluation exercise assumed the mode of a 'social audit' or even 'Jan Sunwayi' by the team members. All our exercises in the NGP evaluation could succeed to generate enormous data from different levels without any difficulties. In short, the methodology we applied for NGP evaluation worked out to be the methodology for this chapter also.

Study Area

NGP evaluation was undertaken by the team in several PRIs from the four states. Number of GPs visited in each State during the period 2004 - 07 is indicated in the following table.

Table-6.4
PRIs Visited for NGP Evaluation

Name of the State	*No. of PRIs Visited by CRM Team*
West Bengal	337
Uttar Pradesh	305
Tamil Nadu	113
Kerala	11
Total	**766**

Source: NGP Records of CRM.

Reflections from Different States in India

In this section, reflections gathered from the four states, in connection with the verification of claims for the award (Nirmal Gram Puraskar), have been presented.

(a) West Bengal

Some of the reflections gathered from the field visits through five districts of West Bengal have been mentioned in the following paragraphs.

Field visits and interactions with the party functionaries at different levels revealed that TSC has been in the political agenda of all major political parties at the local level.[5] Discussions with the party functionaries at the local level indicated that this resulted in minimising corruption in the selection of beneficiaries and provision of scheme benefits to deserving persons. The local leaders are well aware of the guidelines, principles and programmes of the TSC. It is known that progress of the scheme implementation by the PRIs is one of the major agendas of discussion during the meetings of the parties. TSC has been programatised in the agenda of all political parties at the local levels. Interactions with some of the officials in charge of the scheme implementation indicated that 'Politicising

TSC' has benefited by cutting down the expenses in Information, Education and Communication (IEC) activities.[6] Discussions with some of the elected members revealed that even minor punishments were given to some persons for violating the norms/instructions about hygiene and sanitation with the concurrence of party.[7] And some kind of consensus has been noted among all the political parties while dealing with sanitation programmes.[8]

Interactions with number of officials in-charge of the programme indicated that they have given their option to the TSC assignment, fully aware of it as a 'hard option'. A genuine spirit towards the programme has been noted in many of them. Presence of a healthy competition among the officials of different districts has also been observed during the visits. It is seen that wide use of Participatory Rural Appraisal (PRA) techniques during the programme execution has resulted in making them more people-friendly also. Discussions with them indicated that they employed a liberal approach towards the target group of beneficiaries, in providing the scheme benefits. And the continuous rule of 30 years of Left Front Government in the State has resulted in tuning the officials to the left ideology, agenda and programmes. As a result in certain cases, the local bureaucracy assumes the role of a 'Corrective force' in the administration of the scheme in 'Party villages', of course within the permissible limits set by the political party.[9] In addition, a close and constant interface has been noted between the officials and local party functionaries during the scheme execution, mainly due to 'Politicising TSC'. A kind of synergy resulting in flow of information from the offices to the party circles and *vice versa* also has been observed. We came across ample examples of officials taking support of party functionaries in the scheme implementation in some difficult zones/pockets/areas. All these aspects seemingly resulted in the emergence of a committed bureaucracy during the scheme execution in the State. This assessment was based on the interactions with the officials of the State during the visits on three consecutive years.

Number of organisations like Ramakrishna Mission, *Siksha Niketan, Atma Sakthi Sangh, Tubgram Grrammyak Unnayan Samity, Kshithu Kanu Gram Unnayan Samithi*, etc. are playing an important role in the TSC by actively involving in IEC activities, managing Rural Sanitary Marts (RSM) and in various other capacities. It is significant to note that many of them are nurtured and promoted by the left front. A recent development in the state is that with the permission of the political parties, local leaders from different class and mass organisations have floated several NGOs and are actively functioning in the sanitation sector.[10] However, it is noted that most of them are functioning at Block and GP levels only.

It is noted that RSMs function as the hub of sanitation activities at the field level. Most of the RSMs are managed by the CBOs and NGOs. The activities of RSM in the state is undergoing a sea change from construction of sanitary toilets to construction of hollow bricks and other construction materials, low cost housing, water quality testing, purification of water, etc.

A large segment of the schools (especially primary schools) in the rural areas have very poor infrastructure facilities. The status of school toilets in some of the areas visited has been at low ebb. During the field visits, it is observed that the condition of rural pans in many houses has been pitiable. The possibility of deterioration of a rural pan over a period of time is quite high when compared to a ceramic pan. It is viewed that adoption of rural pans in the state has been driven more by ideological moorings than by a pragmatic approach. There is a need for a revisit to the ideologically loaded position of using only rural pans. Absence of appropriate research on the technology and design aspects concerning production of pans and construction of sanitary facilities has been noted in the State.

There is a high degree of exhaustion of ideas and programmes noted among the campaign managers in some of the Districts.[11] It may be because of the inability to sustain the campaign for such a long period. Every effort be made to achieve the targets at the earliest and to bring in diverse programmes and activities towards achieving 'total sanitation.'

A Critic of Midnapore Model

Adoption of 'Midnapore model' played a prime role in achieving the targets of sanitation in many parts of West Bengal. The strategic approach in that model is to provide a small incentive to the poor to construct a low cost sanitation structure and to cultivate a habit of using toilets. It used to be at par with his/her living conditions. It visualises that when the socio-economic status of the poor goes up, there is a natural graduation to the sanitary facility constructed in his/her home as well. It goes without saying that when there is a natural progression to the living conditions of the poor, a corresponding improvement will be made in the sanitary facilities as well, without any further support from the state. However, the field visits through different parts of the state revealed that about 10 per cent of the population who adopted low cost toilets could not achieve the expected economic growth or their growth remained stagnant or deteriorated further. This resulted in the inability to improve the sanitary facilities as expected in the 'model'. As the durability of low cost type sanitary facilities have been deteriorated over a period, they started feeling discomfort, which resulted in leading to open defecation again.[12]

A certain degree of manifestation of self-complacency over what has been achieved earlier has been largely visible among the campaign managers in *Purba Medinipur* and *Paschim Medinipur* Districts. In addition, this has also resulted in a large degree of intolerance towards criticism.[13] Though this cannot be construed as the failure of 'Midnapore model', but points to the need for some changes to be adopted in the strategic approach. It is further suggested that a serious review of 'Midnapore Model' by an external agency need to be taken up as most of the functionaries in charge of the movement have a large degree of sentimental attachment with it and unlikely to make an objective assessment.

(b) Uttar Pradesh

Some of the reflections gathered from the field visits through 21 districts of Uttar Pradesh have been mentioned below.

Interactions with the campaign managers and officials at different levels indicated that the direction of thrust of campaign in the State is given more towards schools than households. This is a strategy to penetrate to the family members (with several illiterate persons) by taking the support of children, as habit formation among them is quite easier. This strategy has been adopted as children can influence other family members, especially the aged people to wean away from open defecation.

During the field verifications, better performance in achieving the targets of TSC has been noted in some GPs where both the Pradhan and the Secretary are women.[14] Interactions with them revealed that provision of sanitation facilities being one of the prime needs of women, they are able to communicate the message of sanitation to the village population especially among women, and work together comfortably.

During the field visits through the villages of UP, it is noted that two types of social exclusion generally prevalent in certain areas have come down owing to TSC interventions. 'Intra-village' type of social exclusion is practised against certain households who practise 'manual scavenging' by different communities within the village. 'Inter-village' type of social exclusion is practised with a village where the concentration of such households who practise 'manual scavenging' is more by the nearby villages. It is observed that such issues of social exclusion could be tackled successfully up to a certain extent during the implementation of TSC in the State.[15] With the introduction of sanitary toilets, manual scavengers have moved to alternate avenues like farming, rearing non-milch animals, cleaning the streets, etc. It is felt that construction of toilets can be used as a powerful tool for inclusion of the excluded communities which leads to an 'all-inclusive village life.'

Dalit mobilisation and assertion in the villages of UP has successfully resulted in generating the demand for sanitation facilities by the marginalised sections of the society during the campaign. Demand for sanitation facilities exerted on the village panchayats have resulted in enabling distributive justice to them as both numerical strength and political equations favours them. It is observed that this has resulted in improving the sanitation conditions of the households in SC/ST colonies.

During the field verifications through some of the villages, it is noted that enabling environment in the area like the active role of number of ex-servicemen has been very much visible during the scheme execution. It is observed that active participation of several former soldiers in the village has given impetus to the implementation of scheme.[16] Even in many remote villages, where no support or intervention from the Block/District officials are available due to terror leashed by the dacoits, the construction activities have progressed well.[17]

During the campaign, number of consultants with specialisation in civil engineering, mass communication, social engineering, etc.

were engaged at the State/Division/District levels. A rapid appraisal of the campaign through different parts of the State indicated that this has resulted in a positive impact on its execution.

During the field verifications, it is observed that several nominations of GPs with even less than 50 per cent of sanitation coverage at the households have been forwarded for the award. These nominations may have been forwarded in the pretext that the targets would be achieved before the evaluation.

Interactions with the elected members, party activists and officials indicated that TSC has been given a prominent role at the State level meetings by the Chief Minister. However, this has not been in the agenda of political parties at the local level. However, of late the young leadership in the villages have started taking more interest in TSC, when compared to the traditional leadership.

During the field visits, it is observed that separate toilets for boys and girls have been made at the schools. However, in some places, it is seen that the construction was not made properly assimilating the philosophy behind this. It is observed that there is only one entrance to the toilet complex so constructed, though there are separate toilets available for boys and girls.[18]

It is observed that most of the efforts made during the campaign by the campaign managers have been more Pradhan-centric or Pradhan-Pati-centric. Hardly any effort was made to involve members of the GP in the planning and execution of the activities. It is also observed that most of the elected members of GPs were not sensitised during the campaign.

It is noted that provision of TSC assistance is not based on a rationalistic formula, but based on the demand from the Pradhan, his/her initiative in the campaign, interest shown by the GP Secretary, proximity to National Highway, demonstrative effect, personal preferences of TSC staff, etc. Influence of district/state level political leaders and chances of patronage distribution also could find their place in providing funds to the PRIs.

During the NGP evaluation exercise, it is noted that political and caste differences between the Pradhan and his/her opponents led to washing of dirty linen in the public at some places. This is mainly due to the reason that in case selected, the award will be received by the Pradhan from the President of India, against the wishes of his/her opponents.[19] It is felt that such attempts were made at number of places when the Pradhan does not belong to a majority community though there are exceptions also.[20] It would be better to address this aspect in such a way that the award is presented to the Pradhan of a GP on behalf of the whole village.

In the State, a specific scheme for achieving total sanitation coverage was initiated in five selected GPs of the State with increased financial support by providing Rs. 5200 as the financial assistance for an IHHL.[21] Due to economic reasons, it is known that such a scheme can never be replicated in other parts of the State. It is viewed that mere announcement of the scheme in some GPs itself has been a de-motivating factor for many other GPs in the same region. It is observed that they have slowed down their activities during the campaign, expecting a quantum jump in the allocations in the subsequent year. And the end-result is that mere announcement of the scheme has been proved to be counter-productive to the cause of TSC.

(c) Tamil Nadu

Some of the reflections gathered from the field visits through seven districts of Tamil Nadu have been indicated in the following paragraphs.

Involvement of NGOs in the construction of IHHLs has been an innovative approach introduced in the State. After an IHHL is constructed, an incentive of Rs. 50 is permitted to the NGOs on the submission of its photograph with the members of the household. In addition, services of Self Help Groups, youth clubs, churches and other religious bodies in their respective areas have been utilised for ensuring maximum outreach of the activities. It is also seen that political parties did not take any active role in the scheme execution.[22]

Government of Tamil Nadu and UNICEF collaborated on scaling up the SSHE programme in the State in December 2006. The strategy was to use monitoring and the collection of data as a tool for planning and managing the scaling up of SSHE by involving the officials from key departments like education, health and rural development at the block level. A survey was initiated in each school in four districts of the state to assess the presence of five basic indicators like drinking water supply, toilet availability, water supply to toilets, hand-washing facilities and training on SSHE. The assessment rated each school on a '10 star scale' and about one-third of the schools achieved 10 star status or came close with 9 stars. The study found that more successful school programmes tended to have trained teachers, active Parent Teacher's Association (PTA) and Village Education Committees (VEC), vibrant student hygiene clubs, effective NGO partnership and a system of mobilisation of financial contribution from communities.

Tamil Nadu has earned wide acclaim for its spectacular performance in improving the sanitation coverage of the rural population from 15 per cent in 2001 to 57 per cent in 2005. A special thrust on Integrated Sanitary Complexes for Women have been built in all village panchayats. A total 13062 such complexes were built at a cost of Rs. 278 crores.[23]

Initiation of Child Friendly Toilets (CFT) is one of the innovations in sanitation movement in the State under the interventions of an NGO. The CFTs were constructed under Water Aid Urban Slums Health and Sanitation Improvement Programme in Tiruchirappalli. As they are constructed adjacent to the community toilets, maintenance is easy. No money is charged from the children for using it and the community pays for soap and other cleaning materials from the income raised from pay and use toilets managed by the women groups. The caretaker of the community toilet teaches hand-washing and its importance to the children and also keeps an eye on the hygienic behaviour of the children after defecation.

Number of technological innovations in the design of sanitation pans was initiated in the State as in 'Kuthambakkam model'. This has resulted in developing cost-effective models of bathroom-cum-toilet, which is generally preferred by women. Designs of mobile sanitation units were also created in the Kuthambakkam village, with most of the items produced by the small scale industrial units in the village itself, which gave further boost to the local economy.[24]

During the visits through the villages, it is noted that the implementation of the scheme in Tamil Nadu is generally bureaucratic-centred. The District Collector and the District Rural Development Agency (DRDA) play the key role in operationalisation of the scheme. At regular intervals, meetings of Village Panchayat

Presidents and Block Panchayat Chairpersons have been conducted by the District Collector.[25] It is seen that the scheme has resulted in reinforcement of bureaucracy in the State, as in the '*Periyar Model*'.[26] One of the IAS Officers from the State on deputation to UNICEF, P. Amudha, was honoured with a Special award for outstanding contribution to the promotion of rural sanitation on 15 August 2005 by the Government of Tamil Nadu.

Gandhigram Rural Institute (GRI), Dindigul has organised number of training sessions for elected members, district officials, and other stakeholders from within the State and outside. It is known that Government of Kerala requested GRI to set up Sanitary Science Parks for State Institute of Rural Development (SIRD).

Number of nominations from the GPs with even less than 50 per cent of sanitation coverage at the households has been forwarded to the Government of India for Nirmal Gram Puraskar. It is known that such nominations are forwarded with the assumption that they will be able to meet the targets at the time of evaluation.

(d) Kerala

Some of the reflections gathered from the field visits through six districts of Kerala have been mentioned below.

According to Census 2001, sanitation coverage of households in the State with latrines is 84 per cent, which is the best available figure among all Indian states. However, there is a difference of more than 10 per cent in the rural and urban settings in the State, favourable to urban. Out of 65.95 lakh households in the State, 55.4 lakh households have sanitary latrines.[27] A recent modest estimate in this sector indicates the sanitation coverage in the State touches 90 per cent. No doubt, the above data on households may include those with unhygienic and unacceptable standard of latrines. Number of latrines without sub-structures (to collect excreta from falling into water) is functioning in the canals, backwater and other inland water ways. Number of field studies are available on the data in the sanitation sector contrary to the aggregate figures at the State level.[28]

PRIs are very much involved in the overall process of TSC in the State—from the selection of beneficiaries to the completion of facilities. It is noted that three tier PRIs earmarked additional provisions from their Plan funds to the central share of TSC, especially in IHHLs and CSCs.[29] PRIs have made provisions in their plan fund itself towards realising the physical targets set during the campaign. It is viewed that the active involvement of PRIs during the campaign has led to enhancing the sanitation coverage. However, it has also resulted in dilution of the demand driven approach to a subsidy driven one as in CRSP.

Sanitation is one of the subjects transferred to the PRIs as part of the decentralisation process and this has paved the way for improving the sanitation scenario in the State.[30] Provision of a significant portion of plan funds to the Panchayats initiated during PPC has resulted in achieving a quantum jump in the sanitation sector in the State. In the Ninth and Tenth Plans, about 600 Grama Panchayats have given top priority to sanitation and more than 100 of them achieved the goal of 90 per cent sanitation coverage. During the period, PRIs initiated several projects for construction of household toilets, school toilets and community complexes during the PPC, as a forerunner to the TSC activities in the State.

SHGs and Kudumbasree units played a significant role in the implementation of TSC at different parts of the State. They were mainly used for creating awareness among the population regarding sanitation aspects. In some places, they were involved in carrying out the base line survey also. Selected members of SHGs/ Kudumbasree units received masonry training during the scheme. It is noted that they have constructed number of sanitary toilets resulting in saving money in selected areas. Majority of the Community Sanitary Complexes in the State are managed by SHGs. It is noted that management of RSM/PC was entrusted to the SHGs in many places.

During the field visits through the State, it is noted that the role of NGOs/third sector organisations during the operationalisation of the campaign has been very limited. In some places, they were used for environment creation and organising capacity building sessions during the campaign. In some places, they were entrusted with the responsibility of running CSC also. However, it is noted that the existing potentials of third sector organisations have not been properly tapped, incorporated and utilised during the campaign.

In the recent times, number of PRIs have started giving more attention to solid waste management in their activities. Government of Kerala brought out an order in 2006 instructing PRIs to prepare a 'sanitation approach document' as part of '*Malinyamuktha Keralam*' (Clean Kerala) project with special attention to solid and liquid waste management in their functional areas.

A sanitation park has been set up at Kerala Institute of Local Administration (KILA) campus as a tool for demonstration of different models and types of sanitary units during the training sessions to elected members and officials of PRIs. This demo park was set up with the financial support from UNICEF, Chennai. However, it is observed that the facility is not utilised on the expected lines during the capacity building sessions for the elected members from PRIs.

Significant strides the state has made in the fields of literacy, health and sanitation, and the 'boast of a relatively high personal hygiene of an average *Malayalee*' have not been adequately reflected in improving the community hygienic standards in the State. This may be a great paradox, which needs further analysis.

The officials/staff involved in the implementation of TSC at different levels were primarily drawn from the Rural Development Department (RDD) of the State Government. Generally it is seen that the assignment with the TSC is treated as a 'soft option' by the RDD officials, which may have its own inherent limitations.[31]

Due to high density of population and land fragmentation issues, a significant section of families dwell in small and even tiny lands, with no space or inadequate space for construction of toilets. In many cases, construction of toilet has been an area of conflict with neighbours whose water sources fall within the distance limits. Panchayats had to intervene during the past for finding out the solution while dealing with such cases. In many cases, scientific and technological options available are limited and not cost-effective. Political expediency may be the deciding factor in settling such issues, either in favour of protecting the water source or permitting the construction of toilet. And it is seen that in majority of cases, the decision is taken at the cost of 'total sanitation.'

Procedural issues stand in the way of enabling the benefits of TSC by the people in the State. In Kerala, a potential beneficiary needs to produce various documents (Title deed, land tax receipt, ration card of the family which includes the name of the beneficiary and BPL certificate) to become eligible for the scheme assistance. In case of non-availability of title deed, he/she is required to produce a certificate from the Village Officer of Revenue Department stating that he/she is a permanent resident of the area for the last 12 years.[32]

By keeping the system for sanctioning of the scheme assistance highly rigid and cumbersome, many potential beneficiaries could not avail the assistance. In such cases, he/she has no other option than to go for open defecation, until a facility is available. Hence, the target of achieving the remaining families cannot be achieved easily. The practice of fixing criteria for a potential beneficiary of TSC seems to have been adopted from housing and other welfare programmes. And the criteria may have little relevance while addressing the issues of health and hygiene sectors. Only by taking a liberal approach in dealing with the issues of sanitary sector, the scheme benefits will reach a certain segment of population living in '*Poromboke*' lands, slum areas, and other common places.

During the field monitoring through the Districts, it is noted that operationalisation of the programme has not been practised as a 'concerted campaign' in most of the places. The synergy expected among various departments/agencies in a campaign approach could not be realised in the field. It is being implemented as another centrally sponsored programme of the RDD in which the existing officials themselves are involved in the implementation. No functional linkages could be seen with the different sectors like health, water supply, women's welfare, SC/ST development, etc. during the execution.

No doubt, sanitation and water supply should go hand in hand. However in Kerala, the Department of Rural Development is implementing the TSC and the Public Health Division of Kerala Water Authority under the Department of Water Resources is implementing the Swajaldhara in most of the Districts. It is revealed from the field that the overall impact of both the schemes could not achieve the expected results, since these schemes are implemented independently, without any functional linkages and co ordination between them.

No active linkage/collaboration with other centrally sponsored programmes could be noted during the campaign in the State. By developing appropriate linkages with those programmes and without losing the identity/ownership of TSC, the overall benefits/ impact would have been much more as a result of co-production.

The campaign activities were also found inadequate, with no specific proposal to address the sanitation issues at hotels, hospitals, water bodies, etc. during the programme. The totality of approach required for achieving tangible results in the sanitation scenario has not been adequately reflected in the programme.

Some level of insensitivity to women has been noted during the campaign in the State. For example, certain illustrations in the IEC materials reiterate the traditional practices adopted in the families like woman cleaning the toilets, woman cleaning the surrounding areas, etc. There is hardly any hint available in the IEC materials as to the need for participation of men during such activities. The traditional division of labour between men and women in hygiene and sanitation tends to be reinforced due to such illustrations in the IEC materials. However, it is noted that a two-day workshop on 'Towards a more women-friendly and child friendly approach' was organised by the Kerala Total Sanitation and Health Mission, Thiruvananthapuram and TSC District Office, Thrissur at KILA. Elected members and officials from Panchayats, representatives from professional organisations and officials from different development departments of Government of Kerala participated in the workshop. The workshop led to wide deliberations regarding the gender and child sensitive approaches and to bring out appropriate strategies, tools, techniques and operational guidelines to overcome the lacunae.

No specific thrust was provided to address the attention of marginalized sections like Scheduled Tribes during the implementation in the State. This has been largely noted during the preparation of IEC materials. Absence of specific thrust on tribals in the IEC activities may have resulted in not sufficiently translating the efforts into tangible results in the selected areas.

The scheme assistance provided in the State (Rs. 2000), includes contribution from plan funds of three-tier PRIs as well, in addition to the central funds. It is viewed that this has been an attractive amount for ineligible beneficiaries as well and several such cases were spotted during the field visits. At the same time, rent seeking behaviour of certain RDD officials is also noted from different parts, especially in geographically vulnerable areas of the State.

Highlights from the States

A scan undertaken through the scheme execution in four states show that there is hardly any common aspect present in them. However, an attempt has been made to derive some of the salient features to make a model out of their experiences. Politicising TSC, support to the campaign by the bureaucracy and active role of NGOs during the campaign could be taken out of West Bengal context. Support offered by consultants from diverse fields like civil engineering, communication and social engineering and the thrust on school sanitation has been noteworthy in Uttar Pradesh. Incentive offered to NGOs for promoting total sanitation and use of diverse technological options has been significant in Tamil Nadu. Pro-active role of three tier PRIs, a recent movement for incorporating waste management into the campaign and the need for a flexible approach towards the target group have been taken out of Kerala context. A convergence of the salient features of these States may lead to the emergence of an ideal approach in other parts of India. At the same time, there is a need to provide ample space for local initiatives and flexibility in approach in diverse settings while operationalising a scheme like this.

'Allegations' Against NGP

Number of 'allegations' about the process and efficacy of selection of PRIs could be heard from different sides, when its pitch was largely heard with the declaration of recent NGP awards. In this direction, a serious debate on NGP experiences from different parts of India was undertaken under the auspices of UN initiative of Solution Exchange for Environment/Water Community and Decentralisation Community.[33] During the session, 26 responses were posted by the campaign managers, social activists and academic scholars about the issues, concerns, and experiences related to the NGP. Some of the major allegations are listed here.

- *(a)* Some villages had received awards on considerations not entirely based on their sanitation status;
- *(b)* Many deserving villages were excluded;
- *(c)* Transparency in the selection process is very low;

(*d*) Emphasis seemed to be on getting the award rather than achieving total sanitation; and,

(*e*) Evaluation in NGP found the emphasis on toilet construction more than its usage.

It is noted that there is some substance in the negative comments cited above. However, we would like to put forward our views in this regard. The very process of NGP award starts with the self-declaration by the Pradhan/President of PRI in the application indicating that cent per cent coverage has been achieved in the area. This would be verified, countersigned and routed through Block Administration, District Office of TSC, District Magistrate/Collector and State Office of TSC. Only then, the nomination is available to the Government of India for verification. This seems to be a manifestation of larger ethical issues in governance rather than the shortcomings in the selection process alone. MoRD has taken due precautions towards addressing the weak areas by taking several steps. Assigning the role of verifying agency outside the state of its functioning, taking strict action against the agencies involved in wrong selection process and ordering of reverification of the claim of PRIs by another agency are some of the steps taken in the direction. However, the practice of reverification has its shortcomings too. The process of reverification has given rise to several claims coming up and in some cases, it is being used as a strategy to get as many awards as possible by staking claims (including several undeserving ones). In addition, it also gave sufficient time to improve the situations after the first visit and then seek for reverification.

The motivational value of NGP has been widely accepted. The evaluation exercise itself can be used as a powerful tool for motivating the different stakeholders for strengthening the campaign. And it cannot be forgotten that the award money is again invested for the same cause in the same area, for improving the existing facilities or initiating unique activities. We would like to argue that there is no limit to the hygiene and sanitation practices and the concept is ever-evolving. Hygiene practices of yesterday, today and tomorrow would be different, and that will depend upon socio-economic aspects and technological advancements.

From our experiences, we can say with full confidence that at no point of time there was external pressure exerted on us from any side — either from the campaign managers at different levels or from political leaders. In this regard, we would like to specially mention the role of UNICEF consultants, as they have supported us in the exercise by presentation of facts and figures, without seeking any undue favour. And the enthusiasm about sanitation in the rural areas has been definitely increased, which helped to move towards achieving 'total sanitation' in their area by adopting multiple pathways.

'E' and 'F' errors are commonly occurred either while fixing targets or giving awards. 'E' error occurs due to 'Excessive coverage including coverage of non-eligible'; 'F' error is due to 'Failure to include all eligible' in the process of selection; and 'S' is the 'Share of non-eligible in the total award winning cases'. By considering the volume and cumbersome nature of work involved in the selection process and number of PRIs applied for the award, both 'E' and 'F' errors are quite negligible. And we admit that in this context, 'E' error has been relatively on the higher side. However, there is an in-built mechanism to correct both the errors in the process. The very logic of investing the award amount in the sanitation sector itself is an in-built measure to check 'E' error. As the award is presented on a yearly basis, 'F' error occurring in one year can be corrected in the subsequent years. However, in this regard, when we compute 'S', it is very less.

Suggestions

Number of suggestions are put forward to improve the implementation of TSC and to make the selection process of NGP foolproof, up to a great extent.

- Training sessions on various technological options be organised for rural masons on a regular basis.
- By making minor structural variations, two-in-one toilets may be constructed which will be a major point of attraction for women. Sociologically, open defecation is not viewed as a great sin in our country; but open bathing is. Towards catering to both these issues, cost-effective designs of two-in-one toilets are suggested, which will be a great relief to women.
- Generally elders carry out open defecation as they are accustomed with the old practice. In addition, joint pains

and difficulty to get up after defecation generally found in aged people, discourage them from using it. This point to the need for a focussed approach to attract elders by creating additional support systems within the toilet and sessions for behavioural changes.

- There is an urgent need for internalising and operationalising the concept of having 'child-friendly toilets' at the Anganawadis.
- Efforts must be made for carrying out an Open Defecation Mapping (ODM) in a participatory method and through which appropriate remedial measures can be taken to check the menace.[34]
- Focussed attempts must be made during the campaign to involve all elected members of the GP towards increasing the programme coverage.
- Necessary efforts be made to actively involve CBOs, business community, retired persons, ex-servicemen, etc. during the scheme execution towards improving the programme output.
- The eligibility criteria for a beneficiary for receiving assistance for construction of IHHL shall be made liberal and flexible. This needs to be treated differently from housing and other welfare programmes, as non-availability of sanitation facilities in one family can lead to far-reaching implications in the health and hygiene of the community.
- Necessary efforts be made to bring TSC to the agenda of the political parties functioning at the local levels.
- Necessary support for Research and Design (R & D) activities be provided towards bringing out cost effective technological alternatives subjected to geographical variations.
- There is a need for scrutinising the nominations for NGP, by a process of graduation from the block, district and state levels. Even an independent verification of the claim can be initiated at District/State levels.
- It needs to be ensured that after achieving cent per cent sanitary coverage, minimum six months may be completed before forwarding the nominations for NGP.
- The MoRD can think of inviting applications for NGP from the PRIs on a regular basis and to carry out the verification of the claim round the year to prevent the rushed process of selection for the award.

- The process of reverification of claims must be used very judiciously. A liberal approach in the reverification of the claims will send out a wrong message.
- The campaign managers must make the message loud and clear to all that the NGP award is for the whole village and not to a single individual.
- During field visits through the UP villages, it is felt that some of the GPs need a focussed attention during the TSC and in the preparation for NGP. Presence of a number of habitations spread over a vast area, drought-affected areas, difficult terrains, dacoit-infested regions, availability of railway lines, national or state highways, presence of river bed, etc. may create number of impediments in the nomination for NGP. Hence a uniform approach is not feasible and practical here and a selective approach can also be thought of during the run up to NGP.
- NGP awardee GPs must be used as resource persons to motivate at least five more GPs in the subsequent years. In this line, some kind of assurance may be sought after the award ceremony. In addition, the Presidents/Pradhans of NGP awarded GPs can be included in the District Sanitation Committees as well.
- Need for a revisit of NGP awarded GPs to analyse the sustainability of the sanitation situation after a period.
- An extensive survey similar to the one undertaken by the Indian Institution of Mass Communication (IIMC) in 1997 as the baseline work for TSC needs to be initiated. Undertaking an extensive study with focus on the specific strategies and activities for High, Medium and Low performing States/Districts can bring further momentum to the campaign towards achieving 'total sanitation coverage' in all parts of the country.

Conclusion

Scanning through different IEC materials, interactions with the campaign managers and analysing the activities carried out, it is realised that Mahatma's perspectives and comments on sanitation have not been properly taken into account during the implementation at different States, though he can be called as 'the greatest proponent' of sanitation and hygiene. It is dismal to note that Gandhian activists and academicians did not give the desired attention to the campaign.

It is expected that the achievement in sanitation sector will lead to a better Human Development Index (HDI) for India. And the initiation of Nirmal Gram Puraskar for the PRIs has definitely given a positive boost to the sanitation drive at every nook and corner of the country. It is believed that this is a crucial move to make India open defecation free by 2012, much ahead of the UN timeframe for achieving the Milliennium Development Goal target for drinking water and sanitation. Only then we can hope to make a 'Swaraj without foul stench' as visualised by Gandhiji.

NOTES AND REFERENCES

1. www.ddws.nic.in (Website of Department of Drinking Water Supply (DDWS), Ministry of Rural Development (MoRD), Government of India).
2. A nation-wide baseline survey was conducted by the Indian Institute of Mass Communication (IIMC) on drinking and sanitation aspects. Details of the study is available in the consolidated report titled 'Water and Sanitation – A Baseline Survey' brought out by IIMC in January 1998.
3. This data on Sanitation coverage in South Asia was taken from the presentation by the DDWS to the Minister for Rural Development, in May 2004 (Downloaded from www.ddws.nic.in).
4 Discussions with Shibashish Banerjee, District Co-ordinator (TSC), Burdwan and Sakthisadhan Maiti, District Co-ordinator (TSC), Midnapore East in West Bengal. Similar comments were made by Wakkeel Ahmed, State Level Consultant (TSC), Dr. R.K. Shukla, Divisional Quality Control Co-ordinator and Pratima Verma, Divisional Co-ordinator (TSC) of Uttar Pradesh.
5. Role of party machinery during TSC was highlighted in a paper on 'Panchayat-Party Interface' presented by Rabiul Hussain, Local Committee Secretary of CPI (M), Khejuri-1, Purba Medinipur District during the Discussion Meet/Dialogue Session on West Bengal and Kerala Panchayat Raj Systems organised as part of the exposure visit to elected Panchayat members from Kerala by SDC-CapDecK and CRM initiative on 23 July 2007. Similar comment was made by Sushantha Mandal, Block Committee President of Indian National Congress (INC), Khejuri-1 and Prashanto Maiti, Zonal Committee Secretary of CPI (M), Khejuri-1 on 24 July 2007.

6. Interview with Shibashish Banerjee, District Co-ordinator (TSC) of Burdwan District in West Bengal on February 24, 2006.
7. This aspect was realised during the discussions with the elected members and political party leaders of number of GPs in Burdwan and Purba Medinipur Districts in West Bengal. Similar comment was made by Himangshu Das, Savapati, Khejuri-1 Panchayat Samithi of Purba Medinipur District in West Bengal and Member of CPI (M) District Committee.
8. Discussions with Sushantha Mandal, Block Committee President, INC, Khejuri-1 Block of Purba Medinipur District in West Bengal on March 9, 2006.
9. Discussions with Shibashish Banerjee, District Co-ordinator (TSC), Burdwan District on 24 February 2006 and K.C. Das, Joint BDO, Khejuri-1 Panchayat Samithi of Purba Medinipur District on 22 July 2007. These two officials were very vocal on the corrective role of the bureaucrats. Many other local officials also expressed similar comments on the issue in a lighter vein.
10. Discussions with Prasun Kanti Das, Savapati of Shaheed Matangini Block in Purba Medinipur, West Bengal revealed that he is the major functionary of an NGO, 'Aamra Susama Jalaprapat', Demarihat, Tamluk, Purba Medinipur, West Bengal. He indicated that the NGO was constituted in 2003 after taking necessary permission from the CPI (M) District Committee. The NGO was instrumental in awareness building activities, preparation of IEC materials and organising training sessions during the sanitation campaign. On similar lines, many NGOs have been floated by party functionaries in West Bengal.
11. This was noted during the field visits through different parts of Purba Medinipur and Paschim Medinipur Districts in West Bengal during April 2007 along with Kumar Alok from Ministry of Rural Development. We have not shared this point with Kumar Alok. However, he is fully aware of the problems of rural pan.
12. This aspect was noted during the interactions with the officials and representatives of Ramakrishna Mission.
13. This issue was realised during the discussions with the campaign managers of Purba Medinipur and Paschim Medinipur Districts in West Bengal.
14. It is known that the understanding and team work displayed by the Pradhan and Secretary (Both women) in Lama GP of Banda District in Uttar Pradesh has been an important factor for the smooth execution of scheme in the area.
15. During the field visits through Hardua Aima GP of Kanpur Dehat

District in Uttar Pradesh, it is noted that manual scavenging could be completely eradicated from the area during the campaign.

16. In Badpura GP of Etawah District in Uttar Pradesh, a group of 30 to 35 ex-servicemen were in the forefront of the TSC execution.
17. In Mavai GP of Kamasin Block, Tera-B GP of Naraini Block and many other dacoit-infested villages of Banda District in Uttar Pradesh, the construction activities in the field of sanitation have been done admirably.
18. This aspect was noted during the field visits through number of schools in Etawah District of Uttar Pradesh.
19. In Sadi Madanpur GP of Tindwari Block at Banda District in Uttar Pradesh, the former Pradhan, who forwarded the last year's nomination for NGP (2006) was in the forefront arguing that the requirements for NGP in the GP area could not be achieved now (2007). Analysing the issue, it is known that he lost the election in the last panchayat elections and now wishes that the present Pradhan should not receive the prestigious award.
20. During the field visits through Rampur Maghila GP in Umarda Block of Kannauj District in Uttar Pradesh, it is noted that the Pradhan belongs to a community which has only two families in the whole village area. However, during the discussions with the villagers, it is felt that they are quite happy with her approach, honesty, efficiency, leadership qualities and functioning.
21. The pilot scheme was introduced in Saifai GP, the home village of former Chief Minister of Uttar Pradesh, Mulayam Singh Yadav and 4 other Grama Panchayats in 2006.
22. During the discussions with Dr. Ponnuraj of Gandhigram Rural Institute (GRI), Dindigul, Tamil Nadu on the administration of sanitation activities in Tamil Nadu, this aspect was highlighted.
23. Excerpts from Tamil Nadu State Budget 2006-07.
24. Discussions with Elango, former President of Kuthambakkam GP and a Gandhian activist from Tamil Nadu on July 5, 2007.
25. This was revealed during the discussions with Dr. Ponnuraj of GRI, Dindigul, Tamil Nadu on July 3, 2007.
26. Details of Periyar Model are available in the book 'Environmental Sanitation, Health and Panchayati Raj' by Bakshi D. Sinha and P.S.K. Menon, published by Institute of Social Sciences, New Delhi in 1996.
27. *Economic Review-2004*, Thiruvananthapuram: State Planning Board (SPB), Government of Kerala (GOK), p.185.
28. Details are available in the DLM reports on TSC in Kerala (2006-07) by

Centre for Rural Management, Kottayam, Kerala and Draft Annual Report (2006-07) and Work Plan (2007-08) by the Research Unit on Local Self Government, Centre for Development Studies, Thiruvananthapuram, Kerala.

29. More than two times of the central assistance on IHHL has been supplemented by three tier PRIs in Kerala from their plan funds.

30. *Economic Review-2004*, Thiruvananthapuram: SPB, GOK, p.186.

31. This point was indicated in District Level Monitoring Report of TSC (January - March 2007) undertaken in 13 districts of Kerala by Centre for Rural Management, Kottayam, Kerala.

32. These issues were highlighted by Rajmohanan Nair, Member, Kumaranalloor GP, Kottayam District, Kerala during the discussions on February 26, 2007. Similar comments were expressed by K.P. Sugunan, President, District Panchayat, Kottayam during one of the meetings of District Sanitation Committee.

33. www.solutionexchange-un.net.in (Website of Solution Exchange, a UN Initiative).

34. An effort was initiated by the Pradhan and sanitation team at Dingwahi GP of Banda District in Uttar Pradesh to eradicate open defecation and it found success.

7

Community Contribution for Environmental Sanitation: Myth or Reality

VEERASHEKHARAPPA

Introduction

In recent years there has been increasing recognition of the limitations on the capacity of national and local governments to manage the rapidly increasing number of development programmes effectively. In response, governments have been assigning greater roles to Non-Government Organizations (NGOs) and the private sector and have actively started encouraging community participation. In the provision of drinking water and sanitary services, community-based programmes involving NGO and private sectors are being encouraged to increase efficiency (Churchil 1994). The major concern in such an approach is sharing/recovery of the cost from the community (Harmeyer and Mody 1998), in process the State gradually withdraw from provisioning of services and the gap will be filled by private agencies and local organizations. Neo-liberal economists argue that the imperfect nature of the State results in 'government failures' in the form of regulatory capture, rent seeking and corruption (Chang 2002). Centralized decision-making and bureaucratic allocation of resources is fading fast to pave the way for decentralized allocation and stakeholder participation (Saleth, and Dinar, 1999), by which peoples, including the disadvantaged, influence decisions affecting them. Institutionalization of social capital and collective action improve efficiency in water supply systems (Narayan, 1993), social capital is essential for implementation and sustainability of the programme (Kahkonen 1999). Thus, there is strong support for structural changes in financing of development projects.

The world over, drinking water and sanitation projects have been viewed as fundamentals for promoting public health. As is well known, sanitation facilities prevent the transmission of oral-faecal diseases at the very source, by preventing human faecal contamination of water and soil. Human excreta are extremely dangerous for health unless disposed off safely (UN-HABITAT 2003). The term sanitation has been interpreted differently; in fact, sanitation involves interventions for reducing people's exposure to diseases by providing a clean environment for living with measures to break the cycle of diseases. This usually includes disposal and hygienic management of human and animal excreta refuse and waste water, control of disease vectors and provision of proper washing facilities for personal and domestic hygiene (WSSCC 2003). Improvement in water and sanitary services has helped control water-related diseases in France (Woods, 2003), Southern Europe, Central America and Several Asian Countries (Das Gupta 2003). In fact, integrated water and sanitation programmes have had great impact in controlling diseases (Esrey *et. al.*,1985). Thus, potable/clean water and sanitation is inextricably linked to prevention of diseases and improves the quality of life and thus reduces poverty. Considering these facts, the United Nations has included the provision of potable water and sanitary services as one of the components under the Millennium Development Goals (MDG) to reduce poverty by 2015 (United Nations 2000). India being a member has agreed to introduce the paradigm shift in policy to involve beneficiaries, NGOs and the private sector. This has been followed by bilateral and multilateral agencies[1] while funding these programmes in a few states, including Karnataka (World Bank 1999).

In Karnataka three major projects were implemented by external agencies (Annex 1), cost sharing and recovery by the community being the major thrust and people's involvement at all stages of implementation, from planning to finally owning the assets for operation and maintenance has been ensured in these projects. The approach critically viewed the premise that communities do not always go together as are heterogeneous in nature and lack the skills required, thus this exercise may become futile.

This chapter tries to investigate how and to what extent a paradigm shift has taken place in the sharing of costs by the community in the provision of potable water and environmental sanitation through user charges. The study has the following objectives:

- to examine aspects of community contribution for environmental sanitation;
- to assess the impact of community role in provision of services equally;
- to examine the role of the community in the operation and maintenance of the assets provided.

Approach and Methodology

In order to pursue the objectives of the study, a multiple sampling method was used to pick the villages for the investigation. Of the total number of villages under the Kantataka Integrated Rural Water Supply and Sanitation Project (KIRWSSP), two sets of sample were selected: (1) about ten per cent of the 1104 project villages, that is, 112 villages spread across 12 districts were selected randomly; all the pilot phase villages spread across State were selected purposively. The required secondary data were collected from Village Water Supply Committees (VWSCs), NGO and Grama Panchayats; primary data were collected from sample households. For household selection, the villages were grouped into two: the first category of villages consisted less than 500 households each; while the second set of villages consisted of more than 500 households each. To ensure equal representation from both the groups, 30 and 15 per cent of households were selected randomly (Table 7.1).

Table-7.1
No. of Households Selected Across Pilot Villages

Name of the Village	*Districts*	*Households*		
		Total	*Selected*	*Selected %*
1	2	3	4	5
Seegevalu	Mysore	250	75	30
A. Nagathihalli	Mandya	238	71	30
Hombadimandadi	D. Kannada	257	76	30
Daginakatte	Shimoga	695	105	15
Kembliganhalli	Bangalore (R)	171	52	30

(Contd.)

1	2	3	4	5
Lakhangaon	Bidar	750	112	15
Yelasangi	Gulbarga	629	94	15
Arkera	Raichur	702	104	15
Madlur	Belgaum	444	66	15
Total		**4136**	**755**	**18**

The tools chosen for data collection involved structured questionnaires and group discussions, wherein the participatory observation method was stressed. This chapter is organized as follows. Section two, in brief, provides a background discussion on changes in policies and strategies towards community participation. Section three examines community contribution and the ensuring of equity and efficiency in the provision of sanitary services. The last section raises certain policy issues concerning the possible ways in which sanitary services should be designed and funded.

Policies and Strategies

Policies

It is estimated that 21 per cent of communicable diseases in India are water and sanitation-related; diarrhea alone killed over 7,00,000, that is, more than 1,600 a day, during the year 1999. In the past ten years, diarrhea has killed more children than all those that lost their lives to conflicts in almost 60 years since the Second World War. To remedy the situation the MDG state that the aim is to halve the number of people without adequate sanitation facilities by 2015. To achieve this target, on an average 3, 50,000 people will have to gain access to improved sanitation every day between now and 2015.

Realization of the need for improvement in sanitation and hygiene is not a new development in India; the need for providing potable water and better sanitation was recognized even during the pre-Independence period for the better health of the British Army (Ramasubban 1982). The Bhore Committee (1944) and the Environmental Hygiene Committee (1948) have provided a blueprint for the implementation of water and sanitary services and stressed their importance in improving public health. This blueprint became a basis for inclusion of these services under national agenda during the First Five-Year Plan (1951-56). However, it was only in 1954 that the Central Rural Sanitation Programme (CRSP) was introduced part of the health sector. The operation, however, did not succeed until the 1980s due to confusion and inconsistency on the sanitation component. General guidelines for implementation of the CRSP, prescribe that each state should develop at least one model village every year under the Integrated Rural Sanitation Programme (IRSP).[2]

Since the beginning of the Sixth Five-Year Plan (1980-85) and the launch of the International Drinking Water Supply and Sanitation Decade in 1980, India deepened its effort to rural water supply and sanitation. Though the provision of water supply and sanitation is the responsibility of each State Government, Central Government funding constitutes nearly 40 per cent of the total investment in the sector. Nevertheless, water supply received greater attention compared to sanitation. The Seventh Five-Year Plan Draft (1985-90) was critical of earlier policies and programmes concerning this sector, due to two factors: first, it was essentially a supply-driven, top-down approach that did not take into account the pattern and intensity of demand for service; and second, the lack of community participation in service provision rendered it inefficient and unsustainable; further, public allocation often did not provide for an incentive structure for the use of services rationally and efficiently. To overcome these problems, it was proposed to involve stakeholders directly in the programme by introducing partial cost-sharing and recovery of user charges. In support of this, the Eighth Five-Year Plan policy paper stressed the need for devolution of responsibility to local governments and recommended changes in the mind-set of people, through four stages of intervention; viz.,

- *(a)* creating awareness;
- *(b)* developing an action plan to facilitate decision making, management and financial autonomy;
- *(c)* strengthening institutions and;
- *(d)* improving the monitoring, accountability and transparency of the sector (World Bank 1999).

The main objective of this policy change was to reduce the burden on the public exchequer. In support of this, policy instances were cited from worldwide experiences showing a positive correlation between stakeholder involvement and efficiency in implementation and sustainability (Harmeyer and Mody, 1997; Pushpangadan and

Murugan, 1998). The 73rd Amendment to the Indian Constitution has vested enormous power in the hands of Panchayati Raj Institutions (PRIs) and its lowest tier, the Gram Panchayat (GP), has been mandated for the service delivery of potable water and provision of sanitary services. In many villages, Village Water Supply and Sanitation Committees (VWSCs) co-exist with GPs, either as sub-committees or independently. Meanwhile, sector reforms have been introduced; the aim of these is to generate more demand-responsive and participatory approaches by empowering local governments and community groups to fully manage their own services without any outside support. In fact, the reforms support and strengthen the process introduced by multilateral and bilateral projects. In support of this, the Ninth Five-Year Plan (1998-2002) Working Group has endorsed it, considering the resource constraints. The sector reform programme is now being implemented as the Total Sanitation Campaign (TSC), involving stakeholders at all stages.

Coverage

Since the First Five-Year Plan, efforts have been made to cover the entire population of the country with potable water and improved sanitation. However, according to the latest official statistics, only 21 per cent of rural households actually have access to some form of sanitation (GOI 1998; GOI 2001). In the relatively poorer states of Orissa, Chattisgarh, Jharkhand and Bihar, more than 80 per cent of all the households have no toilet facilities. In the states of Madhya Pradesh and Rajasthan, the corresponding figure is between 70 and 80 per cent, 84 per cent of the households in Kerala have latrines attached to their houses (GOI 2001).

The reasons for low coverage vary across states, however the common factors are religious beliefs and culture; for instance; an early civilization in the Indus River Valley had sophisticated sewerage systems and among the oldest known toilets. But the advent of Hinduism and its caste system, during later centuries, changed attitudes and practices concerning disposal of human waste (Cooper 1997). The physical structure of the village and lack of awareness of the community about health and hygienic conditions (Veerashekharappa 2002); also the poor policy framework, lack of public health leadership and political will, as other factors acting as constraints for the expansion of sanitary services (Mavalankar and Shankar 2004).

Table-7.2
Availability of Toilets Across States 1991 and 2001 (Per cent)

States	1991		2001	
	Total	Rural	Total	Rural
Andhra Pradesh	18.40	6.62	32.99	18.15
Assam	37.43	30.53	64.64	59.57
Bihar	11.75	4.96	19.19	13.91
Chattisgarh	–	–	14.20	5.18
Delhi	63.38	29.60	77.96	62.89
Gujarat	30.69	11.16	44.60	21.65
Haryana	22.45	6.53	44.50	28.66
Jharkhand	–	–	19.67	6.57
Karnataka	24.13	6.85	37.50	17.40
Kerala	51.28	44.07	84.01	81.33
Madhya Pradesh	15.07	3.64	23.99	8.94
Maharashtra	29.56	6.64	35.09	18.21
Orissa	9.81	3.58	14.89	7.71
Punjab	33.18	15.79	56.84	40.91
Rajasthan	19.57	6.65	29.00	14.61
Tamil Nadu	23.13	7.17	35.16	14.36
Uttar Pradesh	18.02	6.44	31.43	19.23
Uttaranchal	–	–	45.20	31.60
West Bengal	31.51	12.31	43.71	26.93
India	23.70	9.48	36.41	21.92

Sources: Census of India 2001. Series 1, Tables on Houses, Household Census of India 1991, Series 1, Part VII, Tables.

Policies on Rural Sanitation in Karnataka

The Government of Karnataka, has accorded high priority to providing sanitation and has implemented various programmes towards this end. In rural Karnataka, so far as access of households to drinking water sources is concerned, about 59 per cent of them have connection to piped water supply and 64.7 per cent receive adequate water (>55 lpcd). Though we do not have information on the level of community sanitary services such as habitations with proper drainage system, non-existence of stagnant water pools, compost pits etc., data are available on the level of household latrine facility, and accordingly, 82 per cent of rural households do not have latrines (GOI 2001; GOK, 2000).

KIRWSS Programme

Karnataka State is well known for the provision of potable drinking water and sanitary services in general, particularly through the Mini Water Supply (MWS) and Nirmal Gram Yojana (NGY) programmes respectively. Further, the progressive nature of the State, decentralized governance and better network of NGOs, has drawn the attention of external agencies for investment in various sectors including water and sanitation.[3] Among them, the World Bank has sponsored the KIRWSSP covering 1,104 villages, the project integrates water supply, habitat components[4] and environmental sanitation.[5] Under the programme the first two items are provided free of cost, while for environmental sanitation 30 per cent of cost has to be met by the community.[6] Government, NGO, beneficiaries and private sector, all have assumed different roles and responsibilities in the process of implementation. The community is involved at all stages of implementation through the VWSC. The VWSC works as an 'extended arm' of the GP. The State Government has laid down guidelines for the formulation and functions of rural local organisations under the Karnataka Panchayat Act 1993, Section 61A. Villages failing to comply with these guidelines are not eligible for receipt of grants for implementing rural water supply and sanitation schemes.

Community Contribution for Environmental Sanitation

District Aggregate

The first and foremost responsibility of the VWSC is to plan for services and estimate the required finances based on the guidelines of the Engineering Survey Report (ESR). Once the required services and finances are finalized, they have to be shared on a 70:30 ratio basis by Government and the community. To tender water work construction, the VWSC has to mobilize 25 per cent of the agreed amount. Except in Belgaum and Bidar, in all other districts the agreed amount was mobilized. In a couple of districts the mobilization was more than the agreed amount, but in none of the districts was the amount entirely mobilized from household sources only (Table 7.3), hence non-household sources were used as supplements. For instance, the household contribution was 17.6 per cent of the agreed amount in Hassan district. Similarly, in most districts that was below 50 per cent. In the districts of Belgaum, Shimoga Tumkur, Bangalore and Gulbarga it was above 50 per cent. Further, it is observed that except for Dakshina Kannada, Raichur, Tumkur and Shimoga in all other districts the actual amount contributed by the households is much less than what was agreed upon.

Table-7.3
Proportion of Household Contribution

District	*Proportion of Contribution to the Agreed Amount (in%)*	*Household Contribution*	
		As a Proportion of Total Contribution	*As a Proportion of what was Agreed Upon*
Bangalore	142.8	56.7	81.0
Mandya	123.7	45.4	56.1
Hassan	259.1	17.6	45.5
Belgaum	98.6	98.5	97.1
Gulbarga	129.0	54.1	69.7
Bellary	116.6	31.7	36.9
D. Kannada	100	100	100
Raichur	477.8	33.2	148.4
Shimoga	153	73.3	112.1
Tumkur	223	72.	100.4
Bidar	99.6	87.3	87.0
Mysore	151.9	43.9	66.6
All Districts	142.2	56.3	81.1

From Table 7.3, a pattern of contribution emerges where it appears that the community has ability to mobilize the agreed amount, but at the same time it is unable to mobilize the entire amount from household sources. Thus the household contribution constitutes only a certain proportion of what was contributed by the community as a whole and this suggests that the balance amount must have come from other sources. Based on the data obtained and discussions held with office bearers of the VWSC and NGOs, the sources of contribution were broadly classified into two, household and non-household. The non-household sources were GP, cooperative societies, shops and industrial establishments, local leaders and fairs and festivals. Of these, the role of local leaders, contractors and GP was important in that order, because together they filled the biggest chunk of the gap left by households, which amounts to 41.6 per cent.

Table-7.4
Source-wise Distribution of Actual Contribution Across Districts (Per cent)

		Gramapanchayats							
District	*House-holds*	*Loan*	*Grants*	*Action & Property Tax*	*Local Leaders*	*Cooperatives*	*Shops & Industries*	*Fairs & Festivals*	*Contractors*
1	2	3	4	5	6	7	8	9	10
Bangalore	56.7	-	-	4.5	27.0	5.9	2.4	0.4	2.9
Mandya	45.4	-	7.5	-	15.3	3.4	6.4	6.7	15.3
Hassan	17.6	-	1.0	5.0	13.2	-	-	3.7	59.5
Belgaum	98.6	-	-	-	-	-	-	-	-
Gulbarga	54.1	-	1.6	3.7	21.0	0.1	1.4	-	13.6
Bellary	31.7	2.1	-	1.4	51.2	2.8	4.0	-	6.8
D.K.	100.0	-	-	-	-	-	-	-	-
Raichur	33.2	2.9	-	-	-	0.7	-	-	62.7
Shimoga	73.3	3.8	2.5	11.6	3.3	-	-	1.6	3.9
Tumkur	72.0	-		3.3	15.5	0.2	5.5	-	3.5
Bidar	87.3	-	-	4.6	5.9	0.3	1.4	-	0.4
Mysore	43.9	-	1.1	-	40.7	6.2	3.9	4.3	-
District Average	56.3	0.9	2.0	2.8	16.9	1.9	1.3	0.5	19.4

Note: D.K: Dakshina Kannada.

Across districts, the contractors' share in the total contribution was more then 60 per cent. The reasons for this vary across districts, for instance in Raichur and Hassan, the NGO appointed for community management activities was withdrawn due to beauracratic reasons, to substitute which Non-Government Individuals (NGI) were appointed to support and guide VWSCs in the respective districts. The NGIs could not convince households to make the contribution, and as a result most of the agreed amount was mobilized from non-household sources, and within these largely from contractors. Similarly, in districts such as Mysore, Bellary, Mandya, Gulbarga and Bangalore rural, much of the agreed amount was mobilized from other sources (Table 7.4).

However, it is noticed that each village has a different pattern in community contribution. According to Table 7.5, in four villages, households did not contribute at all, followed by less than 30 per cent contribution in 17 villages. Thus, in 21 villages, the household contribution was less then 25 per cent of total amount. In fact, among the selected villages, half the members (53 villages, including 4) were able to mobilize less then 60 per cent of the total agreed amount and in other villages the contribution was more then 60 per cent. The remained amount was mobilized from non-household sources like panchayats, local leaders, contractors and the like. However, as exception to this general rule, of the 29 contractors who did make a contribution, 45 per cent of them contributed amounts varying from 40 per cent and upwards of the total contribution in a village. However, the total amount mobilized at state level from all sources under community contribution was Rs. 130 million against the expected Rs. 300 million (GOK, 2003), thus only 43 per cent of the agreed amount was mobilized. Within that, what was actually mobilized from households was just around 60 crores, thus the community was able in aggregate to mobilize a total of a one fifth of the amount budgeted against it. In fact, the community contribution has been a non-entity in some of villages.

As mentioned earlier, 25 per cent of the agreed amounts had to be mobilized by the tendering villages for water works, but in practice the norms were not followed in all the villages. The reasons attributed were that due to global tendering, for scale of economy, more than two villages were combined as a slice on a cluster basis while tendering for water construction. In the process, villages, which

Table-7.5
Distribution of Villages by Source of Contribution

Class Intervals (Per cent of Contribution)	*Number of Villages*				
	Households	*GPs**	*Leaders*	*Contractors*	*Others***
0	4	75	59	40	73
0.1–10.0	4	17	12	9	16
10.1–20.0	6	5	7	42	6
20.1–30.0	7	5	11	3	5
30.1–40.0	13	6	6	5	3
40.1–50.0	12	1	3	1	3
50.1–60.0	10	2	0	3	5
60.1–70.0	8	0	0	2	0
70.1 and above	48	1	5	7	1
Total	**112**	**112**	**112**	**112**	**112**

Notes: * Under this source loans, grants, proceeds from auctioning of fuel, fodder etc., and property tax are included.
** Under these items sources such as societies and co-operatives, shops and industrial establishments, fairs and festivals are included.

had not mobilized agreed with the amount being tendered on the pretext that the community would later mobilize funds as agreed. However, villagers did not show any interest in mobilizing the funds (Rajsekhar and Veerashekharappa 2003). Further, at the end of the project, in around 80 villages across 12 districts, even when the contribution was less than 25 per cent, yet villages have been tendered. Mysore, Gulbarga and Bidar are among the top districts in terms of number of villages reporting contribution less than 25 per cent (World Bank1999). Based on enquiry in selected sample villages, it is observed that 50 per cent of them could not mobilize the agreed amount in Gulbarga district of Karnataka (Rajasekhar and Veerashekharappa 2003). Sanitation work had not commenced at all and the community rejected the responsibility of operation and maintenance services. Thus, in sum, the community contribution could not take place to the extent that it was planned, particularly from households. What could be the reasons. This is discussed in the following sections.

Village Level Community Contribution

In all the selected villages, except two the agreed amount was mobilized. About 64 per cent of the households have contributed 54 per cent of the total contribution, which was on par with the aggregate figures. However, the proportion of households, which contributed, vary across villages. A smaller number of households have contributed in Arkera (35%) and a large number of households contributed in Seegavelu (93%): similarly, the share of the amount contributed by households in total vary across villages, the lowest being in Lakhangao (35%) and the highest in Daginakatte (88%). In Lakhangao, though the households mobilized a large amount, due to large contribution from non-household sources, the share of households appears reduced.

The methods adopted in mobilization of contribution varied across villages. At the household level, the economic status of the family was considered; accordingly the amount was fixed per household. For instance, in Hombadimandadi and Yelsangi villages the amount was fixed in the range of Rs. 250 to Rs. 1,000, in Madlur, land holders were charged Rs. 100 per acre and the landless Rs. 50. In addition to individual household contribution, funds were mobilized through innovative methods, such as lottery (Lakhangao), musical night (Arkera and Nagathihalli), drama, village fair (Madlur), etc. The reason for less household contributions was the inefficiency of the NGO. In fact, the household reported that they had not been convinced of the benefits from the programme and they were of the opinion that 'none pays' or 'nothing happens even if we did not pay'. Under such circumstances, the role of NGOs was very crucial, for changing the mindset of the people. The failure of the NGOs was an advantage to contractors; in each village the contractor has contributed Rs. 50,000 to Rs. two lakhs (Lakhangao) to meet the target. However, there is tremendous potential in the community to finance capital costs not only for sanitation construction work but also for drinking water supply, if households are convinced about the relation between contaminated water and health profile of the households (Veerashekharappa 1999).

Role of the Community in Implementation

Functions of VWSCs, apart from mobilizing resources, are to liaise between community and other agencies involved in implementation. For this, the committee should hold periodical meetings with the

Table-7.6
Community Contribution in Selected Villages

Name of the Village	*Availability of Water (LPCD)*	*Agreed Amount*	*Per cent Amount Mobilized to Agreed*	*Per cent of Households Contributed*	*Percentage of Amount Mobilized*	
					House hold	*Non-House-hold*
1	2	3	4	5	6	7
Seegevalu	7.7	1,90,000	100.0	93	55.6	44.4
A. Nagathihalli	26.3	1,14,000	91.2	58	79.8	20.2
Hombadimandadi	27.5	48,000	52.0	57	80.0	20.0
Daginakatte	14.1	1,13,420	100.0	45	88.2	11.8
Kembliganhalli	10.1	1,34,000	100.0	53	40.3	59.7
Lakhangaon	26.9	2,19,000	182.0	93	35.0	65.0
Yelasangi	25.9	2,15,000	100.0	86	52.6	47.4
Arkera	38.2	1,50,000	100.0	35	66.7	33.3
Madlur	3	1,10,000	100.0	100	68.2	31.8
Total			**112.4**	**64**	**54.8**	**45.2**

Note: Non-households sources: contractors, donors, lottery, musical nights and village and Gramadevata fair.

community as well as with other agencies, according to norms the VWSC meetings have to be held at least bi-monthly. According to Table 7.8, only 43 per cent of them held meetings according to schedule and 28 per cent at the initiative of officials. The reason for the lower number of meetings held was attributed to factions within the community on the lines of political parties. For instance, in Lakhangao and Seegavelu, the factions were so strong that they hampered the construction of drainage work, even though the agreed amount was mobilized. In both the villages, the animosity between the factions was so intense that any action initiated/proposed by one group, irrespective of its merit and need, invariably met with opposition from the other group(s). Elaborating further, during our visit we observed that if a member of one faction arrived first, members of the other faction stayed away from the meeting. Similarly, if the venue of the meeting was in a particular street, people from other streets used to be absent; hence most of the meetings used to take place during the officials visit at their insistence. Eventually, the VWSC could not gather the confidence and support of the villagers, as the committee members were divided on lines of political parties, though VWSC itself is a non-political entity.

The decisions taken at VWSC have own importance. The office bearers perceived that the decisions were based largely upon the consensus of all members; however, in a few cases, the GP President and NGO staff play an important role in taking decisions. On most of the issues, the Secretary and President can take decisions, but these have to be ratified by the members. Sometimes a general consensus is obtained through open majority or secret ballot. It was observed that women would attend meetings but were not vocal enough in expressing their views[7], though training was provided to them in understanding their roles and responsibilities. A few women had some vague idea about what was happening but did not realize that they had a major role to play in understanding and solving the problem. However, female representation was better in the villages where women organizations were functioning efficiently (Daginkatte, Arketa and Lakhangao). The VWSC was authorized to award contracts for construction of sanitation services. In practice, the contract was awarded to persons who had contributed a large amount. In every village the contractor or political leaders have contributed and cornered the contract for themselves or for the persons they had recommended. In a couple of villages, the households are under the impression that there was a nexus between engineers, contractors and bureaucrats in awarding contracts.

The contractor being a local man and known to the villagers, because of factionalism in some villages the contractors' work was subject to criticism. For instance, in Yelsangi there was a tussle on the location of the Public Stand Post (PSP). Similar conflicts were noticed in other villages as well, such as using low quality pipes and not laying the distribution pipes at the required depth. In some villages, owing to the low capacity of the water storage tanks built, water needed to be filled twice, which was constrained by lack of electricity and other factors. Whenever the households raised these issues in the general body meetings and gramasabha, they have been faced by questions like 'Why should you interfere'? 'Are you going to pay for it'? 'Why bother who gets the contract'? If you want to interfere, why don't you contribute more funds? Moreover, when the contractor is willing to contribute the share on behalf of the community, the VWSC choose to turn a blind eye to the malpractices.

Services Delivery and Sustainability

Under the programme, the objective was to provide potable water and sanitary services to all households in the villages equally and adequately so that they traverse shorter distances. However, it was noticed that despite community involvement at various stages, the services were biased towards wealthy localities, in terms of accessibility and adequacy of water supply. According to our survey, 82 per cent of wealthy households had their sources located at shorter distances. Similarly, 32 per cent of wealthy households draw water 40 lpcd and above, whereas on an average, 17 per cent of the poor draw water less than 40 lpcd. The quantity of water is drawn based on consumption requirements; the consumption or use of water varies across households because of cultural factors. Some households, because of cultural factors bathe daily and mop the house twice or thrice weekly and hence require more water. However, the quantity of water drawn was positively associated with the landholding and wealth status. From Table 7.7 it can be seen that on an average 39 per cent of the households were getting adequate water. Across income groups, households which had annual income in the range of 25,000 to 40,000 were getting adequate water compared to other income groups. In the case of lower income groups, households which were near the source had better access to sufficient water.

Table-7.7
Access to Adequate Water by Income Status

Income per Annum (in Rs.)	*Adequate*	*Not Adequate*	*Total No. of Respondents*	*% of HHs with Adequate Water*
1	2	3	4	5
Less than 15,000	36	98	134	27
15,000 to 25,000	127	175	302	42
25,001 to 40,000	62	79	141	44
40,001 and Above	71	112	183	39
Grand Total	**296**	**464**	760	39

The sanitation services provided under the programme are (1) washing platform, (2) dustbins, (3) cattle troughs, (4) community bathing cubicles and (5) drainage. As mentioned earlier, sanitary services had provided largely on demand from the community. Thus, in many villages some of the components such as community toilets and bathing cubicles, were not proposed during the planning stage. It was felt that those components are not important given the village level contextual factors (location advantages of various services), as normally people prefer to bathe at their houses or at the water source. The review of the ESRs suggests that in most villages, facilities like washing platforms, dustbins, cattle troughs and individual household toilets should be installed. However, most households reported that there were large variations in the components provided in the ESR and proposed by villagers.

However, among sample households, on an average, 17 per cent of them had Individual Household Sanitation Latrines (IHSL), against the targeted 30 per cent. Even in the 17 per cent a cumulative figure of various programmes implemented in the villages, such as Nirmalagrama. Across villages, Daginakatte, followed by Hombadimandadi and Lakhangao had better coverage in providing better sanitation facilities, including drainage, dustbins etc. The reason for better coverage was specific to each village. In Daginakatte, due to NGO commitment; in Hombadimandadi, due to cultural factors and in Lakhangao, due to connection of bio-gas to IHSL. The reason for poor coverage was lack of required land and households were not convinced about receiving the expected services.

Households in some villages pointed out that the provision of IHSLs was biased towards wealthy people. This was explicit as the sanitation services were provided to those households who made a matching contribution of 25 per cent of the total cost. In the villages covered by this programme, it was common to see box type drainage in the wealthy localities and L shaped drainage in poorer localities. Further, in a few villages the VWSC have linked sanction of subsidy to household toilets with community contribution and Private Household Connection (PHC) of water, the beneficiary has to meet either one of these condition. The objective of this decision is to plough back the subsidy amount to the community contribution fund indirectly. This contribution is a pre-condition to sanction latrines under the IRWSS, as per the informal practice observed in

Table-7.8
Households Using Water and Environmental Sanitation Services (Per cent)

Name of the Village	*Water Supply*	*Bathing Cubicle*	*Washing Platform*	*Cattle Troughs*	*Street Bins*	*Sullage Drainage*	*Individual Latrines**	*Individual Latrines Cum Biogas*
Seegavalu	65	NA	neg	NIL	NA	70	8	NA
K. Koppalu	NIL	NA	NIL	NIL	not in use	50	NA	NA
A. Nagathihalli	100	NA	neg	40	not in use	70	16	NA
Hombadimandadi	50	neg	NIL	NIL	not in use	NIL	19	NA
Daginakatte	55	NA	NIL	20	NA	60	9	NA
Kembliganhalli	100	NA	NIL	NIL	not in use	60	7	NA
Lakhanagao	neg	neg	neg	NA	NA	50	1	30
Yelasangi	100	neg	20	20	NA	30	1	NA
Arkera	100	NA	20	20	in use	60	18	NA
Madlur	100	neg	20	20	NA	90	2	NA

Note: Although a number of ISLs were constructed, only a few of them were used.

all sample villages. This undue practice has kept away many households from opting for latrines, as most of them could not deposit the amount. Thus, households face discrimination not only in getting toilets but also in obtaining any sanitation services in their locality. To prevent such unethical decisions, marginal sections of the community were provided a reasonably better representation in the VWSC by reserving an adequate number of seats. However, this could not help in raising their voice, because each proposal was linked to the persons contribution. In fact, many poor households were ignorant about the project, the credentials of the VWSC were questionable, as they have actually been paid to create awareness in general, particularly among the poor, to empower them to participate in the process of implementation.

Under the programme, the community will have a Memorandum of Understanding (MoU) with the government to take up the responsibility of operation and maintenance of assets by collecting user charges. But in some villages (Lakhangao and Daginkatte) even without the MoU the assets had been handed over to one or two committee members. There were cases where most committee members felt that the work carried out was very shabby. Though the replacement of old pipes with new ones was part of the contract, with the nexus between officials and contractors that was not carried out. In Daginakatte, the villagers felt that the construction work was very shabby and a large number of valves were not functioning. On these grounds the villagers rejected taking over the O&M responsibility, but with the help of couple of a few committee members, the officials were able to transfer the assets to the VWSC.

The sustainability of systems depends upon skills in maintenance and timely replacement/augmentation of existing systems, which in turn depends on financial and institutional sustainability. Among these interdependent components, financial sustainability is of the utmost importance. VWSCs should have financial stability and this can be achieved by generating resources through imposing user charges and other charges. To increase the user charges, the number of PHCs has to be increased each year to match the increasing expenditure. Of the total of 755 sample households, 217 had access to PHC, of whom, nearly 70 per cent belonged to wealthy and middle-income categories. This is quite obvious as the deposit had to be paid, in addition to the community contribution, as the share of partial capital cost. However, it was noted that user charges levied did not have any direct influence on water supply efficiency or its rational use. Villages who were paying higher charges also faced problems of scarcity and inadequacy accompanied with inaccessibility. This was discouraging for people, who were opting for a demand-driven approach to water supply services.

As mentioned earlier, in some villages sanitation work was not taken up due to lack of community contribution and in those villages the community could not take the responsibility of O&M. Subsequently, of all the villages under the programme, except for 10 to 12 villages, all other villages were handed over to the respective Grama Panchayat for O&M. Now the GPs are meeting the expenditure from the development fund account of the village, as providing water to the villages is one of the basic responsibilities of the GP.

Lessons Learnt and Alternatives

The above analysis began by elaborating that the concept of community participation through cost-sharing and recovery in development projects has been theoretically established and empirically tested in many part of the world. International agencies are promoting this idea by funding directly and indirectly, and countries are accepting these approaches, as they would reduce the financial burden on the public exchequer.

In India, based on this concept, several programmes were implemented; among these the Karnataka Integrated Water Supply and Sanitation Programme is one. The success of this experiment was subject to the following factors: community awareness, political will of the government including local government, the effective functioning of the VWSC. However, our analysis brings out that the VWSC was ineffective in organization and functioning, owing to lack of statutory power and most of the demerits of the Grama Panchayats were inherited by it. Owning to lack of political will, the progamme was used for the benefit of local leaders rather than institutionalize the programme. In the process, proper institutional framework and collective action does not take place under the programme. In fact, members of the committee acted as licensing authorities rather than facilitators to promote water and sanitation services in village.

Based on our survey findings, it may be held that the VWSC has not been successful in many villages in mobilizing the required community contribution for environmental sanitation. The tendering of villages for construction of water works without mobilizing upfront contributions defeated the philosophy and the essence of the programme. As a result, beneficiary involvement in sharing capital cost and recovery of operation and maintenance costs by levy of user charges could not take place in many villages. Subsequently, this had a negative effect on provision of sanitation services, particularly on construction of drainage services. The amount spent on creating awareness and mobilization of community contribution was more than what was collected as community contribution. If one compares project villages and control villages, the problems are the same or even worse in project villages, because of the lack of accountability among the factors involved.

The lessons learnt from the above analysis is that the concept of need, demand and community contribution were not marketed well. In the sense, NGOs, which had been assigned the responsibility of creating the demand for better service, have not performed their job efficiently. People, with their past experience of existing delivery systems, are unable to believe that services will improve under the VWSC, because the service provider is going to be part of the same local governance. Thus, there is a need to separate the job of service provider from the local governance. This calls for partial privatization of service delivery to improve services. The VWSC can hold the responsibility of regulation on behalf of the GP. Under Sections 100 and 106 the Grama Panchayats or any one appointed by them is empowered to inspect any sewer, drain, privy, water closet, house-gully or cesspool. Considering this legal support, the GP can compel households to construct sanitary latrines. The Grama Panchayat can then outsource the provision part to an NGO or any dedicated organization, similar to Ramkrishna Lok Siksha Parishad, Midn ‹pur. However, these institutions must have a clear structure of goals and methods of implementation. Care must be taken not to duplicate efforts or damage the working relationship between the partner institutions.

NOTES

1. DANIDA, KFW, DfiD, World Bank, UNICEF, UNDP and European Union.

2. These include the facilities like sanitary latrines, conversion of dry latrines, garbage pits, soak-pits, drains, paving of lanes; sanitary latrines in anganawadi schools panchayatghar, health centre; smokeless chullahs; cleanliness of ponds and tanks; clean surroundings around, handpumps and other drinking water sources with platform including washing and bathing platforms etc.
3. World Bank, the Netherland Government and DANID, etc.
4. Washing platforms, bathing cubic, cattle trough and dustbins.
5. (1) Sullage drainage, (2) Road reprofiling and (3) Bye-lane pavement.
6. Out of the total amount required 70 per cent will be provided as grant by the programme and the remaining 30 per cent has to be contributed by the community in the form of cash, material and manpower.
7. The effectiveness community participation is observed looking at the implementation of the decision taken in the meetings and quality of work undertaken. In most of the villages where the VWSCs role was meager in mobilizing the community contribution, the quality of work was very suspect.

REFERENCES

Bhore Committee (1946) This Committee, Known as the Health Survey and Development Committee, www.ndc-nihfw.org/html/Committe and Communications.htm

Cairncross, Sandy (1992) – *Sanitation and Water Supply: Practical Lessons from the Decade,* Discussion Paper Series 9, World Bank, Washington DC.

Chang, Ha-Joon, (2002), "Breaking the Mould: an Institutionalist Political Economy Alternative to the Neo-Liberal Theory of the Market and The State", *Cambridge Journal of Economics,"* 26.

Churchill, Anthony; (1993) *Rural Water Supply and Sanitation – Time for a Change,* World Bank Development Project; See, also, Serageldin, (1994) *Water Supply, Sanitation and Environmental Sustainability, Financial Challenge,* The World Bank, Washington.

Cooper, J. Kenneth *(1997) Human Waste Overwhelms India's War on Disease."* Washington Post, Foreign Service, Monday, February 17.

Dasgupta, Monica Das and Others (2003) Governance of Communicable Disease Control Services: A Case Study and Lessons from India, *Background Paper for WDR 2004 (Unpublished).*

Environmental Hygiene Committee (1948-49), which Recommended a Comprehensive Plan for Providing Safe Water, www.sulabhenvis.in/pages/database_detail.asp.

Esrey, S.A., Feachem, R.G. and Hughes, J.M. (1985) Interventions for the Control of Diarrhoeal Disease Among Young Children: Improving Water Supplies and Excreta Disposal Facilities. *Bulletin of the World Health Organization*, 63(4), 757–772.

Government of India (1999) *54th Round. Drinking Water, Sanitation and Hygiene in India.* National Sample Survey Organization, New Delhi.

Government of India (2001), Tables on Houses and Household Amenities and Assets, Series 1. Office of the Registrar General and Census Commissioner, New Delhi.

GOI (2003),*Towards Total Sanitation and Hygiene: A Challenge for India. Ministry of Rural Development*, New Delhi, Website: www.ddws.*nic. in.*

Government of Karnataka (1998) *Evaluation Study on Water Supply and Sanitation,* Directorate of Economics and Statistics, M.S. Buildings, Ambedkar Veedhi, Bangalore.

GOK (2000) *Strategy Paper on Rural Water Supply and Sanitation, 2000-05,* Department of Rural Development and Panchyat Raj, M.S. Building, Bangalore, October.

Harmeyer, David and Ashok Mody "Private Capital in Water and Sanitation" *Finance and Development*, March 1997.

Kahkonen, Sathu (1999) *Does Social Capital Matter in Water and Sanitation Delivery: A Review of Literature* – Social Capital Initiative Working Paper No. (9), The World Bank.

Khaleghian (eds.) *The Organization of Disease Control Systems: Case Studies from Asia, Africa and Latin America* (forthcoming).

Mavalankar Dileep; Shankar M. (2004), "Sanitation and Water Supply: The Forgotten Infrastructure," *India Infrastructure Report, 2004*, New Delhi: Oxford University Press.

Myles, F. Elledge (2003) *'International Water and Sanitation' Reviewed by Roland Schertnlib* (SANDEL), IRC International and Sanitation.

Narayan, Deepa, (1995), *"The Contribution of People's Participation, Evidences from 121 Rural Water Supply Projects,"* Environmentally Sustainable Development Occasional Paper series No.1, World Bank, Washington D.C.

Pushpangdan, K. and Murgan, G. "User Financing and Collective Action: Relevance for Sustainable Rural Water Supply in India" *Economic and Political Weekly;* April 4, 1998.

Rajasekhar, D. and Veerashekharappa (2003)' *Role of Local Organisations in Water Supply and Sanitation Sector: A Study in Karnataka and Uttaranchal States, India,* Institute for Social and Economic Change, Nargarbhavi, Bangalore.

Ramasubban, Radhika (1982) *Public Health and Medical Research in India.* Saree Report (4): Swedish Agency for Research Cooperation with Developing Countries. Stockholm.

Ruth, Meinzen Dick and Mendeza Meyra (1996), Alternative Water Allocation Mechanisms: India and International Experiences, *Economic and Political Weekly* Vol. 31(12) March 30 p. A-25.

Saleth, Maria R. and Dinar, Ariel. (1999) *"Water Challenge and Institutional Response: A Cross-country Perspective"*, Policy Working Paper No. 2045. Washington, D.C.: The World Bank.

Veerashekharappa (1999), *Karnataka Integrated Rural Water and Environmental Sanitation Impact: An Evaluation Study*, Institute for Social and Economic Change, Nagarbhavi, Bangalore.

UN- HABITAT (2003). *Water and Sanitation in the World's Cities: Local Action for Global Goals*. London: Earthscan Publications Ltd.

United Nations (2000), UN Millennium Development Goals (MDG)" Website http:// un.org/millenniumgoals/index.html.

Veerashekharappa (2002) Community Participation in Rural Drinking Water Supply and Sanitation: A Case Study of Karnataka' *Journal of Indian Water Works Association*, Vol. XXXIV (1) , January-March.

Veerashekharappa (2004) *Promotion of Individual Household Latrines in Rural Karnatka: Lessons Learnt*, Working Paper (160), Institute for Social and Economic Change.

WHO and UNICEF (2000), *Global Sanitation Water Supply Assessment 2000 Report*, Geneva, WHO-UNICEF.

Woods, Robert. (2003). Public Health Service Delivery: The Historical Experience of the Developed Countries in Monica Das Gupta and Peyvand.

WSSCC (2003), Website: www. wsscc.org Related to Water and Sanitation.

World Bank (1999). *Rural Water Supply and Sanitation*. Washington: World Bank and New Delhi: Allied Publishers.

8

Ground Water Governance in Kerala

JOS C. RAPHAEL

Kerala is generally said to be a water rich state among Indian states. But the situation has been changing for the last couple of decades due the population pressure on this tiny landscape with its density of 819 persons per sq.km.[1] It had an abundant rainfall of 3000 mm which is dwindling for the past few decades. Preference for homestead human settlement pattern in the state made severe pressure on forests and wet lands (paddy fields) for want of habitable land plots resulting in land scarcity. Consequently this makes multiple impacts on water scenario viz. land to hold the water reduces spatially. Water demands met by homestead open wells, which are the precious source of water for Keralites, find it difficult to cope up with the supply of water. The state claimed public water supply coverage[2] of 67.52 per cent which is far from satisfactory especially during summer. Rivers of Kerala are exhausted by indiscriminate sand mining for building construction sector. Clay from the paddy fields is also over mined for brick making and building construction to make the situation more badly.

Human settlement pattern in Kerala is peculiar in comparison with the other states of India. Generally, Indian human settlements are in the form of cluster of houses in the villages whereas such clusters are not common in Kerala. Here the people have separate homesteads with clear cut boundaries made up of vegetative fencing or some traditional constructions/compound walls. Kerala has nearly 180 to 200 open wells in a square Kilo Meter on an average. It is estimated that the state has nearly 45 lakhs of open dug wells.[3] Still Kerala faces acute water shortage in the summer which appears like a paradox. Kerala homesteads were self reliant with homestead open wells and ponds. But now the water scenario has altogether changed particularly after 1983, the year in which Kerala faced severe drought in the recent past.

Reasons behind water scarcity in Kerala are numerous. The traditional agricultural practice at local level with water conservation measures is a thing of the past in many parts of Kerala. Nuclear family system requires separate homesteads that fragmented many cultivable lands into small pieces of 0.10 to 0.20 acres or even lesser. These fragmented lands of agriculture turned housing habitats give little scope for the water conservation practice of traditional agriculture. Levelling of paddy fields for house constructions destructed natural eco-systems and this destruction and construction activities necessitated the uncontrolled sand mining from rivers for house and other construction works. Consequently, open wells near the rivers depleted and further, levelled paddy lands gave scope for floods as well[4]. Farmers' collective efforts in the form of cleaning ponds, building minor earthen check dams across the streams at the end of monsoons and other similar activities are now termed as the duties of local governments. As local governments have been entrusted with enough powers and funds for such activities, farmers neither take interest in such activities nor do local governments take it seriously. The reasons for such negligence could be multifarious.[5]

Kerala homesteads were keen enough to conserve the rainwater they get in their own homestead garden soil in the past. And this has been changed up side down to "flush out" all rainwater from their homestead compounds resulting inadequate water in their homestead open wells particularly in summer. The compound walls with rainwater 'flush out holes' are very common in many houses. Ornamental bricking around the house premises instead of traditional cow dung mix flooring become impediments to percolation of rainwater at the homesteads.[6]

The modernization, dams and government water supply systems made them dependent upon government water supplies. The ponds were levelled to sell off their land and perennial open wells often converted to deep toilet pits in many urban centres to accentuate the agony since they get public supply of water. And no new pond making or new tank space is created. Lavish water use of Keralites is known as they get rain for nearly six months from June to November from South West and North East Monsoons. It is often said that Keralites think about water scarcity and conservation during summer and the subject will be in deep slumber once mid summer shower falls in. This has been happening almost every year that paved the way for crores of drought assistance and flood assistance from Central Government and millions from International Development Agencies as loans (nearly 2000 crores) due to the sheer water illiteracy of Keralites[7] The annual state expenditure on drinking water projects through Kerala Water Authority is on an average Rs. 400 crores in the last few years.[8] Often the Contractors, bureaucracy and full time political activists may reap the fringe benefits of such assistance. Over to the quality of water, the situation is worse than the quantity due to co-existence of deep pit toilets and open dug wells of homesteads together. Coli form bacteria found in the open dug wells are often beyond permissible limits in many parts of the state. This invites troubles for Kerala Waters. However, this chapter is making an attempt to appraise the quantity of water available in summer through the "homestead open dug wells and deep tube wells" from the common property resource in ground waters in Kerala. And the ground water is defined as the water which exists below the surface of the ground at any location or at any particular category of locations.[9]

Hydro-Geological Conditions

The topography of the state can be divided into three zones namely, the coastal planes, the mid lands, and the hilly ranges. The major portion of the state is underlain by crystalline rocks of Archean ages. Sedimentary formations of Eocene to recent overlie these crystalline rocks along the coastal belts. The yield of tube wells in the crystalline rocks can be between 6-10 m3/hr. The midland area is covered by laterites where the yield of tube wells may vary from 10-15 m3/hr. In the coastal belts where tertiary formations possess promising aquifers, the tube wells can yield 12-15 m3/hr under free flow conditions. The statistics shows that net annual groundwater availability is 6.23 BCM/Yr. and annual ground water draft is 2.92 BCM/Yr. The stage of ground water development is 47 per cent.[10]

Ungoverned Groundwater Sector

Groundwater is a common property resource. The non realization of this fact by the public causes concern for water security of each family. The present chapter thus deals about ground water sector which normally not governed by government or people's body but separately handled by individual households or firms. If a society is affected by the ground water extraction of a family or business firm that cause concern which is rooted in poor governance of government or the society upon the ground water sector. Much acclaimed ground water extraction of Multinational Company Coca-Cola has been highly discussed in many forums is a corollary of the problem connected with business firm extractions. In the same way, there are unchecked and unnoticed ground water extraction of individual houses, cash crop irrigation, culture fishery, distilleries and many other end uses which are less discussed. The device for ground extraction is either through open dug wells or by bore wells (tube wells). The filter points popularly called *Champu* pipe seen in the coastal belts are not taken for the study in this chapter. And the prime focus of this chapter is on the impact of tube well drilling upon the homestead open dug wells in Kerala which is the main source of fresh water for Keralaites. In this context unscientific bore well drilling and pumping that causes social and economic impacts deserve high attention.

Governance in the Related Water Sectors

The levels of governance varies across other related water utility sectors like piped water supply, canal irrigation, irrigation through ponds, rivers and other bodies. There are aplenty of government schemes which have social capitals that manage mini piped water supply systems such as world bank aided *Jalanidhi*, centrally assisted *Swajal dhara*, local governments' schemes, Dutch aided Community Irrigation Water User Associations, Command Area Development Schemes etc. It seems *Jalanidhi* and Community Irrigation Schemes have got a better project organizational set up than all other schemes. And other schemes are managed in indifferent manner by bureaucracy and farmers. Still there exists governance set up either by government systems or by people's bodies and they are recognized.[11]

Source of Data

The study is mainly based on the discussion with Officers of Kerala State Ground Water Department and Communities of Water Scarce Areas. Secondary data is collected mainly from central ground water board and state ground water department. Author's own professional experience with Dutch aided Kerala Community Irrigation Project added information to the ground water issues and problems in the governance angle. Meeting with large number of members of Panchayati Raj Institutions, communities of water scarce areas and rainwater harvesting campaigns mobilized necessary inputs for research analysis and findings. PRA mode has been applied for the informal group discussion with water scarcity affected people of several blocks of Trichur district in particular.

History

The ground water extraction for agriculture purpose was prevalent from 1970s under the State Agriculture Department of Kerala. The groundwater wing was separated from agriculture to form a State Ground Water Department during 1978. Currently each district of Kerala has got a district level ground water office and necessary staffs which are equipped with usual government vehicles plus two tube well drilling rigs that costs about Rs. 20 lakhs. Also there is mushrooming growth of private tube well drilling agencies in Kerala since the drought of 1983.

Fluctuations of vagary monsoon and sever summers gave wind fall gain for private tube well drillers. Seasonal and saline intruded open dug wells became common in Kerala. Often people found tube well as a strong alternative in getting enough water for summer as well as rainy season. Manual drawing from open dug wells gradually have become obsolete. Energized pumps both for open dug wells and tube wells became common. Centrally assisted scheme of tube well hand pump seen widespread after 1983. Space for tube well requires very less in comparison with open dug wells particularly for public water supply schemes. Land scarcity of this tiny state facilitated the local governments to opt for hand pumps supported by central schemes side by side particularly for scheduled caste and scheduled tribe communities. Non potable and contaminated water from public tube wells with GI pipe had been a mark of poor settlement colonies. Non functional tube wells with rusted iron remain in many locations still invites accidents and environmental hazards. Majority of them were drilled by Government Ground Water Department.

Private Tube Well Drilling

Emergence of private tube well drilling agencies is a mixed blessing where government systems fail on demand and in time for the customers. Indeed private is proud of giving away the service as per seasonal demand. Nearly 30 private drilling agencies operate in each district. It does not mean that each agency have their own drilling rigs. Normally they take for rent from the rig owners of nearby states. Summers are engulfed with rattling noise of tube well drilling in many water scarce regions of Kerala and tube well rigs with pipes are seen run cross Kerala villages. They charge around Rs. 40 to Rs. 70 depends upon the radius of tube well. Also the rate is fixed depends upon the season, demand and other convenience contexts. They are self-righteous to offer "water for sure" with full guarantee in popular terms.

Issues and Problems with Private Drilling

It is quite interesting to study how tube well operators manipulate the facts over households or tube well owners. Once the rate and location fixed by the private drilling agency and tube well owner accepts the terms, drilling machines starts operating. The drilling produces its usual noise and dust that drives away the people around. The most interesting part is the case with assured water. The principle is if no water struck while drilling no money is assured for drilling agency. And therefore, drilling agency will see that water is assured somehow while drilling the tube well. Hence they are very meticulous to see that water is pumped from tube well some how to get money for their effort. This leads to unscientific tube well drilling that affects the open dug wells nearby and society at large.

What is the Common Process of Unscientific Drilling?

As per the scientific drilling process, the casing pipe of deep tube well has to be inserted two to three feet down to the hard rock to pump up the water from the tube well. This way the aquifer that holds fresh water for open dug well located above the tube well aquifer unaffected while pumping the water from tube well. The open dug well aquifer zone is normally located about 10 to 40 feet below in the soil whereas tube well aquifer zone is located much deeper of 200 to 500 feet at the hard rock. Suppose a drilling agency starts drilling the tube well and struck no water in the hard rock, the casing pipe of the tube well will be fixed above the hard rock. There appears a gap between the casing pipe and hard rock (weathered rock space) through which the water from nearby open dug wells around seeps down to this tube well. Under this circumstance, if a powerful pump is installed and pumped up the water from this tube well, the water from the aquifers of nearby open dug wells will seep down to this tube well. Now the water is discharged enough from the tube well. Tube well owner is happy as well as the drilling agency and the agreed rate is given to drilling agency. The problems start later once water level in the open dug wells start decreasing at faster rate than the usual lowering of water table of the nearby areas. Since the public is ignorant about this manipulation of drilling agencies they are unable to complaint due to the information gap. The lowering of water table causes social costs including from the government systems to supply water for all in the summer through pipes. Apart from this social evil, the particular tube well may be collapsed if there exists a gap between casing pipe and hard rock after few years depends upon the hydro geological movements or seismic activities.

Currently there are five development blocks in the state which are over exploited as per the statistics of Central Ground Water Board and they are as follows with their districts in bracket: Athiyannur (Trivandrum), Chittur (Palghat), Kodungallur (Trichur), Kozhikode (Kozhikode) and Kasargode (Kasargode). Moreover, 15 other development blocks are in critical conditions and 30 development blocks are under semi critical stage of over exploitation in the state. Over to the quality, Ernakulam, Trichur and Alleppy districts are affected by saline intrusion in the coastal belts and traces of fluoride contaminated ground water are observed in the Palghat district.[12]

Who Governs Groundwater?

At present, any one can dig a tube well anywhere they wish, pump up water and can sell off. The distance between two tube wells is not practically followed and it is loose in principle too. There is no control of pumping water from tube wells or open dug wells. Nobody govern groundwater sector in Kerala. Panchayati Raj Institutions are ignorant about the technicalities of ground water, tube well and their connection to the homestead open dug wells. This is a stage of zero governance for groundwater sector. Though the digging activities either for tube well or open dug wells require permission in five notified development blocks of the state, it is not keenly attended either by public or the government. The fact remains that the poor households depend upon their own neatly maintained open dug wells loosing water or in other words ground water table is going down at an increasing pace to the extent of half a meter yearly. It costs them further to dig down to maintain the water levels or they need to go for alternatives like collecting water from public supply or joining with Water User Associations or to dig a tube well at their homestead to add competition for ground water table. Water User Associations engineered by World Bank and Asian Development Bank Schemes, the much replicated Indian pattern of centrally sponsored schemes called *Swajaldhara* and many other similar panchayat schemes now promote social capital for water needs that invite more problems while pumping excess water to meet the ever increasing water demand. It costs each user for initial investments and recurring charges to maintain such systems. In turn this high pumping of ground water causes to lower the ground water table in the area that adds further problems for the people who make use of their own homestead open dug wells. Neither the traditional wisdom of homestead rainwater conservation is applied in these scheme areas. Quite often water sources of these schemes are not recharged which will collapse in the near future for this sure reason. Dead bodies of such mini water supply schemes of Kerala Water Authority are aplenty in Kerala. The governments' effort to replenish the ground water tables through watershed development schemes are nullified by the excessive pumping from tube wells and open dug wells. Already there are several instances of spending the fund of watershed development schemes over productive sector of any sort without the focus on soil and water conservation component by the People's Planning Programme carried through local governments. These issues largely are unnoticed by media than reporting much on acclaimed people's struggle over the Multi-national Coca-Cola's ground water extraction in Palghat district which is only a tip of ice berg from the part of industries. What about the extraction of domestic industries and water tankers? Water selling services are an upcoming industry in Kerala and the impact of such extractions to the nearby households are not addressed much in the state. Vociferous organisations which work on environment subjects seem eager about such water struggles that fetch fairly good attention from all audience while blink their eyes on the bigger culprits around every nook and corner of Kerala.

Why this is happening in the highly literate state of Kerala is out of public negligence and ignorance than any high rain-low water paradox. Staff of Government Ground Water Department know about this malpractice and remain silent as they are afraid to come out considering the permission to speak out from heads of departments. Rather drilling operations of private drilling agencies is considered a blessing at large since the Government Ground Water Department is unable to provide the facilities on upcoming demand in time. Neither the meagre number of staff available at the district head quarters is able to check the malpractices of private drilling agencies.

Now let us look at the competencies of private drilling agencies to cope up with the ever increasing demands of public for tube wells. Private drilling agencies not necessarily have any scientific knowledge to fix the tube well location for ground water extraction. It is largely by guessing with some traditional knowledge and physical verifications of traditional means. Government has not sought any specific qualifications for private drilling operators and their water providers. Further, private drilling operators do not require any licence for tube well drilling. They are often considered as 'essential services' in the summer seasons. Hence their actions are uncontrolled. They need not go on as per the guidelines of government. Neither the government is equipped to patrol private drilling nor do the people know the technicalities of drilling and tube well constructions. Call it zero governance of literate Kerala precisely.

On to Scientific Pumping

What is scientific pumping from the tube well? It is based on the pump test from a tube well to fix the capacity and optimum pumping rate from a tube well. As per this a pump test has to be conducted after the drilling using a pump test machine that look almost like a drilling rig. Twenty four hours of continuous pumping is often seen recommended to finalise the optimum pumping rate from a healthy tube well in the dry season. This will help the user to switch on the pump for fixed time with regular intervals which may enhance the water source replenishment in the deeper aquifer. A tube well water resource can be maintained in sustainable manner by optimum pumping. Unfortunately, Kerala Government has only one pump test machine to conduct the test which is highly inadequate. Currently, optimum pumping is fixed on the basis of drilling time tube well water discharge which is rather a guess work or unscientific activity. If this is the position of government system, worst is the experience from the private drilling agencies.

For example, a tube well user has to purchase a motor pump from the local seller to install in the tube well, how to fix the horse power of the pump? Scientifically it has to be based on the pump test and resultant capacity of the tube well. Since it is not practiced with private drilling, helpers/drilling agency will fix somehow a better motor pump with a high Horse Power (HP) or low HP depends upon the financial position of the tube well owner. In other words, private agencies can manipulate the drilling time well discharge and fix for high powered motor which may be expensive for the tube well owner. Or private agencies may not advice the tube well owner about the optimum pumping since it is not known to them on scientific line obviously. There is enough possibility of victimization by the retail seller on the motor pump purchase over tube well owner. If an improper pump is installed in the tube well it may affect the tube well badly or may affect the nearby open dug well adversely. Moreover, installation of unnecessary high power pump can squeeze the finance of tube well owner while purchasing the pump as well as it can rob them while paying high monthly electricity charges. The usage of inappropriate HP pump will cause national waste of electricity too which is an unnoticed grey area by research agencies.

The Ground Water Department of Kerala Government has constructed and identified 864 observation wells for well monitoring which is inadequate; says the officials of Ground Water Department. They opine that since the well density is very high in Kerala perhaps the highest in the world, the present observatory wells for monitoring is inadequate. True that rain gauge exists to measure the available rainwater in the state and no sufficient mechanism in existence to measure the ground water draft from the underground. This is a huge information gap in the water resources planning of Kerala. All it is known that half a meter of ground water table is going down yearly in many places of Kerala.

Kerala Ground Water (Control and Regulation), Act, 2002

This led to the enactment of Kerala Ground Water (Control and Regulation) Act 2002. The Act has several aspects of ground water management but silent about unscientific construction of tube well and unscientific pumping for unknown reasons. Formation of the

Kerala Ground Water Authority is one among the important article in the Act. With the nominal implementation of this article, name of the department is changed to an authority. By and large this is yet another chapter tiger of unimplemented water law in the state.

The most important section envisaged in the Act is the "well registration" by the well owners at the District Level Ground Water Office to rectify the information gap of ground water extraction. As per this the open dug well owners who make use electric motor pump with more than 1.5 HP are to register their wells in the District Ground Water Office concerned. Same way the owners with tube well having motor pump of above 3 HP are to register in respective District Ground Water Offices. The law enforced from March 2003 with limited usual governmental publicity. And the number of wells registered is very poor to the tune of nearly 5000 across Kerala where Palghat district tops the list among all the districts. In nutshell, hardly one per cent of the well owners so far have registered in the District Ground Water Offices in Kerala. Why this happens is worth exploring and found that the information dissemination of this important water law is very poor. It was merely in the nature of pasting the said public notice in the Grama Panchayat Notice Boards or on the window panes and walls. People of below poverty line category normally visit the Grama Panchayats since the most of the local government schemes are for the poor. Many of them might not have such pumps perhaps. Public awareness over the media also was very low. And it was an election period too (summer of 2003) when the government put up public notice regarding the same. Either elected representatives were not willing to insist the well owners for registration since it may affect their votes. Contacted farmers and well owners respond that it is a matter of fear in approaching the Government Offices unnecessarily unless the government insists the same from well owners.

Ultimately, Kerala Ground Water (Control and Regulation) Act of 2002 intends to make a control on the over-exploitation of ground water use remain in chapter thereby underlining the status of zero groundwater governance in Kerala. The upcoming water policy of Kerala state also (draft policy) has not considered the issues of unscientific tube well construction by private drilling agencies and unscientific pumping of ground water by all types of water users. Poor observance of Kerala Ground Water Control Act by the public, its poor monitoring by the government and low media publicity for its public awareness require serious attention by the planners and policy makers for good ground water governance in the state.

Recommendations

The lessons above leads to what could be done next to level the gaps, to fix the mismatches and fill up the lacunas in the ground water scenario of Kerala. The most important is to save the homestead open dug wells of Kerala from unscientific tube well construction and water pumping from it. Though the public water supply systems supplement people's water needs, Census Statistics 2000 notes that homestead open dug well is the main water resource for the state in achieving household level water security. Thus it is imperative to control the unscientific approaches in the ground water scenario of the state and following recommendations are made for the same.

1. Registration of private bore well drilling agencies with the Ground Water Department is essential for licensing them and to issue guidelines to them. The government may incorporate the laws through amendment with 2002 Act accordingly.
2. Insist technical competency and qualification of staff with private drilling agencies to avoid irrational water diving and construction of tube wells.
3. Ground Water Authority and the district level offices must be equipped with adequate staff and vehicles to patrol private tube well drilling to see that guidelines are followed from the government.
4. Pump Test for tube well to be made mandatory including for the government schemes. Private agencies may be allowed to conduct pump testing in the prescribed manner as directed by the ground water authority. Pump test charges may be fixed for private agencies accordingly. It is most important to analyse that how the nearby open dug wells to the tube wells are affected during pumping test.
5. District Ground Water Office should be equipped with adequate pump test machines in every district with adequate pump technicians.
6. The fixation and installation of motor pumps in the tube wells should be scrutinized in consultation with ground

water offices after the submission of well completion reports and pump test reports from private agencies which may be verified after random inspections.

7. Well registration to be made mandatory for the notified pump users with adequate public information dissemination systems. Krishi Bhavans may insist upon well registration documents from farmers while supply subsidies from the government.
8. Sufficient number of observatory wells has to be either constructed or have to be identified for well monitoring.
9. Panchayati Raj and Nagara Palika Members and police are to be given training upon the existing malpractices in the sector, technicalities and possible solutions for the good groundwater governance in the state.
10. Total number of tube wells and filter points of coastal areas are to be measured in census mission formats which remain as a serious information gap for ground water sector in the state.

NOTES AND REFERENCES

1. Census data 2000.
2. Government of Kerala, Economic Review 2005, State Planning Board, Trivandrum.
3. Centre for Water Resources Development Management (CWRDM), Calicut.
4. Various research paper references of Kerala Research Programme on Local Level Development, CDS, Trivandrum, 2001.
5. Raphael, Jos C., Roof Water Harvesting Community Initiatives in Kerala, Kurukshetra, January, 2005.
6. *Ibid.*
7. Bhatathiripad, T.N.N, *Kudivellam* Impressions, Kunnathu Mana Buildings, Trichur, 2004.
8. Government of Kerala, Economic Review 2005, State Planning Board, Trivandrum.
9. Kerala Ground Water (Control and Regulation) Act, 2002, Government of Kerala.
10. Central Ground Water Development Board Statistics, 2006.
11. Raphael, Jos C., Irrigation Management Transfer: A Case Study from Kerala, Journal of Rural Development, Vol. 23, No. 4, October-December, 2004.
12. Central Ground Water Development Board Statistics, 2006.

9

Ground Water Depletion in Kerala: Issues and Concerns

ROSE MARY GEORGE

Ground water is an essential natural resource for human life and is likely to become a scarce resource in future. Due to the paucity of surface water, ground water plays a decisive role in our national life. As population increases, the average amount of ground water available to each person declines. In India around fifty per cent of irrigated agriculture is still dependent on ground water and eighty five per cent of rural drinking water comes from ground water. The advent of Green Revolution with high yielding variety crop technology in the second half of 1960s has also led to excessive usage of ground water[1] particularly in northern parts of the country. Ground water abstraction structures have increased from four million in 1951 to nearly over twenty six million now. During the same period ground water irrigated area has increased to about thirty six million hectares. It is estimated that this rapid pace of development is likely to continue and will reach sixty four million hectares by 2007. The increased demand and unregulated exploitation of ground water caused its depletion in many parts of the country.

Ground Water Depletion

The installation of large number of open wells and bore wells with high power pumps in fresh ground water quality zones from which water is withdrawn will profoundly alter the natural balance of ground water recharge and it will result in ground water depletion. When slow rate of ground water circulation and discharge occurs, the net availability of the ground water remains generally high. The quantity of water available from an aquifer is dependent on groundwater recharge, ground water discharge and available ground water storage. The volume of water in storage will not change when the volume of water discharged from the aquifer equals the aquifer's replenishment. But the perennial overdraft of ground water supplies will result in a progressive decline in the quantity of water in the aquifer. As ground water is pumped from a well, the level of water in the well drops and the surrounding water table is also lowered. In many areas, where many wells are in operation the discharge increases while the recharge remains constant resulting into more lowering of water table (Jeet; 2005). Besides less rainfall tends to less recharge, which accentuates the drought situation.

The indiscriminate use of ground water will lead to serious environmental hazards, as occurred in some parts of India. Both quantity and quality of ground water will affect by the over use. Some of the challenges to ground water quantity associated with its over exploitation are, *overdraft, drawdown* and *subsidence*. *Overdraft* occurs when ground water is removed faster than recharge. This will reduce the storage capacity of ground water. *Drawdown* is the natural result of over pumping and will result in temporarily lowered water table. The water table will recover only when the supply is replenished. In *subsidence* water pressure reduces due to over pumping and as a result the fine particles that held water become compacted. Sometimes the land above the aquifer may sink in addition to the reducing storage capacity. The indiscriminate abstraction of ground water will affect its quality too. Arsenic contamination in pockets of industrial zones is observed as a great threat to health of the people. Another major threat is contamination of aquifer by salt-water intrusion. When fresh water resides from large area heavy saline water will move into that region. In areas where less rainfall, infiltration and surface run off is low, inland ground water salinity occurs because the soluble salt tends to accumulate in the soil. When ground water depletion occurs in these areas quality will reduce to a greater extent due to salinity.

Ground Water Depletion in Kerala

Geographically Kerala lies as a narrow strip of land along the southwest corner of India bordered by Western Ghats on eastern sides and Laksha Dweep Sea on the western side. The state is located between the north latitudes 8° 18′ and 12° 48′ and east longitudes

74° 52′ and 77° 22. The state is divided into fourteen revenue districts and 152 development blocks. Groundwater potential of Kerala differs from place to place due to its varied hydro geological characteristics. Naturally the occurrence and movement of ground water is mainly controlled by the physiography, geological setting and structure.

In Kerala ground water. is the main source of drinking water and about ninety percentage of the rural population depends on ground water sources. Kerala's demand for water is mainly for household purposes, agriculture, generation of electricity, aquaculture and preventing salt-water intrusion. The cropping pattern of Kerala is quite different from rest of India with almost 80 per cent of its land occupied by perennial tree crops necessitates supplementary irrigation during summer season (John, 2003). As such Kerala faces lot of challenges due to greater use and lower recharge causing wide gap between the demand and supply of water in all sectors like drinking water, agriculture and industry. Inspite of the state scenario on the availability of ground water being favourable in Kerala unlike other states, there are certain pockets in the state that faces scarcity of water.

Though Kerala being a lucky state in its availability for rainwater is now facing serious ground water depletion. An increased demand and unregulated exploitation of ground water are threatening to accelerate the depletion of ground water resources in Kerala. The fast depletion of ground water reserves and the failure to enhance recharge facilities may see large parts of the state struggling to meet the demand for water in the near future. There has been a spurt in ground water extraction structures during the last decade and the state shows a heavy imbalance in the availability of ground water over the past five years. The increasing agricultural and industrial exploitation turned many developmental blocks in over-exploited, critical and semi-critical category in the availability of ground water.

Ground Water Estimation in Kerala

The first attempt to estimate the ground water resources of the country was made in the year 1979, by a committee known as Ground Water Over-exploitation Committee. Later the Ground Water Estimation Committee (GEC) came into existence. During 1980s and 1990s this committee recommended a methodology for the computation of ground water resources, which is modified from time to time. In Kerala, the ground water resources was computed during 1989 and 1992 for the first time based on the 1984 methodology and the resources were re-estimated on March 1999 based on 1997 methodology. This Committee was again constituted in 2004 by Central Ground Water Board (CGWB) in association with State Ground Water Department and other central as well as state agencies based on the latest methodology recommended by GEC in 2004, known as Ground Water Estimation Methodology—1997. This new committee consists of the Secretary, Irrigation Department, Government of Kerala as its Chairman, Regional Director, CGWB as Convener and eight others as members submitted its report in March 2004. All the 151 blocks of Kerala were considered for ground water computation except Malampuzha, the new block (because details are not available).

The survey conducted shows that the net ground water availability of the state is 6229.04 MCM (Million Cubic Meters) and Kerala extracts its 46.88 per cent. Palakkad has the highest availability of 750.33 MCM, while Idukki has the lowest of 246.32 MCM. The gross yearly ground water draft for all the uses is computed as 2693.38 MCM for the State. The domestic and industrial drafts account for 40.73 per cent of the total draft (1097.36 MCM) and the irrigation accounts for 59.27 per cent of the total draft (1596.02 MCM). In the earlier methodology the domestic draft is computed separately and is deducted from the total recharge to arrive at an utilizable recharge. But in the present study the gross ground water draft includes the ground water extraction from all existing ground water structures during monsoon and non-monsoon period. The balance of ground water available for future irrigation was also computed after deducting the gross draft for irrigation and allocation for domestic and industrial water supply for next twenty-five years from the annual ground water availability. A balance of 3221.23 MCM is available for future irrigation development as per the new methodology.

The ground water recharge was computed separately for monsoon and non-monsoon season by the committee as per the methodology. The district wise figures of total recharge are given in the following table.

Table-9.1
Dynamic Ground Water Resources in MCM

District	*Recharge in MCM as on 1999*
Trivandrum	308.51
Quilon	495.61
Pathanamthitta	347.00
Alleppey	466.08
Kottayam	521.06
Idukki	269.04
Ernakulam	618.43
Trichur	774.99
Palghat	823.92
Malappuram	557.29
Calicut	366.41
Wayanad	224.39
Cannanore	591.89
Kasargod	376.18
Total	**6840.80**

Source: CGWB, Report, 2004, p. 14.

For ground water development, the units of assessment were categorized into four areas based on two criteria :

(a) stage of ground water development[2] and
(b) long term trend of pre and post-monsoon ground water levels. The four categories thus evolved are,

1. *Safe Areas*, with potential for development, where stage of ground water development at 70 per cent or lower or more than 70 per cent but less than 90 per cent and both pre and post-monsoon ground water levels do not show a significant long term decline. However, in these areas, caution may be exercised in planning future ground water development with regard to quantum of additional ground water withdrawal.
2. *Semi-critical Areas*, for cautious ground water development—areas where ground water resource assessment shows a stage of ground water development more than 70 per cent but less

than 90 per cent and either pre-monsoon or post-monsoon ground water level shows significant long term decline.

3. *Critical Areas*, where stage of ground water development is more than 90 per cent but less than 100 per cent and either pre-monsoon or post-monsoon or both show a significant long term decline in ground water level. And areas where ground water development is more than 100 per cent but neither pre-monsoon nor post-monsoon ground water level show a significant long term decline.
4. *Over-exploited Areas*, where stage of ground water development is more than 100 per cent both pre-monsoon and post-monsoon ground water level shows a significant decline.

   For both critical and over-exploited areas there should be intensive monitoring and evaluation and future ground water development be linked with water conservation measures and micro level studies. In these areas some institutional, technological and financial restriction should be imparted in the ground water practices – the committee suggested.

The study reveals a heavy imbalance in the availability of groundwater in the state over the past five years, with one-third of the development blocks reporting higher exploitation. While all the blocks were in the safe category in 1992, a computation in 1999 revealed over-exploitation in three blocks and six each were classified as critical and semi-critical. Fifty blocks have moved into the unsafe category in the latest assessment, which used a network of monitoring wells to measure the pre and post-monsoon water levels in the blocks. Among the fifty, five blocks were classified as over-exploited, fifteen as critical and thirty as semi-critical. Athiyannoor in Thiruvananthapuram district tops the list of blocks with over exploited resources, followed by Kozhikkode, Kasargod, Chittur and Kodungalloor. Kasargod taps 79.01 per cent of the ground water reserves, the highest rate of exploitation in Kerala and Wayanad comes last with 24.58 per cent. Sixteen blocks show a falling trend in groundwater exploitation indicating a lesser stage of development.

At a meeting of the Estimation Committee, representatives from Agricultural Department expressed concern over the conversion of paddy fields for non-agricultural use and its impact on ground water recharge. Between 1985 and 2005 the extent of paddy fields in Kerala had shrunk from 8 lakh hectares to 2.1 lakh hectares. The committee has recommended restriction on ground water development in unsafe blocks. For proper planning and management of ground water development in a judicious and socio-economically equitable manner, quantification of ground water resources is one of the most important pre requisites – the committee reminded.

Thus the freshwater crisis is not odd to Kerala. It has been in existence in varying scale and intensity at different times of the year. The steep valleys originating from the Western Ghats result in heavy run off and floods during the peak monsoon periods followed by acute water scarcity in other seasons. But water scarcity is not only the result of natural factors, but also caused by human actions. Kerala's changing lifestyle and mounting urbanization increases the need for fresh water. Besides, competition among the agricultural, industrial and domestic sectors is driving the ground water table deeper and deeper. The number of energized bore wells drilled for irrigation of cash crops was rapidly increased, which caused severe ground water depletion. Many farmers have installed high capacity shallow tube wells to meet irrigation needs and even sold the water to other small landholders in that area.

Unscientific agricultural practices, lack of scientific soil and water conservation methods, over use by each individual on the misconception that water is plenty, destruction of water bodies, deforestation, lack of artificial recharge initiatives, etc. caused draught in the land of rain. In addition to this fresh water eco-systems are also degrading. Reliance on well water is showing an increasing trend because piped water at the national benchmark rate of forty liters per capita a day is not available in all areas. The number of open wells in the state is estimated at four million, roughly one well for every eight to ten persons, means well density of Kerala is highest in the world. This indicates that ground water extraction in the state is showing an increasing trend, warranting a systematic and planned response through regulation, artificial recharge and conservation.

Conservation and sustainable utilization of water resources is important to Kerala and initiatives from the part of government are on the way. As an alternative measure more and more techniques of preserving ground water and recharge measures for augmenting ground water can be adopted on top priority. State Government has already been given the propaganda for rainwater harvesting. Watershed development is inevitable in the special context of Kerala, though some of them proved unsuccessful.[3] Many other projects are in its infant stage waiting for success. In recent years various projects for rainwater harvesting were implemented as stated in National Water Policy (NWP) to augment precipitation and thereby ground water recharge. Today states such as Tamil Nadu have made rainwater harvesting obligatory. There every household should install a water-harvesting device, either for roof water harvesting or for ground water harvesting.[4] Ground water recharge is a major programme in the project *Jalanidhi,* recently implemented by Kerala Rural Water Supply and Sanitation Agency (KRWSSA) in some districts of Kerala.

Fresh water is increasingly taking centre stage in the economic and political discourse. Many disputes have aroused between or within states, districts, regions and even communities for securing management and user rights. Attempts to introduce and enforce legislation have by and large failed. Widespread pollution of ground water in pockets of industrial zones witnessed serious uprisings by the people in local areas. This is evident in Plachimada (Kerala) where the uncontrolled extraction of ground water by Coca-Cola Company has resulted into its pollution and depletion.

The Plachimada Issue

Plachimada is an agricultural village, located in the rain shadow region of Chittur Taluk in Palakkad district. Although the area has less rainfall the ground water recharge are better here because of the gently undulating terrain of the region. Plachimada gets lesser rainfall from 1995 onwards. The Hindustan Coca-Cola Beverages Private Limited (HCBPL) is a water-based industry that produces soft drinks using water as the major raw material. This company bought thirty-two acres of land in Plachimada then dug six bore wells and two open wells. As such HCBPL did not buy or bring water from outside and it started production in 2000.

Production of one bottle of coke requires nearly four liters of water, but the exact data on the volume of soft drinks produced by HCBPL is not provided by the plant, so how much water it draws daily remains contested. However the company claims that it draws four to six lakh liters of water per day. The production permit obtained by the company from Kerala State Pollution Control Board (KSPCB) is for producing 5,61,000 liters of soft drinks daily. This would mean that the company would require around 21 lakh liters of water per day. This heavy withdrawal of water for two years has adversely affected the ground water table in Plachimada. Water in the nearby thirty-four wells and twelve bore wells have depleted to a greater extent. As per the estimate of Centre for Science and Environment (CSE) surplus water is not available in Chittur Taluk for commercial use.

Ground water pollution is another area of importance in Plachimada. Since its establishment the waste treatment plant of the company was not functioning well. Wastewater from the plant was continually sprayed on the lawn and garden being raised within the factory compound. This percolated down and reached the water table. Besides, the plant extensively distributed the solid waste as manure to the farmers. The farmers were misled to believe that it is a useful fertilizer and used in the coconut farm, very near to the tribal colony. The solid waste has got spread around through the irrigation channels over a large area and is seeping into the soil, contaminating the soil and ground water. As a result salinity and hardness of the ground water have also increased because minerals from the deeper soil layers moved to upper layers. Women who use this water reported that rice and dhal do not get cooked but become hard and going bad quickly. Water from some of the domestic wells on boiling and subsequent cooling develops an intense milky colour. Many diseases like abnormal hair falling, anemia, vomiting, stomach pain, etc. started among the villagers. Now the women must go two kilometers after normal work hours to collect potable water.

Ground Water Legislation

Regarding ground water legislation we don't have a concrete and comprehensive ground water law to regulate it's over use. What we have is a National Water Policy, framed in 1987, which was reformulated in 2002. In the National Water Policy 2002 the first priority has been given to the drinking water and second priority to agriculture and non-agricultural industries come almost on the bottom of the priority list. But allocation of small scale or large-scale industries on the basis of this policy is rare, because the previous decade witnessed the change of industrial policy together with globalisation. As per the traditional Easement Law prevailing in India, the landowner owns the water below his land and he has exclusive right to extract and use the ground water. It has been said that ground water is attached like a chattel to land and that there is no limitation on how much ground water a landowner may draw. But judiciary in many circumstances has intervened effectively where ground water was exploited on the basis of this law. The court emphasized Public Trust Doctrine in many judgments and prevented monopolization of water for the sake of people. Further the Precautionary Principle enacted by Rio de Janeiro Conference held in June, 2005 was approved by the higher judiciary as part of our national jurisprudence, in many cases against industrial pollution.

The Supreme Court in Kesoram Industries/State of Bengal Case ruled that, "deep underground water belongs to the state in the sense that the doctrines of Public Trust extends there too. Holder of a land may have only a right to use and cannot take any action or do any harm as a result where the rights of others are affected." Besides despite the doubts expressed by Ministry of Water Resources, the Supreme Court mooted the establishment of a regulatory authority that resulted in the formation of Central Ground Water Authority (CGWA) in 1997. But it has not yet become a very effective or fully operational body and its constitutional position is also in confusion like that of CGWB. Because according to Entry 17 in State List, ground water seems to be a state subject and if so, from what provisions did this autonomous organization derive the authority? (Iyer: 2004). However this growing environmental jurisprudence is a great hope of the present globalization era and states should consider it as a guideline in implementing developmental plans.

There is no specific reference to ground water in the constitution. Confusion regarding whether water is a state subject or a national subject has still not come to an end. The relevant positions are Entry 17[5] in the State List, Entry 56[6] in the Union List and Article 262. According to Entry 17, water is indeed a state subject. But it is subject to provisions of Entry 56 of Union List. So water is as much as a central subject and a state subject, particularly as most of the country's important rivers are inter-state. Under Article 262 an institutional arrangement was created to resolve the Inter-State Water Disputes. But such an arrangement for resolving ground water dispute is absent in the constitution. Further the tribunals constituted under Inter-State Water Dispute Act 1956 (ISWD Act) have refrained from entering disputes related to ground water. However it has generally been agreed that the reference to water in the constitution includes ground water. This position was upheld by different judicial interpretations including Article 21, i.e. Right to Life. Right to Life has been held by courts to include Right to Water as a life-sustaining resource including ground water—the very important source of drinking water.

Attempt to introduce actual ground water legislation at the state level have by and large failed. For the first time in 1970 the Central Government circulated a Model Bill to State Governments but the response of the states were poor. The CGWB made some initiatives to set up state level regulatory bodies but only few states have passed the legislation. As per this order Tamil Nadu and Uttar Pradesh enacted such laws and created ground water authorities. Kerala has enacted its law in 2002 namely, Kerala Ground Water (Control and Regulation) Act 2002; as per this Act, the entire power to control ground water use is vested in the Ground Water Authority. But this authority was created very recently and that is not developed in its full swing yet.

As part of the decentralisation initiatives many State Governments have enacted state conformity legislations to cope with the 73rd Amendment. In Kerala, The Kerala Panchayat Raj Act, 1994 (KPRA) was passed with a view to empower the panchayats through people's participation. Though this Act increased the power of panchayats over 'public properties', it excludes ground water, because ground water is considered as the sole property of the owner of the land. In this Act, Section 218 vests the authority over public watercourses in the panchayat. But public water courses include the beds and banks of river streams, irrigation and drainage channels, canals, lakes, back waters and water courses and all standpipes and other water works. Control over ground water through panchayat will remain as a dream until the filling of these legal lacunae.

Thus in Kerala ground water has suffered from under evaluation and neglect. Under both state and private development there is evidence of non-sustainable management and ground water degradation. However depletion is not sufficiently recognized as a major problem in Kerala. Similarly ground water quality issues have taken less importance in most debates about environmental degradation till the Plachimada issue got recognition as a global problem. Access to safe drinking water is a fundamental right and thus state should ensure water rights by preventing violation of water rights. In a positive sense state has the responsibility to provide drinking water in drought prone areas and water scarce urban regions. As far as Kerala is concerned an immediate solution for ground water exploitation rests in the effective amendment and implementation of Kerala Ground Water (Control and Regulation) Act 2002. Thus depletion by over exploitation can be prevented by State interference. Further conservation and artificial recharge initiatives under the auspices of State Government should be made obligatory to the people, at least in draught prone areas, which will benefit in long term.

NOTES

1. Ground water development means the actual exploitation or use of water during the transformation of the neutral stuff into commodity or service to serve human needs and aspirations. The advantage of ground water development for irrigation purpose has been fully recognised in India and has become a significant factor in promoting modern agriculture through high yielding variety crops. Ground water has sizeable distribution and provides an assured and dependable sources of irrigation free from vagaries of rainfall. Therefore increased emphasis is being given for accelerated development of ground water resources in the country. See Jeet, Inder (2005), Ground Water Resources of India, Occurrence, Utilization and Management, Mittal Publications, New Delhi, p. 90.

2. According to Ground Water Estimation Committee, 1984 stage of ground water development is defined as a ratio of net yearly draft to utilizable resource for irrigation. But the report of the Ground Water Estimation Committee, 1997 defines it in little but different way. According to them, stage of ground water development (%) = existing gross ground water draft for all uses/Net annual ground water availability x 100. CGWB (2004), Report on the Dynamic Ground Water Resources of Kerala as on March 2004, Central Ground Water Board, Thiruvananthapuram, Kerala, p. 11.

3. Those are, Western Ghat Development Programme implemented by Planning Commission since the 6th Five Year Plan. The commission was unable to co-ordinate the different agricultural projects of other departments and ultimately resulted into its failure. Another project is

Draught Prone Area Programme (DPAP) that was implemented in a small area of Palakkad district. Water intensive agricultural practices were discouraged by this programme but finally resulted in to its collapse due to lack of people's participation and propaganda. Projects like National Watershed Development Programme for Rain fed Areas (NWDPRA) and OPEC Watershed Project were also failed due to administrative inefficiency and imbalance between project objectives and available infrastructure.

4. Roof water harvesting means tapping of water at the point of rainfall to increase ground water recharge. Ground water harvesting means reducing the speed of run off by constructing structures like rainwater pits (catch pits), contour bunds, check dams, filter strips, side wall, platforms, stone pitched bunds etc.

5. Entry 17 in the State List runs as follows: Water, that is to say, water supplies, irrigation and canals, drainage and embankments, water storage and water power subject to the provisions of Entry 56 of List I.

6. Entry 56 of Union List runs as follows: Regulation and Development of interstate rivers and river valleys to the extend to which such regulation and development under the control of the Union is declared by Parliament by law to the expedient in the public interest.

REFERENCES

Alphons, K.J. (2004), *Water, Environment and Swadeshi,* State Land Use Board, Vikas Bhavan, Thiruvananthapuram.

Burjia, J.S. and Romania, Saleem (2003), *Ground Water Development Present Scenario and Future Needs,* IndianJournal of Public Administration, Vol. XLIX, No. 3, July-September 2003.

CGWB (2004), *Report on the Dynamic Ground Water Resources of Kerala, as on March 2004,* Central Ground Water Board, Thiruvananthapuram, Kerala.

INTACH (2002), *'The Adverse Environmental Impact of the Hindustan Coca-Cola Beverages Private Limited'.*

Iyer, R. Ramaswamy (2003), *Water, Perspectives Issues and Concerns,* Sage Publications, New Delhi.

Jeet, Inder (2005), *Ground Water Resources of India, Occurrence, Utilization and Management,* Mittal Publications, New Delhi.

John, C.P. (2003), *Rain Water Collect and Consume,* Kerala Calling, April 2003, Vol. 23.

KGWCRA (2002), *The Kerala Ground Water (Control and Regulation Act) 2002,* The Law Department, Government of Kerala, Secretariat, Thiruvanan thapuram.

Kokkad, Kamalakshan (2003), *Ground Water Resource Management Rain Water Collect and Consume*, Kerala Calling, April 2003, Vol. 23.

KRPA (1994), *The Kerala Panchayati Raj Act, 1994,* The Law Department, Government of Kerala, Secretariat, Thiruvananthapuram.

Kurian, P.K. (2004), *Question and Answers for Doubts Regarding Rain Water Harvesting*, KRWSA, Thiruvananthapuram.

Report (2003), *Report on Analysis of Water*, Water Analysis Section, Analytical Laboratory, Kozhikkode-9, No: 138/02-03.

Swaminathan, M.S. (2004), *Building A Sustainable Water Security System*, Vikram Sarabhai Centre for Development Interaction and Nehru Foundation for Development, Ahmedabad.

Vikas Adhayn Kendra (2004), *Coca-Cola, Quit Plachimada; Quit India, The Story of Anti Coca-Cola Struggle at Plachimada in Kerala.*

10

Perspectives on the Contours of Multi-purpose Women Cooperatives in India

S. RAJENDRAN AND B.S. CHANDRASEKHARA

Introduction

The third sector institutional framework including cooperatives provides logistic support through 'Bottom Up' approach for transforming the socio-economic fabric of the society (Brett 1993 and Rajendran 2004) to attain overall development. Across the world, voluntary sector has emerged as a complementary institutional framework and sometimes an alternative system for promoting development works (Muttalib 1987) more so in marginalized regions and societies. As an institutional framework, the cooperatives in India inroad into nook and corner and every sphere of economic activities including credit, consumer and women. Third sector has grown both horizontally and vertically and emerged as a powerful tool to deliver the goods especially in resource poor and developing countries. The failure of the state in providing development works often resulted in mushrooming third sector institutions, especially in developing countries like India (Sethi 1993). The private sector on its part heavily concentrates on making profit without concentrating on the societies' economic welfare and development. Consequently, large people have been marginalised from enjoying the fruits of development initiatives and there is a clear vacuum in making the people empowered. Expectedly, this has forced and enabled the third sector including cooperatives to lead development activities especially in developing regions of the world, where the livelihoods are often at stake.

Third sector institutions not only act as catalytic agents between the state and the society but also take lead in delivering the development programmes. Thus over the years, this institutional framework has emerged powerful, changed the development spectrum and there is a paradigm shift in many developing countries for undertaking development initiatives. While some agencies have used the micro-level experience for sustainable development efforts at macro level policy domains (Harper 1997) and on the other it is reverse (Morrissey 1997). Case studies (Aurora and Others 1994 and Rajendran 2004) about the positive impact of the third sector institution on the community are found abundant in the literature; despite there are some degree of apprehensions. Dongre (2004) observed that politicization of cooperative leadership largely led to failure of this system. Other researchers have been critical of the interventions made by the third sector institutions mainly for their poor accountability and lack of transparency. While some have questioned the efficacy of such organizations (Brett 1993) a few scholars like Zaidi (1999) strongly felt that third sector institutional framework failed in its approach and hence suggested to bring back the state into fore.

As reported in the Human Development Report, the states in developing countries discourage community's participation and starting from a 'Top Down' development philosophy, such states generally concentrated in providing food and services rather than enabling people to do more for themselves (UNDP 1993). Means and ends of lopsided 'Top Down' approach by the state for the development initiatives has at times failed in a pluralistic society like India and institutions such as cooperatives especially those managed by women have positively influenced (Kamala 1987), despite there are some difficulties and even failures (Ramanujam 1995). India has a long history of experience for more than one century with regard to cooperative institutional framework. At present in the world, India has the largest cooperative network in terms of membership, share capital and so on. At the same time some cooperatives in India due to various intriguing reasons, do encounter difficulties for their very survival and in coming years this would become much more serious. Empirical studies show that factors like inefficient leadership, lack of accountability, excessive political intervention and poor management of resources have all contributed for the malfunctioning and failure in a few cooperatives. Erosion of values, commitment and ethics is another reason for the defunct of some cooperatives in India (Dongre 2004). However, there are some cooperatives, which stand as models to their neighbourhood.

Against this backdrop an attempt is made to examine the contours of Multipurpose Women Cooperatives (MPWCs) from the Second largest South Indian State—Karnataka. India has a long tradition of cooperative movement and many women cooperatives are successful in their endeavour in changing the socio-economic conditions of their members in respective areas (Chandrashekara 2002). Nevertheless, it is imperative to analyze the operational aspects of such institutions for ushering effective functioning and fostering their ultimate goal of attaining overall development. Hence the present study has two fold objectives; (1) To analyze the growth of MPWCs at macro level, and (2) To examine the dimensions of MPWCs at micro level. This chapter is divided into four sections. Followed by this introductory part, the next section deals with the methodology. The third section provides a detailed account of the MPWCs at macro and micro levels. The last section is devoted to draw major findings of the study and also to give a few suggestions for the better functioning of the cooperative societies in general and the MPWCs in particular.

Methodology

Collating and interfacing the analysis of secondary data with primary information would possibly concretize the whole framework of MPWCs and accordingly, both primary and secondary sources of information have been used for this study. While macro level secondary data for two decades were collected from published documents, primary data were culled out for one financial year from a historical—Mysore—district. The reference periods for the secondary data are from 1980-81 to 1999-2000. Variables like number of MPWCs, financial status and membership from secondary sources and the magnitude of asset holdings; income, employment and related aspects from primary sources were collected. The field level information was enumerated using pre-tested schedules from 24 beneficiaries of two MPWCs and equal number of households were selected as control group for comparative analysis. Further cooperators and local officials were interviewed to know their grassroots perspectives. Simple statistical tools were used for data analysis for issues like growth, dimensions and perspective of MPWCs.

Discussion

This section takes a look at the macro and micro contours and dimensions of the MPWCs both all India and regional levels. The magnitude of MPWCs is high as compared to all types of societies in the state of Karnataka as could be seen from Table 10.1. This is perhaps due to the fact that these societies perform well in this state.

Table–10.1
Share of MPWCs During 1999-2000

Particulars	*India*	*Karnataka*	*Percentage of Column 3 to 2*
All cooperative societies	525310	28462	5.42
MPWCs	8393	864	10.29
Percentage to total	1.60	3.04	–

Source: NABARD (1995) and GOK (2000).

At macro level in India MPWCs form less than two per cent to total societies in the reference year of 1999-2000. With regard to Karnataka this figure accounts to little more than three per cent, demonstrating an important aspect that MPWCs have greater role to play in the state. Similarly, it is observed that the concentration of MPWCs is high as compared to all types of societies in this state. As could be seen from the Table 10.1, while of all societies around six per cent of the total cooperative societies located in this state, MPWCs accounted to more than 10 per cent to total MPWCs. Thus from the above it is evident that MPWCs in the State of Karnataka dominate due to various reasons like encouragement of Self Help Groups (SHGs) like Streeshakthi and the like. In fact to mark the centenary celebrations of cooperatives, recently the State Government sanctioned Rs. 50000 as loan for each Streeshakthi, covering more than 1000 members.

Also a cursory look at the secondary data reveals that the growth of MPWCs in the state is faster than the all India figures. At macro level in these MPWCs the growth of membership, capital and turnover are increasing significantly as compared with all India growth rates. A bird's eye view at the growth rate of various aspects of MPWCs indicates that the State of Karnataka is better as compared with the country as a whole (Table 10.2).

Table–10.2
Compound Growth Rate of MPWCs in Karnataka and India (in Per cent)

Particulars	*Growth Rate*		*Overall Growth Rate (1980-81 to 1999-2000)*
	80-81-89-90	*90-91-99 00*	
INDIA			
1. Numbers	6.28	9.30	13.27
2. Membership (00s)	17.06	5.12	18.41
3. Share capital in (000 rupees)	21.97	8.95	27.97
4. Government share in (000 rupees)	9.77	10.99	19.41
5. Total working capital in (000 rupees)	38.91	0.99	41.04
KARNATAKA			
1. Numbers	21.50	8.89	19.04
2. Membership (00s)	22.59	7.83	21.28
3. Share capital in (000 rupees)	37.56	17.45	32.14
4. Government share in (000 rupees)	33.70	18.80	28.63
5. Total working capital in (000 rupees)	42.46	4.74	30.68

Source: Same as Table 10.1 and NCUI (2001).

The above Table clearly explains the fact that with regard to the volume of cooperatives, membership, share capital; government share capital and total working capital show positive trend for all India as well as for Karnataka. However, a cross sectional analysis on the time series data indicates that the growth rate for the above aspects is more for Karnataka as compared to all India figures. This obviously demonstrates that the MPWCs have better opportunities to expand in the State of Karnataka.

A decomposition analysis would clearly explain the growth performance of MPWCs in Karnataka. For instance, between 1980-

81 and 1989-90 the number of societies grew at the rate of 6.28 per cent in India and for Karnataka this figure works out to 21.5 per cent. However, during the second reference period i.e., 1990-91 and 1999-2000, the figures for all India are 9.3 per cent and for Karnataka they are 8.89 per cent. But the overall growth performance between 1980-81 and 1999-2000 is found impressive for Karnataka (19.04%) as compared to all India (13.27%). Thus with regard to growth performance of MPWCs, it is impressive for the state as compared to India as a whole, thereby demonstrating the dimension that these societies are welcomed by the people in this part of the country.

Similarly, another aspect on the enrollment of members in these societies is found convincing in Karnataka as compared to the country as a whole. While the compound growth rates of membership for the first reference period (1980-81 and 1989-90) for India is 17.06 per cent and for Karnataka it is 22.59 per cent. Even for the second reference period (1990-91-2000) the corresponding figures are 5.12 and 7.83. The overall growth rates for the country and the state are estimated at 18.41 per cent and 21.28 per cent respectively. Thus for the entire study periods the growth of members in MPWCs is higher in the state as compared to all India figures (Fig. 1). This is perhaps more and more members from similar systems like SHGs joining as members in the MPWCs in Karnataka.

Fig. 1: CGR of MPWCs in Indian and Karnataka (in%)

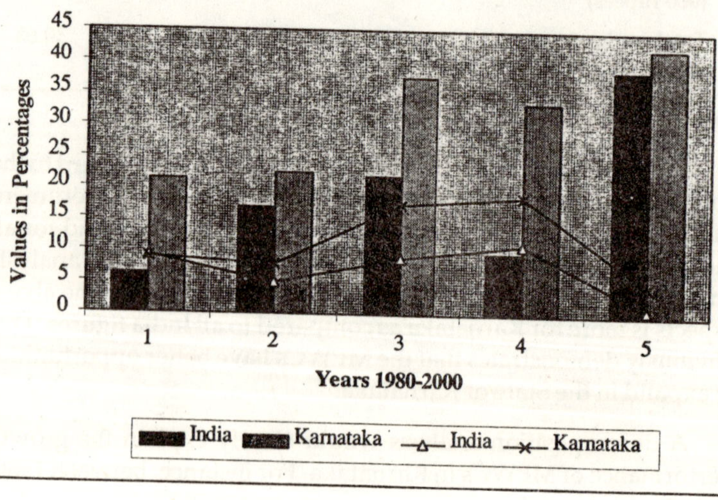

The functional efficiency of any cooperative organization depends on its financial viability and hence an examination of capital available and its growth would throw some light. During both the reference periods it was found that the growth of capital contributions by members is more in Karnataka as compared with the country as a whole. In the first phase of the reference years between 1980-81 and 1989-90, share capital grew at the rate of little less than 22 per cent for the country and the same figure for the State stood at impressive—around 38 per cent. Similarly, during the second phase i.e., 1990-91 and 1999-2000, the corresponding figures are estimated at 8.95 per cent and 17.45 per cent respectively, thereby indicating that the State is ahead of the country. Also the growth rate for the entire reference periods (1980-81 and 1999-2000) for the country is less (27.97%) as compared to the state (32.14%).

The next aspect is the growth of the share capital contributions by the government. Here too the growth performance is better in the state as compared to the country as a whole. During the first reference period (1980-81 and 1989-90) while the growth of the government share capital for the country is around 10 per cent and for the State it is three times higher (around 34%). However, during the subsequent reference period, the growth of government share capital improved marginally for the country as compared with the State, albeit the growth rate is more for the State. The overall growth of the government's share capital for the entire reference periods is estimated at 19.44 per cent for the country and it is 28.63 per cent for the State.

Another dimension of macro picture is the ratio analysis of membership and capital and hence the following is done. Table 10.3 gives details of variations with regard to ratios of members and capital for all India and Karnataka from 1980-81 to 1999-2000.

It is very interesting to note that figures for all India are better for members as low members are available per society at all India level as compared with Karnataka. However, in the State more number of members available per society indicating that more and more members joined the MPWCs. This also shows that such members do have strong faith in the cooperative system for their development action.

Table–10.3
Ratio Distribution of Members (Numbers) and Capital (Rupees)

Particulars	*Years*				
	80-81	*85-86*	*89-90*	*95-96*	*99-00*
INDIA					
1. Number of societies	1568	1353	4054	8171	8393
2. Ratio of members (in Nos.)	47	66	125	85	100
3. Ratio of share capital (in Rs.)	3080	5792	16567	21943	19113
4. Ratio of government share (Rs.)	1930	2971	2775	NA	NA
5. Ratio of total working capital (in Rs.)	7165	16400	218224	172329	138256
KARNATAKA					
1. Number of societies	57	97	402	690	995
2. Ratio of members (in Nos.)	155	179	207	232	199
3. Ratio of share capital (in Rs.)	5912	9619	19920	28852	44849
4. Ratio of government share (Rs.)	2772	5495	7045	11490	16915
5. Ratio of total working capital (in Rs.)	28947	50608	151259	152083	141131

Source: Same as Tables 10.1 and 10.2.
Note: For Karnataka, data for the year 1980-81 was not available and hence for 1981-82 is taken into account.

Another issue is the financial aspect of the cooperative societies and it is found that such resource is more per society in the State of Karnataka as compared with all India data for the study periods. This demonstrates the perspective that this State is financially strong with regard to MPWCs. For instance, for the initial reference period (1980-81) on an average one MPWC had just Rs. 3080 and it increased to Rs. 19113 in the final reference year (1999-2000) for the country as a whole. But these figures are more for the State of Karnataka—the corresponding figures are Rs. 5912 and Rs. 44849. Also the government share capital available per society is high in Karnataka as compared with macro level—India—for all reference periods, indicating that the State is keen in financially strengthening such societies. Similarly, with regard to total working capital per society it is high for the State as compared to all India figures for the reference periods with an exception for the year 1995-96. Thus overall the State is stronger in terms of financial resource as compared with the country as a whole. The next issue is to examine the women cooperatives, which run viably and this is done both for the country and for the state and data are furnished in Table 10.4.

Table-10.4
Distribution of Viable MPWCs (in Per cent) During 1980-81-1999-2000

Particulars	*Years*				
	80-81	*85-86*	*89-90*	*95-96*	*99-00*
INDIA					
1. Total societies (Numbers)	1568	1353	4054	8171	8393
2. Profit making	18	18	62	NA	NA
3. Loss making	24	36	17	NA	NA
4. No loss/profit societies	58	46	22	NA	NA
KARNATAKA					
1. Total societies (Numbers)	57	97	402	690	995
2. Profit making	28	43	42	NA	52
3. Loss making	26	39	41	NA	47
4. No loss/profit societies	46	23	18	NA	1

Source: Same as Table 10.3.
Note: For Karnataka, data for the year 1980-81 was not available and hence for 1981-82 is taken into account.

It may be observed from the above table that by and large maximum number of MPWCs make profit during the reference periods at all India and State level. However, the magnitude varies between these two. For instance, during the initial period of 1980-81, at macro level in the country 18 per cent of the societies generated profit as compared to 28 per cent for the State. However, one has to bear in mind that at the country level 58 per cent of the societies either made profit or incurred loss during the same period as above. This figure is 46 per cent for Karnataka. For all India as well as Karnataka percentage of neutral MPWCs is decreasing considerably over the reference periods. While the percentage of profit making MPWCs is increasing faster for the country, it is slow for the State. Perhaps the excessive political interference, lack of leadership and a host of other issues would have contributed for increase in loss making MPWCs. The foregoing discussion, thus reveals that the growth performance of MPWCs regarding the number of societies, membership and capital, is relatively better at the State level. Nevertheless, the growth of these at the country level is impressive, though less than the State's performance. It enables to conclude that overall the MPWCs are welcomed and expected to perform well in the country in general and the State in particular.

Followed by the above analysis at macro level, the next aspect is to deal with the field based primary information. Before getting into the detailed analysis, it is worth to understand the sample district and villages in brief. Mysore district is located in the southern part of Karnataka and was selected for an in-depth analysis and this district has a long tradition of cooperative movement. This is one of the moderately developed districts in the State and due to long history of princely rule, this part was imbibed with traditional value and cultural system.

Here the cooperative institutional framework is fairly developed and some innovative cooperatives including MPWCs and Banks successfully are being under functioning. Of 62 MPWCs in the district two were randomly selected for this study. In both the societies of Duddagere and Kuragahally MPWCs, 24 member households were selected covering 16 belonging to small and 8 belong to large farm categories. Also an equal number of 24 controlled households spreading 18 small and 6 large farm categories were also selected for comparative analysis (Table 10.5). However, comparative analysis has been made between members and non-members.

The demographic details indicate that the member households are better in terms of literacy level and area operated. Similarly per household asset value also found to be more among the member households. This would possibly influence the income earning capacity

Table-10.5
General Information of the Selected Households

Particulars	*Members*		*Non-members*	
	Small	*Large*	*Small*	*Large*
No. of households	16	8	18	6
Average family size	6.05	6.28	5.02	5.14
Literacy level in per cent	33.25	55.74	28.89	47.83
Total population	61	28	62	20
Per household operated area in acres	4.22	7.46	4.40	8.28
Average asset holding in Rs.	63632	188560	40450	174020

and other social status in these households. Having more assets provided enough economic security to the members for availing institutional finance from the cooperative agencies. Most of the time while the members availed loan at lower rate of interest (12%) others had to take loan varying from 20 to 35 per cent. This in turn viably helped the members to undertake agriculture and other income generating activities. The next aspect is the income generated from the selected households and such details are given in Table 10.6.

Table-10.6
Per Household Annual Income (in Rupees) by Different Sources

Sources	*MPWCs Members*			*Non-members*		
	Small	*Large*	*Average*	*Small*	*Large*	*Average*
Agriculture crops	12830	31652	22241 (27.2)	1904	22547	16076 (36.0)
Sericulture	3986	13683	8835 (10.8)	2657	9793	6225 (14.0)
Agriculture labour	1680	–	840 (1.0)	2940	840	1890 (4.2)
Dairying	24820	15513	20167 (24.6)	9308	6205	7757 (17.1)
Salary		4000	2000 (2.4)	–	5000	2500 (5.6)
Trade and business	–	8260	41309 (5.0)	–	6256	3128 (7.0)
Tailoring	14600	15330	14965 (18.3)	–	–	–
Others	6250	11220	8735 (10.7)	5820	8240	7030 (15.8)
Total Income	**64166**	**99658**	**81912 (100)**	**30329**	**58881**	**44605 (100)**

Note: Numbers in parentheses indicate percentage to total household income. Income from others include brokerage etc.

This Table provides details on the gross annual income generated from different sources as revealed by the member and non-member households. The member households belong to MPWCs generated more annual income as compared to non-member households. On an average member households earned income of Rs. 81912 as compared to Rs. 44605 by the non-member category. A cross sectional analysis on sources of income reveals that member households earned more income from sources like field crops, dairying, tailoring, other sources, sericulture, trade and business, salary and wage labourers. On the other hand non-member category earned more income from agriculture, dairying, others, sericulture, trade and business, salary and wage labourers. However, per household income from different sources for the member and non-member categories clearly show that former group (member) of households received more from agriculture crops, sericulture, dairying, trade and business and others. In fact there is no income from tailoring source for the non-member category of households as this activity is carried out only from the members of MPWCs. Even a comparative analysis across landholding categories, show that households from member categories earned more income by and large in all sources (Fig. 2).

Fig. 2: Percentage Share of Income by Source

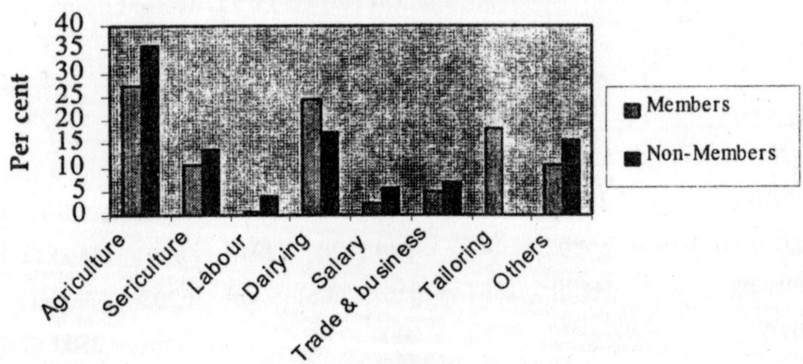

Thus the foregoing discussion clearly reveals that member category earned more income from different income earning activities. This is due to the fact that MPWCs have given a platform for their members to understand new frontiers of developments in different economic activities. For instance, during the field survey it was pointed out by the cooperators, the members of MPWCs have exposure to new farm production technologies and avenues for proper product marketing. This on the one hand enabled to increase the production and productivity in agriculture and on the other enabled them to get remunerative price. It was observed that members do have knowledge of the farm-input subsidy, availability of quality inputs and experts in agriculture for technical knowledge and so on that have resulted in increasing the yield and income. Also the initiative of MPWCs to organize the members for training in tailoring has generated substantial income, which is completely absent in the controlled group. Income earned from tailoring has helped to invest in farm production process.

To an extent the women members empowered themselves in financial matters like investing on farm based assets and growing newer crops. Of course as reported by them, this was possible, as their counterparts were cooperative and compassionate in their involvement in the activities of the cooperative societies. The next aspect is to examine the asset holdings of the selected households in the villages and accordingly data have been furnished in the Table 10.7. It is to study the impact of asset position of households between two points of time. Most of the members joined in MPWCs in 1999 and hence it is decided to estimate the impact of asset holding at 1999 price level.

At macro level, there is an improvement with regard to the possession of asset holding on both sets of households. But the increase in 2002 over 1999 is found more for the member households—almost doubled. Notably, non-member households consolidated their asset position with regard to consumer durable as compared with member households. In both sets of selected households, the change is less with regard to investing on agriculture implements and machinery.

The above Table gives some interesting observations with regard to the distribution of assets in the selected households. The average asset value of the member household was Rs. 63332 in the year 1999 and it doubled to Rs. 126096 in the year 2002. However, the non member category households also improved their asset position but in lesser magnitude. For instance such households had Rs. 68579 worth of assets in 1999 and it increased to Rs. 107235 in 2002. By and large the value of all types of assets increased over the period for

Table-10.7
Per Household Value of Assets in Rupees for Two Periods

Particulars of Assets	*1999*		*2002*		*Percentage Change in 2002 Over 1999*	
	Member	*Non-member*	*Member*	*Non-member*	*Member*	*Non-member*
Implements and machinery	4717	4833	6015	5335	27.52	10.39
Livestock	3875	3394	8800	6250	127.1	84.15
Residential buildings	27200	25500	59500	55500	118.75	117.65
Tractor, trade and commerce building	24000	8781	42781	32250	28.25	26.73
Consumer durable	3040	2603	9000	7900	196.05	203.50
Total	**63332**	**68579**	**126096**	**107235**	**99.10**	**56.37**

both sets of households but the magnitude is more for member category. This is due to the reason that such member households obtained more income from cooperative society based activities like dairying and tailoring. It enables to conclude an important fact that albeit the asset value of both categories increased, members of MPWCs improved their asset position between these periods.

Notably, asset value of livestock, residential buildings, tractors, trade and commercial buildings and consumer durable found more from member category as compared to non-member category during the first period. During the subsequent reference period of 2002, member categories possessed more assets as compared with non-member category of all sources. This clearly demonstrates that the members could substantially improve the asset position, perhaps from the income generated through the cooperatives.

Summary and Conclusions

The above analysis brought out a number of interesting and useful insights of the MPWCs both at macro and micro levels. The macro level analysis shows that there is an impressive performance of MPWCs in India in general and Karnataka in particular. Various aspects like working capital do perform well in the state as compared to India. Perhaps this is due to proactive policy adoption of the State Government to give new twist to the women cooperatives for women empowerment.

An analysis of primary data reveals that members of MPWC generate more income and employment than their counterparts. The asset holding is stronger in the member households as compared to non-member category. Also, the members with their exposure (personal contacts) to modern farm techniques and technology significantly brought down the input cost in agriculture, which in turn resulted in increasing net income from cultivation. Additional income earned from activities like tailoring and dairying in MPWCs helped the members to have sustained and better standard of living. The members engaged themselves in production and marketing of tailoring and dairying activities that have provided substantial employment round the year. Field data and analysis also reveal that members have been considerably empowered with the economic decisions in the household activities which in turn have made an impact on their neighbourhood as well. Also women demonstrated that they have leadership quality for organizational and professional dimensions of cooperatives that may be taken as model for other cooperatives elsewhere.

Thus it is evident from the analysis that participation in the MPWC has improved the economic conditions of the members, which can be emulated in needy and poor resource endowed areas. Nonetheless, there is a scope for further improvement of the efficiency of MPWC and accordingly proper and intensive training on various issues covering the business affairs of the societies and employment oriented programmes could be initiated. Also the control groups for improving their economic development, through intensive campaign shall be initiated to join hands with MPWC. There were a few operational difficulties like poor marketing, non-availability of subsidized inputs and poor realization of remunerative price, encountered by the women members have to be looked into by the policy makers for effective and sustained functioning and management of MPWC in India. Efforts may be made by the policy makers to collaborate MPWCs with noted NGOs in the respective locality for providing training for product making, value addition and above all for marketing. Committed SHGs managed exclusively by women may be encouraged to work with MPWCs to increase the efficiency.

REFERENCES

Aurora, G.S., V.S. Parthasarathy and V. Ramaswamy (1994): "Voluntary Organizations and Rural Development," *Institute for Social and Economic Change*, Bangalore, (mimeo).

Brett, E.A. (1993): "Voluntary Agencies as Development Organizations: Theorizing the Problem of Efficiency and Accountability," *Development and Change*, 24(2): 269-303.

Chandrashekara B.S. (2002): "Critical Analysis on the Working of Women Multipurpose Cooperative Societies in Karnataka," *Ph.D., Thesis* Submitted to the University of Mysore, Mysore (Unpublished).

Dongre Y. (2004): "Cooperatives at Cross Roads," *The Hindu*, October 11th, Chennai.

GOK (2000): "Cooperative Movement at a Glance in Karnataka," *The Office of the Registrar of Cooperatives*, Bangalore.

Kamala (1987): "The Role of Women and Youth in Cooperatives", *The Cooperator*, XXIV(21):627-35.

Harper Caroline (1997): "Using Grassroots Experience to Inform Macro Level Policy: An NGO Perspective," *Journal of International Development*, 9(5): 771-8.

Morrissey Oliver (1997): "Micro-Macro Linkages: An Economist's Perspective," *Journal of International Development*, 9(5):755-60.

Muttalib M.A. (1987): "Voluntarism and Development—Theoretical Perspectives," *The Indian Journal of Public Administration*, XXIII(3):399-419.

NABARD (1995): "Cooperative Movement in India," *National Bank for Agriculture and Rural Development*, Mumbai.

NCUI (2001): "Cooperative Movement in India—A Profile," *National Cooperative Union of India*, New Delhi.

Rajendran S. (2004): "Non-governmental Organizations and Sustainable Agriculture Development in India", Paper Presented at the *Sixth ISTR International Conference, Held at Ryerson University, Toronto, Canada* from 11th to 14th July.

Ramanujam, K.M. (1995): "Women Cooperatives and Economic Development," *Kurukshetra* XLIV(2):11-4.

Sethi H. (1993): "Some Notes on Micro-Struggles: NGOs and the State," *Asian Exchange Arena Bulletin*, 9(1 and 2).

Zaidi S. Akbar (1999): "NGO Failure and the Need to Bring Back the State," *Journal of International Development*, Vol. 11, 259-71.

UNDP (1993): *Human Development Report*, New Delhi.

11

The Way Forward of SHG-Bank Linkage Programme

H.S. SHYLENDRA

Introduction

The Self Help Group (SHG)-Bank linkage Programme is the major form of microfinance intervention being implemented since 1992 in the country, the National Bank for Agriculture and Rural Development (NABARD) being its chief promoter. The main aim of the Programme is to mainstream SHGs to bring banking services to the doorsteps of poor, especially the women who have been neglected by the formal agencies. The vision of NABARD for the programme is to empower the rural poor by improving their access to the formal banking system in a cost effective and sustainable manner. NABARD has set for itself a goal of reaching 100 million poor through one million SHGs by 2008. Till March 2002, 4.61 lakh SHGs have been linked to the banks for accessing credit and savings facilities with an estimated outreach of 7.9 million poor households.

So far the results of the programme far exceed the set target. This appears to be the outcome of the efforts of NABARD in mobilizing large number of NGOs and financial institutions to participate in the Programme. Totally about 444 financial institutions like commercial banks, Regional Rural Banks (RRBs) and co-operatives and 2,155 Non-Government Organisations (NGOs) and other developmental agencies in the country have been involved in the Programme.

NABARD has followed a two-pronged strategy in main-streaming the SHG-Bank linkage Programme. Besides providing cheaper refinance support to financial institutions and NGOs for on-lending to SHGs, NABARD has taken various measures both to sensitise the various stakeholders and build their capacity to take up promotion, nurturing and linking of SHGs. The refinance for the purpose is provided at 6.5 per cent to the financial institutions. Capacity building of the stakeholders has been attempted mainly through training of large number of staff of banks, NGOs and government personnel at various levels. At the SHGs' level a large number of members have been trained to equip them with skills to handle SHG management in a better way. Special assistance has been given to select RRBs and NGOs to emerge as Self-Help Promoting Institutions (SHPIs).

In terms of reaching its physical targets, the Programme apparently has been quite impressive. The available studies on the Programme indicate to a positive impact being experienced by the poor in terms of getting easy access to formal savings and credit facilties leading to improvements in their socio-economic conditions. For the banks, the Programme seems to have helped in reducing their transaction cost and in improving recovery of collateraless loans lent to the poor. At the same time, the Programme is faced with problems like uneven spread across and within different states, inadequate response from the banks, rapid promotion of SHGs leading to large number of them becoming defunct and prevailance of high rate of interest charged to ultimate borrowers raising questions about the ability of the intervention for poverty alleviation.

Given the progress achieved by the Programme and also some of the problems confronting it, the present note makes an attempt to assess the Programme and arrive at possible strategies to take it forward. For the purpose of simplicity the assessment is done separately for each of the major stakeholders involved in the Programme.

Role of NABARD

NABARD is one of the key players in the SHG-Bank linkage Programme. It is the Chief Promoter of the Programme. Hence the onus for the future success and sustainability of the Programme to a great extent lies on NABARD.

Not as Core Banking Strategy

Based on the rationale identified for micro-finance intervention,

NABARD's aim is to develop the SHG-Bank linkage model as the core strategy which could be used by the banking system for reaching out to the poor households. However, because of economic reforms the banks are compelled to constrict their rural lending. Can the Programme attain the desired results under such a contradictory scenario?

Moreover the outreach of households and the quantum of credit flow achieved till March 2002 accounts for only a very small proportion of the total need. The cumulative bank credit flow of Rs. 10,264 million attained through the Programme accounts for only about 1.6 per cent of the ground level rural credit flow in the country. Besides the gap, the mainstream financial institutions cannot ignore their direct responsibility of providing banking services to the poor. Also the concept of SHG as such has certain limitations like low capacity for pursuing higher and diverse savings and credit business.

Not to be Target Oriented

SHG promotion and nurturing is a time consuming process. Any kind of target fixing in SHG promotion is likely to go counter to the basic principles of SHG formation. Apparently, the SHG-Bank linkage Programme is tending towards becoming target oriented. While one can set bigger goals for the Programme but target based approach is not consistent with the basic nature of SHG formation.

Creating Enabling Environment

Since NGOs have become one of the major players in the whole programme and are likely to play a significant role in future, it is necessary that legally their role is clearly recognized and clarified. In order for the Programme to attain both credibility and accountability, NABARD on a priority basis should make efforts to get the necessary enabling legal provisions enacted for MFIs and NGOs as recommended by the Task Force on microfinance.

Encourage All Models and Other Strategies

Three models of linkage have emerged under the Programme. Under the first Model, the financial institutions both promote and finance SHGs directly; under the second Model, NGOs promote and nurture SHGs while the banks provide the credit support and; in the third

Model, NGOs both promote and finance SHGs using funds borrowed from outside agencies. However, a major chunk (84%) of the linkage is accounted together by first two models. It becomes necessary for even spread of SHGs, NABARD emphasis on all the three models.

NABARD has started direct refinancing of NGOs. This is a good strategy as it is likely to reduce the borrowing cost to the ultimate borrowers. NABARD must continue with its strategy of giving special focus to backward areas. The training programmes should now become more focused and aim towards professionalising the microfinance sector.

Role of Banks and Co-operatives

The Programme visualizes financial institutions to provide linkage to SHGs promoted both by themselves and by NGOs. However, as revealed by the available studies there has been a highly varied response from the banks to participate in the Programme. There were also many operational hurdles created by banks like insistence of collaterals and impounding of deposits for linking. The slow progress of the Programme in the initial phase has been attributed to such difficulties posed by the banks. Further, of the total SHGs, the proportion of SHGs directly promoted and financed by financial institutions accounts for only about 15 per cent.

While in those areas where NGOs are present, the banks can take the help of NGOs in promoting SHGs; in other areas banks must come forward on their own to form and nurture SHGs. For this to happen in a major way, the banks need to create SHG cells in their zonal or district level offices for providing continued thrust and monitoring. Like specialized officers, they should appoint and post professionals trained in micro-finance and SHG concept in rural branches so that they are able to promote SHGs in a significant way. They can even open exclusive SHG branches.

The banks must come out with new savings and credit products to suit the changing needs of the SHGs including extending cash credit facilities.

For co-operatives which are lagging behind in the Programme, even under the existing laws there is enough scope to take up financing of SHGs with suitable amendments to their bye-laws. SHGs can be constituted internally for weaker sections.

Role of NGOs

The major credit both for introducing the SHGs as financial intermediaries as well as for the results achieved so far under the Programme goes to the NGOs. That NGOs have emerged as the prominent players in the Programme is evident from the fact that they have been involved in the promotion and financing of bulk of the total SHGs linked in the country. NGOs also have been able to largely target their SHGs exclusively for very poor and women. A large number of NGOs are either trying to promote or even transform themselves into full-fledged Micro-Finance Institutions (MFIs). In terms of the future role of NGOs with regard to the SHG-Bank linkage Programme the following suggestions are made.

Widen and Deepen SHG Base

There is a wide variation among NGOs in the number of SHGs promoted. At the all-India level, the average number of SHGs promoted and linked per NGO comes to 214. The number of SHGs formed by NGOs receiving support from NABARD varies from just 6 to 2502 in the country. Some of the leading NGOs have restricted their SHG formation only to limited area. In order for the NGOs to make significant dent on poverty alleviation through financial intermediation they need to increase their outreach by forming in a phased way more and more SHGs within and across the villages. They can also increase the outreach of households by encouraging wherever possible the existing smaller SHGs to include newer eligible members. Efforts also could be made to revive defunct SHGs.

Co-ordination Among NGOs

In order to avoid any unnecessary duplication and competition in SHG formation, NGOs in a particular block or district must co-ordinate among themselves before and during scaling-up. Such a co-ordination would not only help in orderly growth of SHGs but also in increasing the outreach of SHGs in newer villages. Through such co-ordination NGOs will also be in position to exchange ideas about best practices.

Integration of SHGs

Many NGOs have promoted large number of SHGs spread over many villages. Ideally NGOs should try for linking their SHGs with the nearby financial institutions as it would enable them to automatically get integrated with the financial system.

A large number of NGOs these days are trying to federate their SHGs. Many have even formed formal federations which are emerging as autonomous micro-finance institutions. NGOs must ensure that any new entity created should not become a burden on the SHGs. Formation of federation should be attempted only when an NGO has been able to promote a significant number of SHGs with minimum threshold level of savings and credit.

Protecting the Credibility of SHGs

There have been many reported instances of financial irregularity by SHGs. Such instances are likely to have a contagious effect putting the whole system to disrepute. Since NGOs and SHGs are not regulated by any agency with regard to their savings and credit activities, it becomes the primary responsibility of the NGOs to ensure credibility and soundness of the financial system created. The SHPIs must take up preferably through some external agencies, periodic verification/auditing of the SHGs' books of accounts. Again periodic grading of SHGs may be taken up in a very simple and participatory way. The SHPIs also may make use of IT for streamlining the accounting and financial system of the SHGs functioning under them.

Role of SHGs

If the vision of empowering rural poor through the Programme is to be realized, the SHGs which are the key in the entire linkage system must be enabled to emerge strong and vibrant. SHGs should evolve both as strong financial intermediaries and as peoples' institutions capable of managing their own affairs in an autonomous and participatory way. The responsibility for this lies with all the agencies like government, banks and NGOs directly or indirectly connected with SHG promotion.

Financial Intermediary Role

The SHGs must be enabled to mature as financial intermediaries capable of meeting all the basic savings and credit needs of the poor. The required financial services may be provided either directly by the SHGs or channelised through them by outside agencies. The financial institutions and NGOs must enable mature SHGs through training and orientation to launch savings and credit products which can suit the needs of the members. Providing cash credit facility by the banks to the SHGs could be one way of enabling them to provide dependable loan services. Allowing members to partially withdraw savings during emergencies and periodically distributing even partially income/interest earned by the group to members would add great value to SHGs.

SHGs and other Programmes

The NGOs promoting SHGs are also trying to utilize them as instruments for delivering other services like health, literacy, farm inputs etc. In many cases, the SHGs themselves have taken up such activities based on members' demand. Such activities should be taken up only when they are approved by the members and that they do not come in the way of carrying out savings and credit functions in a sound manner. NGOs and government agencies are trying to form separate groups for poverty alleviation programmes so that the existing SHGs are not disturbed by the subsidy and concessional loans. However, if members of the existing SHGs are eligible for such assistance, NGOs must ensure that the SHG members not only get such assistance but at the same time are able to function in a cohesive way through their SHGs. This would require the capacity building of the SHGs.

Updating Members' Skills

With the increase in savings and credit transactions of SHGs, the burden of maintaining proper records may increase. Many SHGs, are dominated by illiterate or semi-literate members. They may find it difficult to maintain their records systematically on a continuous basis. Such weakness may also give scope for irregularities. SHPIs must ensure that the skills of the SHG members are upgraded for accounts keeping and record maintenance.

Retaining Basic Features of SHGs

SHG system though meant for the poor also has shown tendency for leakage. It is the responsibility of all institutions promoting SHGs to ensure that the SHG membership remain confined to the poorest.

Theoretically and practically, the advantage of SHGs for financial intermediation has been very well established. The members of a SHG assess jointly the need and repayment capacity of the borrowers based on the collective information. Through peer pressure the SHG tires to ensures proper utilization of loan and its recovery. The ability of members to take crucial decisions regarding sanction and recovery of loans is central to the success of a SHG. Any undue attempt to disturb this feature is likely to affect the loan recovery. With the creation of federations or separate MFIs, the basic decision making role of the SHGs is likely to be usurped by such outside agencies. To the extent possible the basic decision making power is retained with in the SHGs.

Conclusion

All the past attempts to provide the poor with easy access to formal savings and credit have had only a limited success. Going by the experience so far, the prospects for the poor to obtain their due share in the formal finance appear relatively better under the linkage Programme. But the Programme still has a very long way to go if it has to become the core strategy of the banking sector. The response of financial institutions to the Programme in general has been very tardy. All the key stakeholders need to take stock of their experiences and make a concerted effort on the lines identified above to take the Programme forward. The key to the success lies in retaining the basic character and strength of SHGs along with integrating them appropriately with outside systems to meet the needs of the members in an endearing way. What is needed for its future success is a higly co-ordinated efforts among all the stakeholders at different levels.

12

Governance and Social Inclusion: Case Studies of Bhoomi, Power Sector Reform and Decentralized Teacher Management

NEERU SHARMA

The last 25 years have seen remarkable shifts in the theory and practice of public administration reform, both in developing and industrialized countries (Birner 2006). The period of structural adjustment of the 1980s was marked by the downsizing of the public administration, which was followed by a rediscovery of the role of the state in the 1990s. The current debate is characterized by an emphasis on good governance and a political struggle over the question of which tasks are best performed by a reformed state, the private sector and/or civil society. Hybrid governance structures that are characterized by partnerships between different sectors have also become important. Against this background, the chapter has three objectives: (1) to link the trends in public administration reforms during the past two decades with the political value—and belief-systems that form the basis of different reform trends: neo-liberalism, welfare-state and "third-way" politics, and communitarianism; (2) to present a conceptual framework that can be used to assess reform initiatives in public administration and their implications for the poor; and (3) to provide empirical examples to illustrate recent reform trends based on the framework.

This chapter uses three examples *(a)* the reform of the power sector in Andhra Pradesh as an example of a reform within the public sector and *(b)* the decentralized teacher management in Madhya Pradesh and *(c)* the growing role of the private players particularly the case of online delivery of the land titles to the rural farmers in Karnataka. The review of different approaches in undertaking these reforms underscores the need to acknowledge the political basis of reform initiatives, even though such reforms are often promoted in a technocratic fashion, especially by international financial institutions. The three cases indicate that neo-liberal, welfare-statist and communitarian reform models may differ in their scope for contributing to poverty reduction and social inclusion, but no reform approach can be assumed to lead "automatically" to these goals. Without paying special attention to the poor and disadvantaged groups of society in administrative reform, it is unlikely that any type of administrative reform will contribute to social inclusion and poverty reduction to the extent it could.

Reform of the Energy Sector in Andhra Pradesh

This case deals with the reform of the energy sector in the State of Andhra Pradesh in India. This case is based on a study by Birner, Neeru and Palaniswamy (2006). The power sector reform in Andhra Pradesh has to be seen in the context of a period of general economic reforms in India, which started in 1991. The power sector has been subject to a rather controversial reform process, in which questions of unbundling and privatization were particularly contested. In Andhra Pradesh, the reform process started under the rule of the Telugu Desam Party (TDP) led by Chandrababu Naidu, under a high-level committee report in 1996. In support of the recommended reforms, the Andhra Pradesh State Electricity Board (APSEB) made efforts to reach out to the public, e.g., by distributing various bulletins in English and Telugu, and by distributing a film to reach illiterate audiences (World Bank, 2003). ABSEB also managed to successfully negotiate with all but one labour union. As a consequence, 90 per cent of the more than 70,000 electricity sector employees could be brought on board to the reform process by guaranteeing that none of the employees would loose his or her job or benefits. In 1998, the AP Electricity Reform Act was passed. In February of the election year 1999, APSEB was restructured into two independent corporations, one for transmission and distribution, and one for generation, and in March 1999, the independent AP Energy Regulatory Commission (APERC) was formed. In the process to reform the power sector, the Government of Chandrababu Naidu also took unpopular measures, such as increasing electricity prices to all sectors. Resistance from the farming community took violent forms. In 1997, the response to a spontaneous farmers' uprising in the Coastal Belt was police gunfire, in which three farmers' lost their lives. Nevertheless, Naidu won the 1999 state elections on a reform ticket. His major opponent had promised to make electricity free to the farmers, but Naidu won the elections without making a similar promise.

Andhra Pradesh received US$ 210 million loan from the World Bank in 1999 to support economic reforms. The government decided to reduce the subsidy to the electricity sector. In July 2000, the regulatory commission APERC issued a tariff order, increasing average tariffs by 15 per cent, agricultural tariffs by 50 per cent and residential tariffs by 69-300 per cent. The government pointed out that more than 60 per cent of the households (with usage below a certain amount) were not affected, but this was not sufficient to prevent the massive public protest fuelled by the announcement of the tariff hike. Eventually, the demonstrations turned violent and three activists of the Communist Party CPI (M) were killed in police fire. While the government did not roll back the tariffs, it made no major efforts for further cost-recovery in subsequent years. Otherwise, however, the government continued with its power sector reform programme, which included the creation of four distribution companies, institutional capacity building and other measures to increase the efficiency of the sector.

In 2004, the Congress Party won the state elections in a landslide victory. Opposition leader Y. Rajaskekhara Reddy (YSR), who again had promised free electricity to the farmers, became Chief Minister. He made electricity free to the farmers the day he was sworn in. Later on, he introduced a measure according to which the 5 per cent richest farmers have to pay for electricity. After the elections, the Agricultural Labor Unions, which represent the poorest section of the rural society, complained that they had to pay for electricity, while the farmers, who are in any case better off, received electricity free. Subsequently, electricity was made free to agricultural labourers, but only for a basic consumption level.

While YSR's Congress-led government did not further pursue the privatization of the power sector, it has remained committed to reforms that improve its performance. The World Bank dropped its conditionality regarding the need for privatization and abolishing the free power policy. In terms of the models described, the reform largely follows a managerial approach, which is supported by technical assistance from the international consultancy KPMG and funding from the British Development Agency DFID. As mentioned above, some activities such as billing were outsourced. In the public discourse, YSR emphasizes that power sector reform and free electricity to farmers are highly compatible. In 2006, Andhra Pradesh's power sector performance was rated for the second time to be first among all Indian States. The rating was conducted by CRISIL, an independent rating agency.

Implications for Poverty Reduction and Social Inclusion

At first sight, the power sector reform in Andhra Pradesh appears to have fulfilled both the objective of creating a more efficient and effective public administration in an important sector, while taking social concerns—such as the farmers' unfavourable income situation—into account. However, some caveats remain. The CRISIL rating captures the perspective of an investor, which is quite different from the perspective of poor rural households. While APERC made progress in measuring and documenting the quality of electricity supply to urban households, similar performance measures are not available at a disaggregated level for rural areas. One of the major farmers' organizations conducted a study, which documented that the quality of electricity supply in rural areas is in a very unsatisfactory state, due to problems of underinvestment and mismanagement in the maintenance of power lines. According to interviews conducted with various stakeholders, households with political connections, or households who are able to pay bribes, are in a better situation to get power lines repaired. Such concerns are not reflected in the CRISIL rating.

The policy of providing free electricity to the farmers has certainly contributed to addressing the problem of agrarian distress in the state. However, it is obviously not the most effective way of using public funds for poverty reduction and social inclusion, and this measure does not contribute to increasing equity among the rural population. Obviously, only farmers who were able to invest in wells and pump sets are able to benefit directly from this measure, and the larger the farm holdings the larger are the benefits. Moreover, the agricultural labourers, the poorest section of the society, who mostly belong to Scheduled Castes and Tribes, were initially totally neglected in the free power policy. As indicated above, these problems were addressed to some extent. Still, the fact remains that only the richest 5 per cent of the farmers pay for electricity, while all other farmers receive electricity free of charge, independent of their consumption, while the agricultural labourers need to pay above a basic minimum level.

Decentralized Teacher Management in Madhya Pradesh

The 1991 census had revealed very high rates of illiteracy in MP: 56 per cent for the population as a whole and 70 per cent for the females. Only 35 per cent of the State Scheduled Castes population was literate and 21.5 per cent of its large tribal population (Vikram Chand, 2006).

In 1993 the newly elected government of MP began major reforms in the primary education system. The first step the new government took was to engage in participatory school mapping exercise that involved a door-to-door campaign conducted at the Panchayat level to : secure household-level data on the number of children of primary school age, whether enrolled or not enrolled; understand the reasons for the non-enrollment; develop a village education register to track the educational progress of the school children under the Panchayat; and develop a village plan to address challenges in the schooling. The Lok Sampark Abhiyan (LSA)-the formal name for this survey — revealed that about 32 per cent of the state's village lacked adequate primary schools; moreover compared to the official statistics, GER for the primary school age group (6-11 years) was 20 per cent lower (Clarke 2003: 9). Lok Sampark Abhiyan I and II not only yielded more reliable information on the state of primary education but also mobilized communities around the issue. In 1997 the Madhya Pradesh launched the Education Guarantee Scheme (EGS). The heart of the EGS was a guarantee given by the State Government that if a panchayat forwarded a list of at least 40 children without access to the school within walking distance, the state would ensure a functioning school within 90 days. Under the programme, local communities were expected to contribute physical space for a school, choose a teacher and supplement resources. The government bore the cost of the teachers' salaries, provided teaching and learning materials as well as seed money for the infrastructure, and took responsibility for teacher training. Parent Teacher Associations were charged with monitoring the functioning of the EGS schools and reporting to Village Education Committees (VEC).

Another noteworthy feature of the decentralized teacher management was that MP also introduced a more decentralized system of teacher management to improve the accountability. Regular teachers had been recruited by the State Government and could be transferred across districts. In order to make teachers more responsive to the Panchayats the government introduced a new category of the teachers, Shiksha Karmis (SKs) , in 1996. EGS teachers known as the gurujis, did not constitute a cadre at all; they were recruited to fulfill a particular post in the particular school and could not be transferred. They were contract employees who could be removed at any time by the PTA in conjunction with the VEC. In 2001, the government introduced a category of the contract teachers known as the Sanvida Shala Shiksha (SSS) who were slightly paid better. The appointment of the SKs and the SSSs helped the government fill vacant teaching posts in the backward region. As most of these teachers—unlike many regular teachers—were local residents, they were willing to be posted to such regions and communities. Local teachers possessed a greater bond with the communities, which in turn increased motivation. The limited transferability of the SKs and the non-transferability of the gurujis and contract teachers also stemmed the flight of the teachers from the rural to urban areas and reduced absenteeism. Finally the fact that the gurujis and the contract labourers were removable, while the SK's could not be confirmed for at least three years, made it easier for janpad panchayats to enforce discipline, including regular attendance and accountability for learning outcomes. MP also strengthened the supervision process in another way, by introducing the Cluster Resource Centres (CRCs) covering schools within a radius of 8 km. within a block. CRC provided a forum of peers to discuss the problems and find the solutions. Clearly these wide ranging institutional reforms played a key role in containing primary teacher absenteeism, despite MPs status as one of the poorest States in the country. In order to institutionalize the reforms, the State Government passed a landmark Education Act 2002. The Act formalized the role of the PTAs, VECs and CRCs. The purpose was to spark greater interests among politicians in improving the learning outcomes in their constituencies.

No other State has gone so far as MP reaching out to deprived communities in so short a time, in reshaping the teacher service conditions, or in creating legal framework for the primary education.

In MP the political leadership's commitment to decentralization and participatory processes in service delivery played a major role in the shaping the reform of primary education. The appointment of the Para-teachers under the PRI control allowed for the extension of a more accountable system of primary education across the State, with local teachers subject to tight monitoring by the local communities.

Implications for Poverty Reduction and Social Inclusion

Recent field visits analysis (Vimala Ramachandran, September 2003) and qualitative micro-studies (Aarti Sahijee, 2002) reveal dramatic improvement in the access to the primary education—especially for children from very poor households and in scattered settlement. All EGS schools were found to be regularly functioning with one or two teachers. Community leaders admitted that several children moved from the government primary school to the EGS schools—partly because of the convenient location and partly because of the regular functioning and empathetic teachers. Yet one of the main issues that emerged in most discussions on decentralization is whether Panchayats are truly representative? Did it create space for effective participation in the poorest of the poor-dalits, tribal groups (especially the more disadvantaged)? This is indeed a fiercely contested issue in Madhya Pradesh. While there is no doubt that devolution of the funds to the Panchayat has made a difference on the ground, there is bound to be considerable variations across districts and even within districts. The formal representation of the socially disadvantaged groups or women does not guarantee representation. Like other states in the country MP also has its share of dummy representatives. It is therefore difficult to say whether decentralization has been effective in giving dalits and poor women a voice in the local governance.

Bhoomi-Online Delivery of the Land Titles to the Rural Farmers in Karnataka

India's system of land records is crucial for improving the ownership of one's land. Indeed creation of accurate, complete land information systems is one of the key challenges for governance today. A study carried out by Mackenzie in India shows that India loses 1.3 per cent of its potential growth because of badly maintained land records. The Central and the State Governments have been long aware of the need to reform the land record system. The breakthrough came when the State Government of Karnataka mandated that 'Bhoomi-Computerization of the land records 'would have to be undertaken and finished in all sub-districts by March 2002. It was also decided to fully support the development of the citizen centric land records system even if it meant substantial investment by the State Government for those components of the projects, which were not being funded by the federal government. The political mandate was backed by full administration efforts at all the levels. The Karnataka Government's Department of Revenue planned to set up computerized land record Kiosks (Bhoomi Centres) across 177 taluk offices. These kiosks were to provide farmers with the records of Rights, Tenancy and Cultivation (RTCs) – a document needed for obtaining bank loans, giving proof of ownership, etc. The Bhoomi project was expected to speed up delivery of the RTCs without delays, harassment or bribery.

The phases in which Bhoomi project was implemented included: The first and most important step to kick-start the Bhoomi system was to capture legacy data records in possession of the Village Accountants numbering about 20 million. For this purpose, a comprehensive data entry software "Bhoomi" was designed after exclusive discussions at various workshops in division, district and the state level. The feed back from these workshops helped the department in designing the data entry software. The manual records were withdrawn from the field in the entire State in a phased manner. A print out of the computerized records was individually signed by the Village Accountants, Revenue Inspectors, Shirasthedar, Tahsildar, Assistant Commissioners and Deputy Commissioners after comparing with the manual registers to authenticate the data. The farmers get the copy of their records on the payment of user charges of Rs. 15. When a change of ownership takes place through sale of inheritance, farmers can file an application for a mutation of the land record at the Bhoomi centre at a separate operator assisted counter that held the mutations. The unammended Karnataka Land Revenue Act did not provide for the Computerized System. The Act has now been amended and provides for the storage of data on the storage devices and use of Bhoomi software to be notified by the government from time to time.

Maintenance of the equipment at 177 centres, many of which are located in far flung rural areas; dealing with the isolated incidences of fraudulent certificates being presented at Banks; mitigating the problems of the farmers that have to travel long distances to reach a Bhoomi Kiosk; lack of currency and poor quality of crop survey data; the problem of the illiterate farmers in filling the mutation forms are some of the challenges that the project team has grappled with. Many actions have been taken to improve up the time of computers at the Bhoomi Kiosks. The processing of the payments to the facility managers has been decentralized so that the facility manager become more responsive to the needs in the field. The printing process is being made more secure to deal with the problem of fraudulent certificates.

Impact on the Social Exclusion and Poverty Reduction

Ironically, while the Bhoomi aims to help the poor, in regions like the Bijapur in Karnataka, which has the highest demand for the RTC's, it is the poor who appears to be struggling most with the new system. "We spend Rs. 10 as bus fare to reach the town from our villages and pay Rs. 15 for an RTC. Sometimes it takes two days because the queue is so long. The VA was better, "complains Mehboob Modi Patel. Another farmer, Amsidda Irrapa Karnal says, "I am illiterate, who will help me fill the application form (for the RTC) here?" Some of the early reports (based on the small sample interviews and anecdotal evidence) also pointed to problems and other limitations. For example Handstand and Lokesh interviewed 23 users of Bhoomi in January 2001 in one centre and reported that 20 of the 23 farmers favoured the old system. Teething problems (like the kiosks had been working for 6 months) like power outage for 5-6 hours at the kiosks seemed to be the main reason for the dissatisfaction with the new system. Bhoomi as a transparent land record system is a vast improvement over the manual system that it has replaced. Yet there is lack of data to isolate and assess the direct impact of the Bhoomi system on the poverty reduction. There was some concern in Karnataka among the small farmers about raising the user fee to Rs. 15 from Rs. 2 in the manual system, particularly if the services were genuinely improved. Soon after the initial success, elected representatives, district officials and farmers made demands that Bhoomi be extended to sub-taluks level. Presumably the project was considered as unqualified success. Projects that intend to benefit the rural populations need to recognize the high level of effort that is needed to make rural population aware of the reforms that have been instituted. There is some feedback that inspite of the considerable publicity of the Bhoomi; farmers may still not understand the implication of all reforms that have been carried out. The farmers need to be made aware that there is no need to pay the bribes because the functionaries would be no more be able to misuse their authority to benefit or wrongly penalize any one.

One also needs to be sensitive to the gender equality. Landownership has long been a bastion in India-in Karnataka women just own 12 per cent of the land-and this is reflected in Bhoomi, where women have not heard of the new system. Many women say that they have not seen computerized RTC, issued free by the revenue department in 2001 for personnel verification. Some of the reports also points out that there could be lack of awareness about how Bhoomi system works. For example, even though there are no forms to be filled in Bhoomi to get a RTC, some reports in media quote complaints in this regard.

Conclusion

The review of different approaches to the public administration reform in this chapter underscores the need to acknowledge the political basis of reform initiatives, even though such reforms are often promoted in technocratic fashion, especially by International Financial Institutions. Notwithstanding the difference in the modes of the different models, there existed similarities in the approach of three different States in the reforms.

First is the role of political leadership, the literature on the reform cites the importance of the strong political leadership being clearly associated with the successful policy change (Haggard and Williamson 1993). In case of electricity reforms, Andhra Pradesh's Former Chief Minister Chandrababu Naidu is an interesting case. From the perspective of the market-oriented paradigm, he is widely considered as an example of a strong political leader who was prepared to pursue reforms, including unpopular reforms, in the wider public interest. The fact that Naidu lost the 2004 elections by a large margin is not necessarily a proof that this strategy does not work at all. Naidu won the 1999 elections, even though he had already started a widely publicized reform agenda and even though he did not adopt the "free power" election promise that the Congress Party had put forward. Naidu's case is rather an example that "reform by strong political leadership", while not impossible, requires considerable political judgment and skills. The tariff increase pursued by Naidu in 2000 can be interpreted as an example of serious political misjudgment. Political leaders and parties differ considerably in their ability and their approaches to have an "ear on the ground." The approaches that parties and political leaders use include *(a)* close contact with the electorate "to feel it out," *(b)* use of Party structures to get feed-back from the grassroots level, and *(c)* more "scientific" methods such as issuing opinion surveys. Whatever approach is used, having "an ear on the ground" seems to be an important prerequisite to pursue a "strong political leadership" strategy successfully (Birner *et. al.*, 2006). The political executive in Karnataka was also completely involved in the computerization project. The State Chief Minister and Revenue Minister highlighted the importance of the project in many public forums. The Chief Ministers wrote regularly to all the District Deputy Commissioners, exhorting them to get fully involved in the computerization, and inaugurated a large number of the land record kiosks. Meanwhile the Revenue Minister regularly reviewed the computerization process and also inaugurated the large number of kiosks. A Committee of the Members of the Legislative Assembly visited the kiosks of Deputy Commissioners; invited MLAs of their districts to witness of the functioning of kiosks. All this helped to demonstrate that there was a strong political will for the computerization of the land records – desire to project the pro-poor image of the government led the politicians to lend full support to the project. In Madhya Pradesh the fact that Chief Minister believed in the decentralized and participatory programmes, and remained in power for two successive terms with a large majority in the state assembly, helped empower the civil servants associated with the RSGM to implement reforms that would otherwise will be difficult.

Institutional innovations in MP and Karnataka and Andhra Pradesh were another major factor that accounted for the success of the reforms. The education guarantee scheme created institutional structures and statutory mechanisms for the inclusion of the excluded (poor and rural children who had no access to the primary school within one kilometer walking distance) by providing a forum for the articulation of the demand for education through panchayat, a mechanism to forward the demand through local-self government structures, public commitment by the government to establish EGS primary schools and finally mechanisms for continued participation of the community and panchayat in the management and supervision. The forging of the mutually supportive links between the State Government, local self government institutions and civil society was another breakthrough, ensuring convergence and synergy between the administrative/financial wing and the academic arm of the education. Further, making the system responsive and accountable to the Gram Sabha (the entire village—as the basic unit of the democratic decentralization) effectively flipped the accountability pyramid. External analyst played a key role in the reform. The EGS school is today owned by and accountable to the Parents Teachers Association and Village Education Committee—who in turn are elected by the Gram Sabha. Funds allocated by the government for the EGS programme are managed by the Panchayat and allocation/expenditures are supervised by the Parents Teachers Association of each school. The government, the panchayat and the school form the three corners of the management pyramid. Other institutional management strengthens the decentralized teacher management and quality monitoring. The experience suggests that the structural reform in one sector cannot be sustained unless reforms in governance follow. On the other hand in Bhoomi project the resistance from field staff was anticipated and conscious step was taken to lessen the resistance. To allay the fears of the field officials that their job descriptions will change in a major way, twelve state level information seminars were organized for 1,200 senior and mid level officers. And four division level workshops were organized to train 800 officials. These seminars emphasized that computerization will remove the drudgery of maintaining these records manually. Revenue Officers would continue to be responsible for the field inquiry. Selected field level personnel were invited to participate in the software development process for various Bhoomi modules through a formal state level Bhoomi Committee. Field supervision is critical to rollout of any new system. The project leader in-charge preferred to appoint four independent consultants who could tour sites randomly in each division and report problems and progress of Bhoomi. The Village Accountants who would be in-charge of the new kiosks were chosen carefully and mainly included the young person fresh out of college and were recruited and trained in the headquarters. Partnerships were forged with many different agencies. Agencies like the NIC and private data entry agencies played an important role during the phase of the implementation. Since the department was reluctant to enter the data, private data entry agencies were used. Similar is the case in Andhra Pradesh, in support of the recommended reforms, the Andhra Pradesh State Electricity Board (APSEB) made efforts to reach out to the public, e.g., by distributing various bulletins in English and Telugu, and by distributing a film to reach illiterate audiences (World Bank, 2003b). APSEB also managed to successfully negotiate with all but one labour union. As a consequence, 90 per cent of the more than 70,000 electricity sector employees could be brought on board to the reform process by guaranteeing that none of the employees would loose his or her job or benefits. These examples clearly demonstrate the necessity of the institutional innovations and structural reform before undertaking the governance reforms.

Thirdly, the role played by the external catalyst has led to the successful governance reforms in all the three States. Right from the start, the EGS was designed to forge enriching partnerships between the Panchayat, the larger community and administration. Given the project was steered by the Rajiv Gandhi Shiksha Mission, all academic and administrative linkages were ensured. The programme also built on the mutually supportive external linkages-the Government of India allocated the European Commission DPEP funds to Madhya Pradesh. As a result, the programme was included in the joint review commissions of DPEP and specific appraisal missions jointly fielded by the World Bank, European Commissions, DFID India, Royal Netherlands Embassy and UNICEF. This facilitated National and International Exchange on a range of pedagogy, management and mobilization issues. As the programme matured, initial apprehension with what was described as a low cost programme soon led to the realizations of the potential of the EGS model in the educationally backward regions. As a result the EGS programme received national and international attention.

The State Government of Karnataka would have not taken up the project of this magnitude involving an upfront investment of Rs. 200 million. Central Government was the key catalyst that enabled the project champion to sell the idea within the State. World Bank, which has provided a Structural Adjustment Loan to Karnataka, has also been quietly supportive of Karnataka's e-government programme. The Bank has been providing technical assistance in the form of periodic review of the major e-government initiatives. The project leaders have been open to feedback from the Bank's team. Some of the new initiatives like the connectivity to the rural kiosks had a strong Bank endorsement. A bank funded evaluation conducted by an independent agency was seen as a very useful exercise for establishing the credibility of a fledgling system. External recognition in the form of awards and positive feedback has been a major motivator for the Bhoomi Team. Andhra Pradesh received US$ 210 million loan from the World Bank in 1999 to support economic reforms. In terms of the models described, the reform largely follows a managerial approach, which is supported by technical assistance from the international consultancy KPMG and funding from the British Development Agency DFID.

The timing of the reforms plays an important role in overcoming the political resistance. Trying to reach a consensus on what a policy solution would look like may be an important condition for policy change so that windows of opportunities can be used more effectively, when the other conditions (problem pressure and political situation) are met. Moreover, to learn more about "windows of opportunity" for reducing agricultural subsidies, it might be useful to study cases where such subsidies were, in fact, reduced or abolished. One could look at other countries, but for comparability, these should also be democracies where farmers have voice. In case of electricity, the tariff increase in Andhra Pradesh in 2000 is an example where a reform was pursued even though only one of the three conditions was met. Since Naidu won the elections on a pro-reform platform, the political conditions were suitable for reform efforts. However, fiscal stress – the problem that this reform measure intended to address – was not what citizens perceived to be the major problem. For the farmers, the major problem was their declining income, aggravated by the drought. Moreover, the proposed policy solution – tariff increases without any link to quality improvements – was not very convincing for obvious reasons.

EGS also emerged as a response to both the need for the educational access as well as balancing the precarious fiscal situation of the state. The very foundation of the MPEGS – community demand channeled through Panchayat to an administration that was obligated to provide a school within the 90 days. Lastly even the case of the Bhoomi suggest that the collection of the land revenue and the existence of the institutions of the state have been co-terminus. The Central and the State Governments have been long aware of the need to reform the land record system and the breakthrough came when the State Government mandated that 'Bhoomi Computerization of the land records' would have to be undertaken and finished in all the sub-districts by March 2002.

While these factors account for the success for the factors the study indicates that as the more empirical analysis of the effects of public administration on different groups of the society would be useful to better understand the implications of different reform models for the poor and for the disadvantaged groups of the society. As long as the rigorous studies on the distributional effects of different types of public administration reforms are not available, the debate will remain ideological. The three cases indicate that neo-liberal, welfare-statist and communitarian reform models may differ in their scope for contributing to the poverty reduction and social inclusion but no reform approach can be assumed to lead "automatically" to these goals. Without paying special attention to the poor and the disadvantaged groups of the society in administrative reforms, it is unlikely that any type of administrative reform will contribute to social inclusion and poverty reduction to the extent it could.

REFERENCES

Birner, Regina (2006) : "From Public Administration to Governance : International Trends in Public Administration Reform and Their Implications for Poverty Reduction and Social Inclusion," Paper Presented at Conference on Poverty, Inequality and Access to Justice for the Poor in South Asia from 7-9 November 2006, Centre for the Study of Law and Governance, Jawaharlal Nehru University, New Delhi.

Birner, R., Sharma, N. and N. Palaniswamy 2006: "The Political Economy of Electricity Supply to Agriculture in Andhra Pradesh and Punjab," Unpublished Manuscript. IFPRI, Washington, DC.

Chand Vikram (2006): "India Reforming Public Services in India; Drawing Lessons from the Success Report No. 35041-IN", February 28, 2006, Poverty Reduction and Economic Sector Management Unit, South Asia, World Bank.

Ramachandran, Vimala and Bose Sumit (2004): "Education Guarantee Scheme; a Community – Government Partnerships that gets millions into school in Madhya Pradesh," paper presented at Reducing poverty, sustaining growth – What Works, What Doesn't and Why a Global Exchange for scaling up the success, Conference at Shangai, May 25-27, 2004.

Chawla, Rajeev and Bhatnagar Subhash (2004): "Online Delivery of Land titles to the Rural Farmers in Karnataka, India", paper presented at reducing poverty, sustaining growth—What Works, What Doesn't and Why a Global Exchange for scaling up the success, Conference at Shangai May 25-27, 2004.

Haggard, Stephan and Robert Kaufman (eds.) (1992): *The Politics of Economic Adjustment*, Princeton University Press, Princeton.

ICRA and CRISIL (2005): "Power Sector Rating," Consolidated Report to the Ministry of Power, March 2005. New Delhi.

Handstand and Lokesh quoted in Chawla Rajeev and Bhatnagar Subhash (2004): "Online Delivery of Land Titles to the Rural Farmers in Karnataka, India" Paper presented at Reducing Poverty, Sustaining Growth -What Works, What Doesn't and Why a Global Exchange for scaling up the success, Conference at Shangai, May 25-27, 2004.

13

Good Governance and E-Governance: The Case of Revenue Department in Karnataka

G.M. DINESH AND B.S. BHARGAVA

Good governance has become a buzz word in the development literature. Conventionally, both government and governance go together as they are very closely associated (sometimes used as a synonym), but now governance has acquired a wider meaning and scope. The government refers to the formal institutions of the state and their monopoly of legitimate coercive power. It also refers to formal institutional processes, which operate at the level of nation-state to maintain public order and facilitate collective action. There is a redirection in the use and import of good governance. Governance signifies 'a change in the meaning of government, referring to a new process of governing; or a changed condition of ordered rule; or the new method by which society is governed'. The process of governance leads to outcomes that parallel those of the traditional institutions of government. Governance is ultimately concerned with creating the conditions for ordered rule and collective action. The outputs of governance are, therefore, not different from those of government. It is rather a matter of difference in processes.

It is asserted in theory that good governance is when the state retrenches, becomes less powerful, assumes a low profile and operation in a network with private interests and groups as a partner scarcely more important than the other. This kind of approach is tantamount to a transfer from a 'top-down process of Government to an inter-active process'. Again, good governance is characterized by the move away from supervision to contracting out; from centralization to decentralization from the state that redistributes to the state that regulates; from public services management to management following market principles; and from state, 'guidance to co-operation between the state and the private sector'.

The World Bank has identified a number of aspects of Good governance, which have assumed significance for the developed and developing countries. These are:

- Political accountability, including the acceptability of political system by the people and regular elections to legitimize the exercise of political power.
- Freedom of association and participation by various religious, social, economic, cultural and professional groups in the process of governance.
- Bureaucratic accountability ensuring a system to monitor and control the performance of Government Offices and Officials in relation to quality of service inefficiency and absence of discretionary power. The related determinants include openness and transparency in administration.
- A sound administrative system leading to efficiency and effectiveness. This in turn, means the value for money and cost effectiveness. The effectiveness includes the degree of global achievement as per the stated objectives and also the administrative system, which is able to take secular and rational decisions and the system, which is self-propelling to take corrective measures.

73rd and 74th Constitutional Amendments, taken together, make a landmark in the history of local self-government, more importantly they visualize third level of governance/strata. The imperative of good governance at this level assumes more significance as Panchayati Raj Institutions (PRIs) have yet to acquire a desirable level of sustainability (unlike National and State level governance). Therefore, in addition to the sustainability aspect all the three levels in the Indian polity need serious attention and concerted efforts for achieving the goal of good governance.

The definitions given below may be accepted by many (Bhargava, 2003).

Good governance is a combination of appropriate institutional mechanism and processes for achieving efficiency and effectiveness in administration within a democratic polity.

E-governance will involve the application of information and communication technologies to bring about more speed, transparency and responsiveness to the various areas of government activities resulting in enhanced accountability and consequent empowerment of the people. E-governance would cover transactions and information exchange between government and citizen, government and business and within government itself.

E-governance is the application of information technology to the process of Government functioning to bring about 'SMART' governance at all levels. It stands for Simple, Moral, Accountable, Responsive and Transparent governance.

The Government of Karnataka was a pioneer in this area and had setup the computer centre as early as 1971. Since then, various initiatives in e-governance have been taken and completed.

One of the primary objectives of Mahithi—the Millennium IT policy announced by the Government of Karnataka (GOK) is to use *"e-governance as a tool and deliver a government that is more proactive and responsive to its citizens."* The GOK believe that the effective implementation of e-government will take IT to the common man.

Era of e-governance aimed at demystifying the role of government, simplifying procedures, bringing in transparency, making need based, good quality and timely information available to all citizens and providing all services in an efficient and cost-effective way and identified services on an online basis. E-governance allows direct participation of constituents in government activities. E-governance will allow citizens to communicate with government, participate in the government's policy making and citizens to communicate each other. The e-governance will truly allow citizens to participate in the government decision making process, reflect their true needs.

Today Karnataka is the foremost state in the country with extensive implementation of the system of e-governance. The department of information technology, which monitors and spearheads the entire system of e-governance, operates as the nodal agency supporting every government department in their activities helping them to implement projects successfully. The prestigious Bhoomi e-governance project was undertaken by Government of

Karnataka (GOK), under the centrally sponsored scheme of computerization of land records. Under this project all 20 million-land records of 6.7 million landowners spread over 27,000 villages in 177 taluks of Karnataka have been computerized. This system works with the software called "BHOOMI" designed fully in house by National Information Centre (NIC), Bangalore. Land record is a crucial document in the lives of people. It is essential for security of loan tenures, crop loans, bail applications, betting scholarships for children, planning rural development programmes etc. kiosks have been set up under these projects provide information and deliver various services to the rural public.

Brief History of Land Records

The land records have a long history behind them, as long back as the history of the revenue administration. The earliest efforts to prepare land records on systematic lines and also to adopt innovative methods began with Sher Shah Suri, the Emperor of Northern India, for just five years (1540-1545). During his regime land records were, prepared recording the holdings of every cultivator that also showed the extent of area cultivated under each crop in every season. Sher Shah Suri not only changed the system of assessment of land revenue but also introduced some improvements in the methods of its collection. He gave instruction that leniency was to be shown at the time of assessment, but not at the time of collection.

The process of revenue administration started by Sher Shah Suri was continued and improved upon under the reign of the Moghal Emperor Akbar (1556-1605). Todar Mal--the greatest revenue expert, who started his career under Sher Shah Suri joined in the service of Akbar, is remembered even to this day for evolving a system of revenue assessment and survey – a system which drew a balance between the demands of the State and needs of the subject.

Under the Vijayanagara Kings, the revenue administration had reached the high level of efficiency, who determined the extent of land by the quantity of seeds sown. The Marathas in the integrated areas of Karnataka appointed officers like Deshpande, Kulkarni, Deshmukh etc., to revenue accounts. The Keladi Nayakas in the north introduced the land revenue system called *the sist*, which was perfected by Shivappa Nayaka who classified the lands into five categories according to their fertility taking into account the average yield over a period of 13 years.

Tipu Sultan introduced a new system of revenue administration who divided the territory into *tukadis* of 5000 *pagodas* each. On the restoration of the Mysore state to the Wodeyar Royal Family (1799), Dewan Purnaiah attempted to rationalise and stabilise the various rates of assessment and conferred property rights of soil and allowed the collection of revenue both in cash and kind.

The Raitayatwari system laid down by Lord William Bentinck was followed by Cubbon while administering the Mysore territory. In 1862, when Bowring took over the reign of administration, an orderly process of reformation set in. In November 1863 the Revenue circular was issued for systematizing revenue procedure.

The Mysore land revenue code (Act V of 1888) was promulgated and came into force from 1st April 1889. The rules framed under the code were first published in July 1890 and revised in August 1901. In the year 1958 the Karnataka Land Records of Rights Act, 1858 and the rules thereunder came into existence.

After the recognition of the state the need of adopting a uniform code regarding the maintenance of land revenue records and revenue administration was much felt. As a result evoked a new act to consolidate and amend different laws relating to land and revenue administration in the state. The Karnataka Land Revenue Act, 1964 (Karnataka Act 12 of 1964) was enacted and various Rules were framed under the Karnataka Land Revenue Rules, 1966, Sections 127 to 136 of Chapter XI of the Act, and Rules 38 to 71 of Chapter VIII and IX of the said rules deal with record of rights. The act is in force till date.

Importance of Land Records

Land records form the base for all land reforms and therefore regular periodic updating of land records is essential in all states.

In ancient times land revenue was possibly the only source from which the entire income of the Government was derived. Further, its incidence was on a large section of the population as a major proportion of the people relied on land for their livelihood and existence. This, tax on land proved to be the primary source of the

State's wealth. The revenue collected varied from region to region and also depended upon the regimes. Broadly speaking it was a share of the produce paid in kind or cash.

The mode of assessment and collection underwent a change when the British took over the administration. Lands were measured roughly and village records of lands were gradually built up. Thus, closely linked to the collection of land revenue was the creation of an array of land records wherein collection of revenue could be income for the Government.

However, the importance of land records cannot be undermined due to fall in the importance of land revenue. The entire structure of land records management that was associated with revenue collection now had to sustain its relevance suo moto. The shrinkage in the relevance of land revenue collection does not undermine the importance of the land records in the governance paradigm.

Thus, the concept of collection of revenue necessitated the maintenance of land records, in a rudimentary form in ancient times and a more systematic form during the British Administration. Maintenance of land records has now become more vital for administrators and creation of a land information system is one of the key issues facing governance today.

Land records itself is a generic expression and could include, in Karnataka State, records like the Register of lands of Khetwar Patrika, Records of Rights, Tenancy and crop inspection register (RTC)– Form 16, khata register (Form 24), khirdi (Form 25), Mutation Register (Form 12), disputed cases register (Form 8) and the like...

However, certain types of information relating to land play a very important role. These may include primary information about land presented in terms of its geological information like the shape, size, land forms, soils; economic information related to land use irrigation and crops; and the information pertaining to the legal rights, registration and taxation. No improvement in land can be made without acquiring rights to land. These rights cannot be acquired until ownership is established.

Land records form the basis for assignment and settlement of land titles. These records must stand the test of legal scrutiny. Land is a very precious source and the land records system must safeguard the rights of the legal owner of the land.

As all type of data related to land, as explained earlier, is available in these land records, they are used for various planning processes although the manual maintenance of this land record does hinder in effective collection and analysis of the data contained in them.

The importance of land and land record in affecting people's livelihood is an indisputable fact. Issues of land rights not only raise legal complexities but also have socio-ecomonic dimensions. If the state has to address these questions a sound land information management system has to be put in place because information is the key to power.

Problem of Manual Systems

The manual system of land records maintenance was highly opaque. 200 lakh records were maintained which were subject to following defects viz.,

Opaque System

The manual system of land records maintenance was highly opaque. Over 9000 village accountants maintained 200 lakh records. The sub-district office did not have any updated copy of such records. Thus a situation of virtual monopoly of village Accountants over these records was prevailing for many years. Records were not open to public scrutiny and were updated many times only on various considerations.

Prone to Manipulations

Manual Record Administration was prone to manipulation. There have been large instances of government land being shown in the name of private parties. In fact, in Bangalore division alone 25 billion worth of government land had been manipulated and shown in the name of private influential persons. Opaque manual system facilitates such manipulation very easily by unscrupulous officials.

Harassment and Extortion

Many a times farmers faced harassment and extortion for not only provisions of land records to them by the village officials but also for processing requests for change in land title.

Delay in Delivery of Land Records

On many occasions such delay was unintentional. Even if a village accountant was willing to give such records in time, he was not available when farmers wanted him most as he was manning more than 4-5 villages. Therefore, there was no certainty about timely availability of such records when a farmer required them.

Cumbersome Mutation Process

The process of mutation (change in land title) was very cumbersome. Applications were being given to village officials who virtually enjoyed discretion of either processing them or not. As records were maintained in decentralized manner, there was no reporting mechanism available at sub-district level about the pending of such applications with village accountants. Lack of any monitoring mechanism in manual system made farmers amenable to all pressures from hierarchy of the department.

Lack of Timely Data for Planning Purpose

Land records contain various useful data like soil type, irrigation details, trees, crops grown, crop yield etc. All such data is very valuable for various administrative purposes including various development schemes and programmes to be implemented at the grassroots under the control or supervision of PRIs. As data was manually maintained, it was not possible to collate and analyze such data resulting into mine of such useful data not being used in any meaningful way.

Cumbersome Crop Loan Mechanism

Banks often asked various land records before lending crop loans to farmers. Farmers in turn had to hunt village officials with no guarantee that banks would not ask for any more records. This made crop loaning process prone to delay and resulted into harassment of farmers.

Delay in Disposal of Civil Litigations

The courts often required various land records for disposing land based civil litigations (which formed more than 70% of total litigations). Records were not forthcoming from village accounts easily and in time resulting into delay in disposal of civil litigations. Farmers had to often spend, in many cases more than 5-10 years for disposal of their land litigation cases in absence of these records.

Earlier Efforts Towards Computerization of Land Records

The federal government, realizing the importance of well-maintained and updated land records database, launched the scheme of computerization of land records in the year 1991. Gulbarga District was one of the pilot districts chosen by the federal government among 24 districts in the country.

By 1996 for the computerization of land records was extended to cover all the districts of the state. While the funds under the project were sanctioned for capturing of the legacy land records data in digital form, there was not enough clarity about its validation and subsequent updation. No funds were allocated for sub district computers where the data could be update. The project therefore fizzled out without achieving its objective.

The reasons for failure of the earlier attempts of computerization of land records were studied in detail with reference to Karnataka. The following reasons emerge out of sufficient probing.

Lack of Clarity

The federal government did not have the clarity about strategy for implementation of the scheme. It was not clearly spelt out in the scheme as to what has to be done with the digitized data, how would that be updated with time? How would these records be distributed to the farmers? What would be done with the manual records?

Lack of Involvement

Perhaps the lack of clarity led to involvement of the Revenue Department Officers and District Administration in the project. The lack of training of village accountants on data entry process led to wrong and defective database. Further validation of data was not properly done leading to errors in database. The printed records were distributed to the farmers in some of the district without paper validation and then updation or any use of the database forgotten about. The distribution was itself regarded as computerization of land records.

The Bhoomi project was a breakthrough in the computerization of land records launched on 6th February 2001. The result is evolution of a transparent and effective land record delivery system which fully addresses the insecurities and concerns of the farmers and which is now in operation in nearly all sub-districts of Karnataka.

Banning of Manual Records

It was clear that two parallel systems would always work at cross-purpose with each other and probably even making the computerized system a casualty. The manual system suffered from malafides was exploitative and inefficient. The successful pilots had given the required confidence to the department that manual system can be disbanded in phases in such sub-districts where scheme was being operationalized. Banning manual system did put pressure on the system, as it required computerized system to perform at least as good as manual system to start with. However the Bhoomi team, District Administration and National Information Centre (NIC) rose to the occasion as single team and withstood such pressure successfully.

Bhoomi Project in Karnataka

The Bhoomi computerization of land records in all 177 taluks of Karnataka under Bhoomi has been implemented by revenue department. Deputy Commissioners of respective districts have been implementing Bhoomi in the field.

Features of Bhoomi

Bhoomi is a very comprehensive software designed by NIC, Bangalore. This software provides for printing of land records as and when required. It incorporates process of online updation to ensure that the Record of Rights Tenancy and Crops (RTCs) provided to the farmers is in synchronize with the time. The manual land records in operationalised taluks have been declared illegal. All the mutations to the land records database are done on the computer itself so as to ensure that data on computer remain current with time.

It incorporates the state of the art bio-logon metrics system from Compaq, which authenticates various users on the Bhoomi software on the basis of fingerprints. This ensures that no body can hack the system by imitating other users. The replacement of password security system by fingerprint authentication system would go a long way to ensure that database is free from any hacking and that the non-repudiation system is in place. This software also has the provision of scanning of original mutation orders of the revenue inspector (who is the authorized person to pass orders in the mutations in the field) and notice served on interested parties. Both documents are scanned to ensure that not only responsibility can be fixed on officials by showing the original documents signed by them but also to ensure that the interested parities do not claim in the court that they were not served with the notice before effecting the mutation. The software enables the administrators to generate various reports based on type of soil, land holding size, type of crops grow etc. This information would enable administrators to take informed policy decision.

Highlights of Bhoomi

- Fully online system to carry out mutations on land records data.
- Finger print biometrics authentication to ensure fool proof authentication system and to enforce the concept of non-repudiation.
- Facility to scan the field mutation order passed by revenue authorities and the notice served on the public.
- Land record centre in each taluk office for public interface.
- Synchronizes with the regular field work done by village accountants and revenue inspector.
- Provision for interfacing of Touch Screen Kiosk at taluk office.

Benefits of Bhoomi

- Farmers can quickly get their land records from Kiosks and are protected from harassment and extortion. As against time delay of 3 to 30 days they now get their records in less than 2 minutes. No overhead cost is to be incurred. No application is required to be submitted at the kiosk. The records are authentic and legible. Use of biometrics authentication system for updation of records has freed farmers from the worry of probable manipulation of their records by some unscrupulous officials.

- They can lodge application for mutation (change in land title) to their land records at the computerized kiosks, get acknowledgement for the same and can monitor the progress using touch screen kiosks available in some Bhoomi centres. They would then get their updated land record in a fixed time frame without the need of approaching any authority. As against earlier time of 70-200 days, mutation would now require less than 35 days.
- Farmers can also get the official status report of their request for mutation, which would let them know the stage at which their request is pending. This status report would help them in enforcing their right of getting the record mutated in the prescribed time.
- Access to farm credit would be less cumbersome. Online connectivity to banks would ensure farm credit to farmers in less than 5 days as against 25-30 days in manual system.
- It would be easier for the farmers to pursue land-related litigation in the court.
- Easy maintenance and updation of land records documents. In manual system land records updation used to get delayed by as high as 1-2 years in some cases. Now it would always be in synchronize with time.
- Support for development programmes, based on valuable land records data like various crops grown in a village or a sub-district, the fertilizers and pesticide requirement in a season etc., to departments like Agriculture, Industries and Planning. Such data in earlier system became available to departments only after 2-3 years. It is now available almost immediately.
- Accurate and timely preparation of annual records like land revenue etc.
- Monitoring of government lands and prevention of their encroachments. Lack of monitoring had costed a reported loss of Rs. 25 billion to State Government by way of officials tampering with records.
- Courts would be able to make use of land record database for adjudicating various civil disputes related to ownership, possession and cultivation in various courts.
- Online connectivity to financial institutions would help

banks in planning for their farm credit related activities. In manual system they worked on 2 years old data or just guessed the farm sector requirement.

- Online connectivity would also helps banks to ensure that revenue administration is indicating bank's charge on land records of such farmers who have availed crop loans.
- Facilitates creating change on land of farmers who take crop loans.
- Private sector had complained of absence of crop and land data for their planning purpose.
- Bhoomi data would help supplier of various agricultural inputs like seeds, pesticide, fertilizers etc. to plan their activities.
- Details of irrigated lands and pattern of land holding could be used by private sector for more informed decision-making. In manual system such data was just not available.

Bhoomi Will Open Gateway to Villager's World

Today, the Bhoomi project connects 177 taluks (distribution points) earns a revenue of Rs. 1 crore a month with about 7 lakh people shelling out Rs. 15 each to get a printout of the land record. If you take this amount (Rs. 1 crore) and divide it by 1000 villages, each village gets Rs. 10000. On a revenue sharing basis of say, 60:40, Rs. 6000 would go into the villager's kitty. No doubt he will have to pay the rental and 0.50 paise for each printer paper, but at least some money is ensured every month as well as ease of access to records at the village level itself.

User Charges Generated by Bhoomi

The total cost of the Bhoomi project is Rs. 40 crore. Out of which the variable cost incurred from 2001-03 is Rs. 18.5 crore. Number of farmers who availed services since its inception are 1,76,29,721 which work out to 122 per cent (Rs. 22,58,74,196) of the total variable cost (see Table 13.1). This has been covered within two years. Hence it indicates that the project is economically sustainable over a period.

Flaws in Bhoomi

Karnataka's Bhoomi project, which computerized 20 million rural land records, was designed as an instrument of equity. But is IT reinforcing inequality. "At present IT is reinforcing more than attacking inequality; men are benefiting more than women; the rich

Table-13.1
Revenue Department GOK. Statement Showing User Charges Collected from Bhoomi Kiosks

Sl. No.	*District*	*User Charges Collected During the Month of December 2003*	*Cumulative User Charges Collected*	*No. of Farmers Who Availed Bhoomi Services During the Month of December 2003*	*No. of Farmers who Availed Bhoomi Services from the Inception*
1	2	3	4	5	6
1.	Bangalore (Rural)	428955	7784995	28597	519000
2.	Bangalore (Urban)	456015	7818608	30401	521241
3.	Bagalkot	1845900	14262935	123060	950862
4.	Belgaum	1784550	20745180	118970	1383012
5.	Bellary	324075	6970190	21605	464679
6.	Bidar	173455	4912600	11564	327507
7.	Bijapur	2248755	12530180	149917	835345
8.	Chamrajnagar	151095	2705070	10073	180338
9.	Chickmaglur	373975	6919470	24932	461298
10.	Chitradurga	598140	6841306	39876	456087
11.	Dakshin Kannada	518910	9514405	34594	634294
12.	Davanagere	317960	8283921	21197	552261
13.	Dharwad	1038645	6708910	69243	447261
14.	Gadag	1199690	5265130	79979	351009
15.	Gulbarga	522840	9867059	34856	657804
16.	Hassan	1036215	12127539	69081	808503
17.	Havery	484670	6390895	32311	426060
18.	Kodagu	134395	3493975	8960	232932
19.	Kolar	162745	8094859	30850	539657
20.	Koppal	601230	4862477	40082	324165
21.	Mandya	462535	9292750	30836	619517
22.	Mysore	450515	9049285	30034	603286
23.	Raichur	416895	5957921	27793	397195

Contd.

1 2	3	4	5	6
24. Shimoga	329520	8966960	21968	597797
25. Tumkur	545955	12448165	36397	829878
26. Uttar Kannada	388046	8571661	25894	571444
27. Udupi	334040	5487750	22269	365850
Grand Total	**17629721**	**225874196**	**1175339**	**15058282**

Source: Computed from the records of Revenue Department GOK, as well as website, www.revdept.kar.nic.in

are benefiting more than the poor. The challenge is to create the conditions for 'reversing the polarities'; but that is a task for social movements more than computers" (Richard Heeks).

If the Bhoomi in Karnataka is to serve the total needs of the farmer in the state, it has to go beyond just land records and treat the farmer as a valuable customer. (Manu. N. Kulkarni, 2003). Bhoomi, unfortunately, stands as an island, there are too many medium sized and small projects that are floating around, almost rudderless one must say. The right hand, often, does not know what the left hand is doing. For example, one of the major projects was to include GIS features (Geographical Information System). It was dropped, subsequently, at the implementation stage it was told, because the software required to create digital maps of the districts was too expensive. Interestingly, under the ages of another project, one of the government departments had already engaged a vendor to create digital maps of districts. They could have as well been used by this project but they had no idea of its existence. Information sharing across department is minimal.

The idea of Chief Information Officers (CIOs) is yet to take off in Karnataka and there doesn't seem to be much enthusiasm about it. In the worlds of software development one speaks of measuring oneself on the Capability Maturity Model. It has five levels – the lower level most, called 'Initial' is at level 1 and the highest, called 'Optimizing' is the level 5. He would say that Karnataka is at level 1 and Andhra Pradesh is at level 2 (called the 'Repeatable' level of maturity). Translation Karnataka's development in ICT is 'ad hoc' and that Andhra Pradesh, while not fully mature, is one level higher. 'Repeatable' implies some procedural discipline. (S. Jagadish 2003).

Mallaiah Prabhaker, Director of Karnataka's treasury department admits that IT cannot address fraud in primary data that is put online. The concern is echoed by G.N. Nagaraj, a prominent left wing politician in Karnataka who says the State Government has not bothered to tackle fraudulent land records that went online in the Bhoomi project.

Concluding Observations

In short, a model for success that seems to work, depends on the following factors such as Political will, Bureaucratic commitment, Leadership in projects, Appropriate organization structure and Required business process, will go a long way in fulfilling the set objectives in the e-governance projects in India in general and Karnataka in particular.

REFERENCES

B.S. Bhargava, "Governance, Good Governance and the Indian Context," Governance, (Journal) RCVP Noranha Academy of Administration and Management, Bhoopal, Second Issue, October 2003, pp. 25-29.

India Today (2000) "Is e-Governance for Real?" Weekly, 11 December, pp. 70-5.

Jagadish S. (2003) "The Ice has Broken with ICT". *Deccan Herald,* May-12.

Manu, N. Kulkarni. (2ra003) "Rural Beyond the Bhoomi", *Deccan Herald,* June - 19.

Ramachandraiah C. (2003), "Information Technology and Social Development," *Economic and Political Weekly,* March 22.

Dr. Richard Heeks, e-governance expert, Britain's Manchester University.

www.bangaloreit.com

http://www.bhoomi.kar.nic.in/

http://www.revdept-01.kar.nic.in/

14

Globalization and Good Governance in a Democratic Society: The Indian Predicament

B. VENUGOPAL

Recent years have seen a major shift in political discourse. From development and welfare concerns, there is a rapid switch over to concern for good governance. It is curious that 'governance' should become so much of an obsession with such a diverse range of people as politicians, administrators, academicians, researchers, businessmen and even non-governmental organizations. Fascination for the term has resulted in its being used as an objective, explanation or even rationalization for almost every action and inaction on the part of the state, on the one hand, and nearly every demand/expectation of intervention / withdrawal made on it, on the other.

The concepts of Governance and Good Governance are not new; they are as old as civilizations. It is stated by many scholars that these terms are seen in ancient classics. But these terms started gaining importance only after the emergence of Globalization culture. When the role of the governments and the state began to decline and government has become just one of the actors in governance, the scholars on administration, politics and philosophy have started to discuss the relevance, importance and aspects of governance.

This chapter is divided into two parts. The first part discusses the theoretical aspects of good governance and its relations with globalization. The second part is an attempt to link the concept with the Indian context. For reasons obvious, this chapter does not make a specific search into the problems or maladies of Indian administration, but makes a general view of the need for good governance in India in the age of globalization and what are the specific situations we have to develop for achieving good governance in India.

Governance

The term governance has wider meaning and implication than those of the term Government. Government refers to the machinery and the institutional arrangements of exercising the sovereign power for serving the internal and external interests of the political community, whereas governance means the process as well as the result of making authoritative decisions for the benefit of the society.

A large number of International Relations literature on governance emerged after the collapse of Communism and the bi-polar world order. It accepts that inter-dependence is an increasingly important feature of a new World Order and argues that facilities this calls for commonly accepted norms, rules and patterns of behaviour that facilitate international cooperation. Contrary to the realist or the neo-realist approaches to international politics that stress the overwhelming importance of perceived national interest, governance is typically associated with a constructivist approach in which rules as regimes are viewed as key ingredients for stabilizing international relations. Co-operation across both national and issue boundaries require the initiation of a process involving factors ready to transcend narrow national interest concerns. Governance, therefore, is a process involving multiple factors in the international arena that produces new norms and rules for working together to solve global problems or conflicts.[1]

Interest in governance among students of Comparative Politics has also emerged as a result of collapse of communism. Their study of the rules of the game is associated with an increasing concern about the world to bring about democracy. In this context, governance is studied as a part of regime transition. Their view of governance is related to institutional frameworks for the realization of democratic ideals.[2]

A comprehensive explanation for Governance is given by Anne Kjaer who says that Governance is about managing rules of the game in order to enhance the legitimacy of the public realm. Legitimacy may be derived from democracy as well as from efficiency.

Regarding Governance theory in general, the focus has been on efficiency, but there is a growing literature on democratic accountability which should not be ignored.[3]

The World Bank has its own interpretation of governance that is of special interest because its official mandate prevents it from dealing with political issues. To cope with this, the World Bank makes a distinction between governance as an analytical framework and governance as an operational framework, leading it to identify three aspects of governance:

1. the form of political governance
2. the process by which authority is exercised in the management of a country's economic and social resources for development and
3. the capacity of governments to design, formulate and implement policies and discharge functions.[4]

The World Bank has professed to confine itself only to second and third aspects of governance, but it has found itself under increasing pressure from Western bilateral donors to address also to the first. Its recent recognition of human rights as an essential aspect of governance seems to be a manifestation of this extended operational use of the concept.

Good Governance

Good Governance connotes certain value assumptions, where as governance as a process denotes value free dispensation. Good Governance is associated with efficient and effective administration in a democratic framework. It is equivalent to purposive and development oriented administration which is committed to improvement in quality of life of the people. It implies high level of organisational effectiveness. It also relates to the capacity of the centre of power of political administrative systems to cope with the emerging challenges of the society. It refers to the adoption of new values of governance to establish greater efficiency, legitimacy and credibility of the system. Good governance is, thus a function of installation of positive virtues of administration and elimination of vices of dysfunctionalities. In short, it must have the attributes of an effective, credible and legitimate administrative system—citizen friendly, value caring and people sharing.

O.P. Minocha, by quoting World Bank guidelines, defines Good governance's criteria as "political accountability, availability of freedom, law abiding, bureaucratic accountability, information available transparently, being effective and efficient and cooperation between government and society."

The concept of Good governance derives its relevance in the context of misgovernance which includes nonfeasance, over-feasance and malfeasance. In many countries, the democratic form of government has proved to be ineffective for checking swindling of public funds for private gains by the elected leaders as well as bureaucrats. Misuse of power, fraud, chicanery and embezzlement of funds are systematically perpetrated by the leaders of the government and their unions. Misgovernance is found all around, especially in the developing countries in rampant degree. The concept of Good governance becomes attractive as a remedy against this state of affairs.

In 1989 the concept of Good governance was for the first time high lightened in a World Bank document on Sub-Saharan Africa. This concept was introduced in the agenda by the World Bank because it needed to explain why a number of countries failed to develop, inspite of the fact that they had adopted the neo-liberal adjustment policies imposed on them by the IMF and the World Bank. The answer was "bad governance" understood as self serving public officials and corruption in the public services. Thus the recipe for the developing countries was to increase transparency and accountability in the public sector. The overall model to be 'transferred' was one of expenditure reduction, privatization and public service reform, that is, not only less, but also better government. During the 1990's the bilateral donors also put increasing pressure on recipient governments to hold democratic elections. Hence the model of Good Governance promoted by the donors and international Institutions was built upon the Anglo-American liberal democratic states.[5]

The preliminary conditions of Good Governance are the establishment of the rule of law supplanting the rule of whims and caprice of the power that be. Good Governance demands that government must be not only representative but responsive as well as to the needs of the governed. A strong sense of responsiveness and commitment to serve the governed – the customer and the client of the government would ensure efficient delivery of services to the people.

Thus Good Governance shares on aims and ethos of a cohesive and responsible democratic society. Good Governance provides moral legitimacy, apart from constitutional validity and credibility to the goals as well as instrumentalities of government. Good Governance comprehends within itself all sections of governance and all sections and regions of society.

The main constituents or attributes of Good Governance are rule of law, accountability, decentralization, honesty or probity in public affairs, independence of judiciary, human rights, people's participation, equality of treatment as needed in a pluralist society, absence of discrimination on the basis of religion, colour, race, language, place of birth, faith, sex etc., administrative responsiveness, social sensitivity, ethical approach or conduct, effectiveness, willingness to learn and having an urge to improve as well as evolve capacity to anticipate the nature and direction of change to cope with the challenges as they arise from time to time.

The basic thrust of the concept is to motivate people in government so that they can make full contribution of their capabilities in serving their nation and community. The objective of Good Governance is to create an environment so that public servants as well as politicians in government are able to respond to the challenges of Good Governance. That challenge involves a notion of duty, vocation and service to the public, as well as the caring responsibility for their welfare. And it strengthens the values of liberal democracy. That ideal, based on vocation, duty and service, also draws upon the concept of sacrifice – a concept which rises above self-interest, placing individualism over collective good and greed. The concept of service also creates a shared feeling or spirit of public duty among those who govern.

Good Governance and democracy are synonymous to each other. All the characteristics of Good Governance are possible only in a democratic polity. Democracy integrates participation into the political life of the country and provides a basis for legitimacy of government. Important linkages exist between the features of democratization and other aspects of participatory development and

Good Governance. Good Governance and democracy include the basic values in their own right, such as human rights and principles of participation and others such as accountability, transparency and high standards of public sector management, which are also means to developmental ends. Some of the objectives, such as the rule of law, must be viewed as both ends in themselves and means to viable development. In a democratic system, the legitimacy of the government depends on the existence of participatory process and the consent of those who are governed. The accountability of the political and official elements of government for their actions depends on the availability of information, freedom of the media, transparency in decision making and the existence of mechanisms to call individuals and institutions to account for their conduct. Accountability also exists at the political level through representative government and political process. The competence of government is also needed to formulate appropriate policies, make timely decisions, implement them effectively and deliver services. Respect for human rights and rule of law, to guarantee individual and group rights and security, provides a viable framework for economic and social activity and allows and encourage individuals to participate.

Globalization and Good Governance

Globalization is a world wide process which is unfolding in different parts of the world with different meanings and different connotations. It is neither a singular condition nor a linear process. It is a multi-dimensional phenomenon involving diverse domains of activities and interactions including the economic, trade, political, technological, cultural and environmental spheres. Similarly, the significance of globalization also differs for individuals, groups and countries. Globalization, as a universal process has two distinct characteristics, first, it suggests that many chains of political, economic and social activity are becoming inter-regional and inter-continental in scope: and second, it suggests that there has been an intensification of levels of interaction and interconnectedness within and among the states and societies.[6]

Globalization is a process with multifarious implications and it cannot be fully understood in terms of economic and trade activities only. It has globalised the world economy and now the states are increasingly becoming its part and parcel but it cannot be restricted to merely economic and trade spheres. It will also have consequent implications for the states in the spheres of socio-cultural domains. The policies and programmes within the states will be subsequently affected with the process of globalization and, therefore, its philosophy and practice should be understood and analyzed in its totality. Globalization has significant dimensions in terms of identity, community, knowledge and ecology. It is a broad process of restructuring of the state, civil society, political economy and culture.

Globalization has direct bearings on the concept and practice of Good Governance. At the outset, it should be clearly understood that Good Governance in the context of globalization has many connotations and, therefore, there is no commonality regarding its definition or practices. Globalization has posed many challenges in this regard; however, effort is being made to highlight few of them for further discussions.

First, the end of sovereignty in the emerging international context need not be the end of the state in the foreseeable future. The state is still a unit factor as well as the supreme factor in the international system and bears the main responsibility for governance of its people within its territorial limits. But, at the same time it is subjected to various kinds of interference and interventions directly or indirectly from outside states and supra state structures which do not allow the states to independently decide what is good for their governance. Hence, the prescriptions from outside are imposed upon them that determine the definition and practice of Good Governance which may or may not be suited to their indigenous genius, conditions and requirements. This conflict between the "North and the South" may pose new challenges in the 21st century in this regard.[7]

Second, globalization with its accompanying trend of privatization is impinging upon the state systems to wind up public sector and to open up opportunities for private sector with least interference and least taxation and duties. So, if the state sources of revenues are shrinking, the objectives of people's welfare and social justice will be difficult to realize and it will pose new challenges of social unrest , upheavals in different forms in different parts of the world. In the bolstering global competitiveness, the governments all over the world are rolling back their policies and programmes of social democracy and people's welfare. Under the compulsions of liberalization and privatization, the states are abandoning the regimes of progressive taxation and accepting that growing inequalities of wealth and income are unavoidable side effects of increased economic efficiency and financial viability.[8]

Globalization is also bringing forth new trends such as movements towards civil society increasing role of NGOs, greater efforts towards new awareness for global environment, human rights and protection and emancipation and empowerment of weaker or marginalized sections.

Globalization encompasses contradictory trends. On the one hand, the unaccountable forces of globalization such as cross border flows of undocumented workers and modern communications with instantaneous speed are partially beyond the control of effective state regulations. To adjust, the state responds to the globalization process by more fully integrating the domestic economy into the world markets. On the other hand, the state pulls in the opposite direction by using a variety of government interventions to create a competitive edge. All countries industrializing late rely on large scale interventions-most important, direct involvement in the production process establishment of social and economic infrastructure, generous in terms of credit and material support for shifting from imitative to indigenous technological capacity. The options are clearly restricted and the question is not whether the state should intervene in the economy but what type of state and what interventions are most appropriate in a specific context? And policy initiatives in whose interest? Will state intervention be subject to popular control?

The challenges posed by globalization to the state and governance are not just of maintaining a fine equilibrium between economic growth and securing a higher place in the new international order and upliftment of poor masses and development of backward regions but also to fight the new strongholds of the so-called "economic constitutionalism" which reduces the autonomy of the state from providing protectionist policy and insular regime to poor citizens.[9] In this Economic Constitutionalism, rules and constitutional mandates are being redesigned to sustain neo-liberal arrangements so as, for example, to give greater veto power to the minority interests of capital and to make certain kinds of political change in the future more difficult. Innovations to constitutional provisions mean new constraints that circumscribe the maneuvering room for future politicians to manipulate monetary and fiscal policy or trade protectionism. The NAFTA, Maastricht Treaty and the GATT Uruguay round agreements are the examples of this type of Economic Constitutionalism. The new structural reforms and strings attached to international funding institutions pressurize the recipient nations for removal of subsidies on even essential sectors like health, water, agriculture, electricity and the free use of public infrastructure. This creates a situation of potential social tension between the rich and the poor. Because governance does not mean addressing felt needs of people only rather the felt aspirations. The global media has increased these felt aspirations of common people. Another problem relates to the question of quantity versus quality of services. New quality services like toll highways and hospitals to the sections of the people who can afford to pay has also increased the level of felt aspirations among the poor masses for getting quality services. Thus the fundamental challenge of globalization to the state and governance is to become accountable and responsible to the ruled and also play to the gallery of global market forces. This tight rope walking between the expectations of these two distinctively different masters—the ruled and the global market forces—is the most significant challenge to good governance.

Good Governance in India

In India, self governance and good governance (common good) was the core of our freedom struggle. After the attainment of independence, good governance became synonymous with the constitution under the caption, "we, the people of India," through the guiding star, the Preamble of the Constitution. Since then, the search has been on for the seemingly elusive goal of good governance by setting up of various committees and commissions to revitalize public administration. However despite all these efforts, we have failed to make a significant impact on public psyche against the institutional deterioration and decline of values in general because of lack of Dharma, common good and our leadership. In fact our political system could not promote and sustain common good of the governed for the last fifty seven years.[10] And it cannot be realized unless for generating good governance both democracy and bureaucracy are willing to change themselves. Their present form is totally out of tune with the demands of the 21st century. We must accept the truism that the final test of democracy lies in the patterns and processes of governance.

The condition of India's public services is utterly deplorable. We are passing through difficult times in terms of eroded credibility and effectiveness of the civil services, growing public perception of unholy nexus between certain elements among politicians, civil servants and criminals and increasing criticism of the low level of honesty, transparency and accessibility to the political and bureaucratic elements.

C.P. Bhambhri observes that global capitalism has found a powerful social constituency in India which expects social and economic benefits at the cost of state sovereignty. Consequently, inequalities are increasing at various levels and contributing to the miseries of the poor. This collapse has left little scope for the adoption of more compassionate development policies with beneficial social and economic contents for the poor. But both sides are not coming with substantive remedies.

The Constitution of India is the oldest functioning legal document in the third world and we may feel proud of the achievements of the country. Yet there are numerous major ailments that have afflicted the functioning of political system in India. They are: proliferation of political parties and political instability, criminalization of politics, steep fall in values and degeneration in politics, unaccountability of bureaucracy, allocation of undue perks and privileges to elected legislators, prevalence of problems like poverty, illiteracy backwardness, overpopulation, lack of amenities, lack of administrative and judicial accountability and work culture, lack of an efficient grievance redressal mechanism and inadequacy of the administrative justice system.

Our Constitution is formulated on the principles of the 19th century. It is further kept intact by judiciary which is made of judges who are independent of every thing and are accountable to none. The masses are taught to evaluate only on the basis of its neutrality, impartiality and appealability on every point. None is allowed to judge its performance in terms of cost, time, effectiveness, capacity to help the poor and the exploited and satisfaction to the aggrieved parties. Members of judiciary hardly realize that about 85 per cent aggrieved persons, instead of knocking at the doors of justice, like more to suffer because of judiciary's limitations and unbearable costs of litigation. Sufferings of the people cross all the limits when MNCs and other international forces enter the scene. None is permitted to question the acts and performance of the judiciary. Decisions can hardly be taken in time by leaders, political parties cabinet and legislative bodies, even in very urgent situations. Every political decision has to pass through parliamentary committees, discussions and anarchic media agencies. Elections are contested not on specific issues and their solutions, but on the basis of manifestoes which contain thousands of empty and generalized statements. We see political leaders and representatives becoming rich overnight. Political leaders know little about the role of intraputs, but pretend to lead the country in unknown directions.

The legislative organs of the country have become out dated. They survive only because of the absence of any viable alternatives. Hardly any one of them uses modern scientific knowledge, including IT.

The bureaucracy is surviving simply by sitting behind the fortunes of elected leaders. They have constructed their own world of rules and regulations, files, records, special procedures and subjective forms of implementation. Bureaucracy has become irresponsible, careless and self centered.

In the Indian context, good governance was a causality due to the absence of mission or vision and lack of leadership. It became totally perverted by pervasive and incisive corruption in every department of social life, in general, and political life, in particular. The canker of corruption in top echelons of government systematically destroyed the entire fabric of social and economic life in this country, caring little for bearing responsibility and throwing to the winds the ethical values of public life. The result is that people are compelled today to "eat corruption, sleep corruption and drinking only corruption." This was the scenario, which the Vohra Committee's findings on the nexus between politicians, bureaucrats and criminals focused.

Administration as a specialized field of government activity has marked a significant turning point in response to globalization. Many acts and regulations regarding economics, trade and commerce have either been amended or are in the process of amendment. Many Acts, like the Indian Patents Act have been drastically changed in character and quality. The ministries and institutions governing economic policy making have also experienced considerable changes. Even the Planning Commission, once known as the Super Cabinet has experienced erosion in its role in policy making. The governing pattern in public enterprises has also been experiencing changes due to reform initiatives such as granting of more autonomy and introducing effective accountability in public enterprises through initiatives like autonomy packages, bringing more public enterprises under Memorandum of Understanding and professionalizing the board of directors by inducing part time non-official members.

The aim of these new initiatives in the field of administration is to attain a higher rate of growth on sustainable basis through efficiency and profitability in the economy by relaxing grant control over domestic economy to foreign trade , capital and technology. But the changes have not succeeded in attaining the desired results. First, the Indian economy since the beginning of globalization has not experienced a higher rate of growth on sustained basis. The rate of growth has oscillated between 4 per cent and 8 per cent. The industrial sector and foreign trade which are the central focus of amended and new economic laws have remained more volatile. Secondly, changing economic laws governing both internal and external sectors simultaneously have not helped the Indian industries to improve efficiency and productivity. Rather these have helped MNCs to enter India in a big way and take over most of the lucrative industrial activities. Thirdly, the administrative ministries and the political leadership and bureaucracy have made consistent efforts to thwart the implementation of new initiatives in the field of governance. The recent decisions by the central as well as the State Governments about privatization and the establishment of Special Economic Zones suggest that policy makers have no clear opinion on the issue of changes in governance. Fourthly, India has not made adequate institutional arrangements to reap the benefits of globalization particularly originating from the World Trade Organization.

The case of the initiatives in issues like efforts to establish a citizen friendly government, implementation of transparency in the Government, implementation of the Right to Information etc. also meets with the same fate. These initiatives have also not succeeded in fulfilling the laid down objectives.[11]

The key question is how to retrieve the dismal situation of our political system. Of course the country needs a change. A package of remedial measures will have to be evolved incorporating huge investments in building our social infrastructure simultaneously with equally demanding needs of physical and economic infrastructure. While the existing administrative apparatus will need to be subjected to in-depth administrative reforms, including electoral reforms on an extensive scale to cover comprehensively procedural, structural and attitudinal aspects, there is also an urgent need to enlist active involvement of NGOs and voluntary agencies and people's co-operative bodies and such other forms of associative democracy in carrying out functions of administration on an increasing and widening scale ensuring a smooth roll back of administration and effectively curtailing administrative expenditure. For, the surest way of realizing good governance is through promoting more and more people's participation, both at policy formulation level as well as implementation level, even though it is through a wasteful process of trial and error.[12]

Administration is to become more and more citizen friendly and citizen caring, responsive and accountable, effective and efficient, just, reasonable, air, open, and impartial. The institutions of governance must be alive to the complaints of citizens. There should be effective and efficient complaint redressal system which must be inexpensive, transparent, impartial and rational. The internal grievance redressal system in the various government organizations needs to be restructured and reoriented to make it citizen friendly. A well organized complaint system for redressal of citizens' grievances is a must not only to provide continuous feed back on the state of affairs prevailing in government but also to ensure correctional opportunity for review, correction and reform.

The government must be open and ready to provide information. In a democracy, it is supposed that the people will participate and offer creative contribution in the process of governance. Or this, it is essential that they must be provided reliable information. Any effort in the direction of creating the culture of good governance must start from creating the system of ensuring openness in the functioning of government. No claim, howsoever tall, for good governance would be accepted as sincere in absence of right to information.

One of the criteria of good governance is that the government lays down its standard of performance and is prepared to be evaluated against those standards. Though the trend of setting standards of performance has recently been started in different strata of government, much more is required to be done. The setting of standards of performance and linking it, in case of non-performance, with personal accountability will no doubt, enhance the efficiency and there by bring responsiveness in the government. The setting of standards of performance with a well organized complaint system will no doubt enhance the credibility of the governance process in people's minds.

The World Bank has identified the need of political and bureaucratic accountability as one of the requirements of good governance. The need for accountability is always linked with the concept of power. There is no power which is not linked with accountability. The power must always be disciplined for its rational and purposeful use. It may also be pointed out that the earlier belief that if power is vested in high authorities, then it may not be misused and abused has proved wrong. Therefore, we have to devise a system to check the abuse, misuse and malfeasance of public power.

In the global scenario of privatization, deregulation and degovernmentalisation, the issue of ethics in public service will occupy a position of priority. In government contracting, there is considerable potential for conflicts of interest, particularly in sensitive areas. In private sector, there is no duty of independence or impartiality as their primary concern is shareholders' interests and not the public interest. There is also the question of the effect of private sector contribution to politicians and political parties which might compromise neutrality of those employed in public service. The issue of independence, impartiality, integrity, objectivity, accountability and neutrality were the ones which led to the establishment of the public service. The issue that will continue to dominate this era is ethics, particularly ethics as a metaphor for an increasing concern for democratic values and public purpose. This calls for ethics law, ethics boards, ethics commissions, committees, education ethics, evolving of professional codes of ethics and various other measures to reduce public corruption and greater discipline in resource use.

Civil Society Organisations and Good Governance

It was the World Bank who first laid emphasis on the role of the importance of NGOs in the process of good governance, thus rolling back the role of the state. On account of the neo-liberal account, withdrawal of the state should make room for voluntary services, namely NGOs. This shift to NGOs has frequently been justified as an expression of the emphasis on popular participation and participatory development.

The civil society should articulate its social response to issues, which vitally influence the society or a large section of the society. In the western world, this civil society has been strengthened and activised by the organized efforts of the church and a host of civic groups, which contribute to the richness of social life in varied ways. These liberal societies keep their political governments in check and the constitutional government of the liberal state represents a mirror like reflection of the civil society, so laboriously built by social efforts. In sum, a civil society should:

(a) Have a sprawling middle class as a buffer to balance the social convulsions of the affluent and the deprived groups.

(b) Have a strong base of law abiding people, capable to manage their own affairs with voluntary effort.

(c) Have a network of NGOs, dedicated to self help as agents of change and agents of delivery.

(d) Have an alternate sector of charitable, developmental and participative institutions to create an infrastructure that supports and supplements the popular politics and efforts of welfare state.

(e) Have a wide spread awareness of human rights, a will to secure and ensure the basic dignity of the individual in his or her civilisational struggles in society.[13]

In India we have a long tradition and history of civil society organizations encouraged mainly in the period of freedom struggle. The civil society organs in India has exhibited special strength mainly in two tasks.

1. in criticizing the government policies and development plans
2. in opposing development projects.

But our civil society remains in the following areas.

1. in analyzing scientific and technical issues, which are extremely important in the context of governance.
2. in making policy interventions .

In the Indian context, the government is the most powerful and coercive institution in governance, which believes in concentration of authority, whereas NGOs lay emphasis on decentralization, free market, contracting out of good service, deregularisation, sustainable development, employment and result oriented outputs. That is why, these NGOs are becoming increasingly important elements in governance in the new era.

The emergence of the NGOs represents a "corporate sector" which includes both national and trans national co-operation of public importance. So far India is concerned; her economic reforms need to give good bye to the regulatory regime in order to strengthen the participatory role of people in sustainable development and to entail accountability in our democratic set up. For democracy to be successful at the national level, the grassroot organizations have to be made stronger for the cause of good governance as participation warrants every kind of citizens' interventions in administrative actions. It involves a factor of determination and decision making.[14]

What is the nature of the role to be played by the NGOs in India? Social mobilization, enabling and empowering the people to receive fully and fruitfully what is intended for them, is the central issue in good governance. Such social mobilization can be done only by agencies that are not bureaucratic. In this task of preparing the people to receive effectively, what is intended for them, the NGOs have a crucial role to play and as such they become agents of change as well. The role of NGOs, therefore, is a role both as agents of delivery and agents of change.

Coming to the role played by NGOs in good governance, it could be said that the most important role of the NGOs is to create political awareness among the people at the local level. In doing so, they should be guided by three principles:

(*a*) charitable (*b*) developmental and (*c*) participative. To achieve this, they have to fulfill some prerequisites, (1) they themselves should be people's organizations, (2) they should help in the development of grassroot organizations to become self reliant through local leadership, (3) they should not attempt to operate projects directly (4) they should be able to create motivation and opportunities for self employment among people, (5) there should be complete co-ordination among the NGOs to avoid duplication and wastage.[15]

To sum up, it may be said that the challenge before the NGOs is clear and quite big. The question before them is how to take full advantage of the environment created through the process of decentralization and democratization at the grassroot level. We must not forget the fact that in the emerging situation, if the civil society is not strong, governments will get far more influenced by the powerful special interest groups, especially economic interest groups, and this influence will become ever stronger with further economic growth. Finally, it may be said that formal participation by the masses and effective and constructive role played by NGOs may prove to be lamp post of good governance at the local level.

Conclusion

The analysis of the performance of our governance since independence reveals that in India's context, the roles of politicians, civil servants and the peoples in achieving good governance have brought to the fore many problems so far as globalization is concerned. In fact, our system, under the Nehruvian model could not recast a balance between the rights and responsibilities of individuals and of government for achieving the target of good governance, though the issue of social justice emerged as an important ingredient of good governance, wherein our political system failed to transfer mass poverty into mass prosperity, nor could it re-order the balance of rights and responsibilities between individuals, private corporate and government agencies. The model proved ill—digested, dishonest and cumbersome. A lot of debate on the centre—state relations was there but hardly anybody cared to undertake examining of the administrative incompetence, political partnership checking huge black money etc., which frustrated most of our fiscal policies.

In brief, the minimum requirements for achieving good governance include rule of law, decentralization of governing authority, governmental accountability and responsiveness, and transparent administration. Unfortunately, none of these has been satisfactorily established so far. India has failed to create a vibrant civil society capable of transforming mass poverty into mass prosperity. Unless there is a close and honest rapport between the government and civil society it is next to impossible to achieve good governance. At least this is the lesson of developmental experience of West Europe, USA and Japan and the modern East Asian states. Today, globalization forces are irresistible and it will be futile to try to check the globalization process on grounds of doctrinaire and ideological purities. A far more pragmatic approach will be to engage in intense and honest bargaining for deriving the maximum advantage of globalization in technology and finance in order to serve India's basic national interests. In the 21st century context, India does not have the option of achieving economic development through regimented political system; the civil society conscious of its rights and privileges would not simply allow it. The challenges to good governance in contemporary India are formidable indeed. Good governance is not an ideological luxury nor is it a lolly -pop which we can dangle before a lisping child; it has today become an inexorable necessity like an oxygen cylinder to a suffocated patient.

NOTES

1. Goran Hyden, Julius Court and Kenneath Mease—Making Sense of Governance, Viva Books, New Delhi, 2005.
2. *Ibid.*
3. Anne Mette Kjaer—Governance, Atlantic Publications, New Delhi, 2004.
4. Governance and Development, World Bank Report, Washington D.C., 1992
5. Kjaer, *op.cit.*
6. See Anthony G. McGrew, Conceptualising Global Politics, Cambridge University Press, 1992.
7. Roop Singh Bareth, 'Globalization and Good Governance' in B.M. Sharma and Roop Singh Bareth (ed.), Good Governance, Globalization and Civil Society, Rawat Publications, Jaipur, 2004.
8. *Ibid.*
9. Aravind Kumar Agrawal, 'Globalization: The New Challenge to State and Governance' in B.M. Sharma and Roop Singh Bareth (ed.)–*op.cit.*

10. N.S. Ghelot, 'Good Governance and Its Relevance in Indian Democracy in B.M. Sharma and Roop Singh Bareth, *op. cit.*
11. B.S. Ghuman, 'Impact of Globalization, Liberalisation and Privatisation Policies on Governance: The Indian Experience' – in S.N. Mishra, Anil Datta Mishra and Swetha Mishra (ed.) – Public Governance and Decentralisation, Mittal Publications, New Delhi, 2003.
12. M.K. Gaur – 'Political Stability and Good Governance' in T.N. Chathurvedi (ed.) – Towards Good Governance, IIPA, New Delhi, 1999.
13. P.D. Sharma, Civil Society, Administrative Culture and Public Governance in India in S.N. Mishra and others (ed.), *op. cit.*
14. N.S. Ghelot, *op. cit.*
15. S.N. Mishra and Swetha Mishra, 'Good Governance, People's Participation and NGOs', in T.N. Chathurvedi, *op. cit.*

15

Good Governance through Electoral Reforms

T.M. JOSEPH

A country with several socio, economic, political and administrative maladies, India presents itself a typical scenario to test the indicators of good governance. With large scale prevalence of poverty, unemployment, illiteracy, malnutrition, corruption, nepotism, communalism etc., the citizens of this country look forward to better governance in all respects. While it is evident that the crisis of governance in India is very deep, the present chapter holds the view that the health of a democracy depends on the quality of representatives elected by the people. It is important to know that the electoral systems hold the key to the quality of any system of governance. Elections are critical to the maintenance and development of democratic tradition because at one level, these are influenced by the political culture in which they operate, but at another, they also generate strong influences that can improve or distort this political culture. Therefore, the scope of this chapter is limited to an analysis of the problems related to the conduct of elections and suggests possible recommendations to reform the electoral system.

The process of general election in India is a gigantic exercise. It has been said that holding general elections in India is equal to holding polls in Europe, the United States, Canada and Australia all put together. Statistically, the number of voters in India is in excess of 600 million. The number of polling booths all over the country adds up to about 900,000 making an average of 667 voters for each booth. However, the population is not so uniformly spread over unequal territorial constituencies and usually a polling booth caters to no more than 1200 voters even in highly populated metropolitan areas. Five persons are needed for each polling booth making a total of 4.5 to 5 million election personnel to be mobilized and administered. These polling personnel are drawn from the Central and State Governments and other bodies. In addition to this about 2 million security personnel need to be used to maintain law and order on polling day. These basic figures give some idea about the enormity of the exercise to elect some 545 members of parliament. Once you take state and local elections into account the figures become truly staggering. India has upwards of about 3.2 million (32 lakhs) directly elected peoples' representatives spread over various tiers of governance.

Over fifty years of our experience with successive elections at various levels has established beyond doubt that our electorate is capable of delivering electoral verdicts in a democratic way. But this general impression is not without certain substantial irregularities at the micro level. In fact, our experience with elections has also brought out to fore many distortions, some very serious, that have crept in either due to loopholes in the electoral laws or due to the incapacity of the system to punish deviant and in many ways unacceptable behaviour. There have been constant references to 3 *MPs*—money power, muscle power and mafia power—and to 4 *Cs*—criminalization, communalism, corruption, and casteism. Basically all of these have vitiated the political atmosphere in the country and even compromised the legitimacy of the political process.

In full recognition of the problems that lead to the malfunctioning of our electoral system, in recent years there has been many exercises aimed at reforming it. In the last ten years, there have been at least three major formal exercises by the government addressed to electoral reforms. These are:

- The Goswami Committee on Electoral Reforms (1990).
- The Indrajit Gupta Committee on State Funding of Elections (1998).
- The Law Commission's report on Reform of the Electoral Laws (1999).

In addition, the National Commission for Reviewing the Working of the Constitution (NCRWC) and the Election Commission has also documented its own thoughts based on the recommendations of these three organizations as well as based on their own experience of ground realities. These agencies have dealt at length on the diverse aspects of existing electoral laws; but in this chapter the attention is limited to the apparent distortions in the electoral verdicts and making some suggestions for reforming the existing electoral system.

Winning on Minority Vote

Among the multitude of problems that confront our electoral system, the most serious one is the disproportional representation in legislatures. The multiplicity of political parties, combined with our Westminster based first-past-the-post system results in a majority of legislators and parliamentarians getting elected on a minority vote. In other words, they usually win by obtaining less than 50 per cent of the votes cast *i.e.* with more votes cast against them than in their favour. There are States where 85 to 90 per cent of the legislators have won on a minority vote (*i.e.*, by having obtained less than 50% of the votes cast). In many cases candidates have won by getting less than 20 per cent of the total votes cast in their constituency. To quote a few examples: in Uttar Pradesh, over the last three Assembly elections an average of only 11 per cent legislators won on a majority vote. In other words, almost 90 per cent legislators won on a minority vote. The same proportion for Bihar is 18 per cent and 82 per cent; for Madhya Pradesh it is 40 and 60 per cent; for Assam 29 per cent and 71 per cent and for Karnataka 31 and 69 per cent. Only Tamil Nadu displays a different characteristic where a large proportion of legislators have won on a majority vote—1991-90 per cent, 1985-83 per cent. At the national level, the proportion of MPs who have won on a minority vote is over 67 per cent at an average for the last three Lok Sabha Elections. This means that at an average, at the very least, two-thirds of our legislators all over India win on the basis of a minority vote. (NCRWC 2001).

In a highly divided society like ours, this practice of winning on minority votes has created a vested interest for political parties to progressively appeal to parochial loyalties. If a candidate can win on less than one-third share of the total votes polled, he does not need to generate a wider appeal. In the long run, this has even more serious consequences for India, as the existing cleavages will only deepen thus dividing the society further. We have certainly seen it on the communal and caste fronts. By making caste and community a factor for political mobilisation, we have made the divide even wider and deeper in the Indian society and made it nearly impossible for Dr. Ambedkar's vision and wish of a casteless and classless society ever coming true.

Since we have territorial constituencies from which voters elect a single representative, it is strange that most people of the constituency do not vote for a particular candidate yet it is he who becomes their representative. In such a situation, the question often asked is: whose representative is he when a majority of voters did not want him?

Mixed Member Proportional System

The seriousness of this issue has generated suggestions from many quarters with a view to correct the disproportional effects in the existing electoral system. One major change proposed by the Law Commission was the introduction of the "Mixed Member Proportional System" as practiced in the election to the German *Bundestag*. The German system is designed to fill 50 per cent of the *Bundestag* (Lower House) with constituency MPs and 50 per cent with MPs drawn from party lists. The former is elected on 'first-past-the-post' (FPTP) basis, essentially the same as that in India, and with equivalent disproportion in the pattern of results. The latter 50 per cent are allocated 'correctively' so that FPTP distortions are ironed out and the final composition of the *Bundestag* is (with limited exceptions) in proportion with how the electorate cast its votes for each party. There are two central features of the system:

(1) Voters have two votes, both of which are on a single ballot paper. One vote is the 'constituency vote'. This part of the ballot paper shows the names of all the candidates contesting for election as the Member of Parliament to represent that constituency. The candidate who wins the most votes becomes the constituency MP. The second vote is the 'party vote'. This part of the ballot paper shows names of all the registered political parties that have nominated lists of candidates drawn up separately in each region. Somewhat perversely, it is the 'party vote', which is the more important. The 'party vote' determines the final, proportional composition of the *Bundestag*; the first has an impact only in the constituency concerned.

(2) However, a political party has to clear one of two 'hurdles' – gaining at least 5 per cent of the 'party votes' nation-wide or three constituency wins – in order to receive a proportional allocation of seats in the *Bundestag*. Votes for parties, which fail these two hurdles, are disregarded in calculating the composition of the *Bundestag*. If a party does cross any of these hurdles, its total number of MPs will be made up of any *constituency MPs* it has plus enough *list MPs* to reach its final share of total membership in the House. If a party crossed the 5 per cent votes hurdle but wins no constituency seats, all its MPs will be *list MPs*.

It should also be noted that the total number of constituency seats won by independent candidates and by candidates for parties that are not on the 'party vote' are deducted from the total number of seats before seats are allocated according to parties' shares of all the 'party votes'. So in a 100 member House, if 5 independents have won from various constituencies, 95 seats will be available for proportional allocation.

The Law Commission suggested that the number of MPs in Lok Sabha should be increased by 25 per cent, instead of the 50 per cent in Germany, and this additional number of MPs should be made up of candidates pre-nominated by political parties. Thus the Law Commission suggested that the strength of the Lok Sabha should be increased to 688, with about 138 candidates nominated on the basis of a list to be provided by various political parties. The Commission also suggested that political parties that secured less than 5 per cent of the valid votes cast in the Parliament or Legislative Assembly Elections would not be entitled to any seat, based on their list system, in that legislature. It was also suggested that while bigger States would constitute a territorial unit for this purpose, the smaller States should either be clubbed with a bigger State or they should all be clubbed together for forming a territorial unit for elections to the Lok Sabha.

The suggestions of the Law Commission, however, are not without certain inherent flaws both on grounds of principle and practicability. It is argued that the adoption of the partial list system would create two very unhealthy long-term trends in a multi-faceted society like India (NCRWC: 2001). In the first place, it would create even more difficulties in providing a stable government. Proportional representation is famous for creating non-majority legislatures where coalitions are a rule rather than an exception. This has serious implications for governance in India, as already borne out by our experience of the past few years. Because each coalition partner wields negative influence, the government may have to ignore even flagrant abuse of political positions by coalition partners. The idea of the "List System" runs against the grain of attempting to provide stability in the government because with many parties present with small but sometimes determining numbers it potentially enhances horse-trading to create artificial majorities for forming and maintaining governments. The result is weak governance. Also, the suggestion would create two classes of members of Parliament in Lok Sabha—those elected directly by the people and those coming through party lists.

Secondly and even more important, elections should be used to unite our very divided society, which is progressively getting more divided because individual players are constantly mobilizing support based on narrow loyalties. The idea of any form of proportional representation will aid in the divisive tendencies, as it will now pay the politician to appeal to a small group if he feels that he has a good chance of getting their vote en-bloc. The moment political parties are given the opportunity to have representatives in the Lok Sabha or the State assemblies based only on the number of votes that they obtain, it takes away the incentive to make their electoral appeal broader. Also, the parties which can have the resources to put up a large number of candidates even in areas where they do not hope to win will have a distinct advantage under any scheme of additional seats through list system. It will then pay the political party to address itself to narrow interests because that may be the only safe way for it to ensure itself a few seats in the house. It should never be enough in such a diverse society as India to maximize support among a narrow grouping and then rely on being needed as a part of a coalition government. On the contrary a party must appeal broadly across the electorate.

Proportional representation of this kind assumes a well educated and aware electorate and a type of matured political behaviour from both the electorate and the elected representatives and can only work for good governance if there are very strong conventions of behaviour that cannot be transgressed at all. India is really very far from it at the moment.

The Run-Off Election

The next possible alternative to ensure that the winning candidate gets more than 50 per cent of the total votes polled, is the introduction of the run-off election. If, in the first round, nobody gets over 50 per cent, then there should be a run-off contest between the top two candidates so that one of them will win on the basis of over 50 per cent of the votes polled. To save on the cost and trouble of a run-off, another suggestion made is that of each voter being asked to give an alternative vote so that in case of no one getting 50 per cent + votes in the first count, the alternative votes get counted. With Electronic Voting Machines (EVMs) and technology available now counting of alternative votes need cause no delay or other problem.

Several eminent persons, including the distinguished former President Shri R. Venkataraman have proposed that the option of electing only candidates with over 50 per cent of the votes cast in their favour is a far better way to achieve the objective of better representation. Each legislator should be elected on a majority vote and can therefore be said to be a representative of the majority of voters from his constituency. The Law Commission, who evaluated this suggestion in their report albeit with the inclusion of a "negative vote" did comment in their report that this was an excellent suggestion but they felt that there might be insurmountable practical difficulties with implementing it because of the run-off election that will happen at least in 2/3rd of the cases at present. But with the advancement in computer technology, it seems that the Election Commission can manage the run-off elections without much difficulty. In fact, the run-off vote is like a re-poll in certain constituencies. There is no revision of electoral rolls, no fresh nominations, no fresh campaigning or the like. It is the same polling booth with the same administration and therefore it should not be complicated.

The NCRWC has cited two substantial advantages of following the policy of 50 per cent+1 vote. On the one hand, it resolves the problem of representation. On the other, it also makes it in the self-interest of various political parties to widen their appeal to the electorate. It can help push political rhetoric in a direction that the mobilizing language might take on comparative 'universal' tones as opposed to 'sectoral' tones of the present day. Currently the possibility of winning on a minority of votes polled has encouraged parties to function on caste, communal or other sectoral bases. When such parties get into positions of power, they also follow a sectoral agenda. With the need to be more broad based in their appeal, issues that have to do with governance rather than with cleavages and narrow identities might start to surface in the vocabulary of the politicians. On this count alone it may be considered worth pursuing.

The second ballot system is also not without its own drawbacks. The main worry is that once a run-off is decided leaving only two candidates in the fray, it may lead to a matter of do or die for each of these two candidates; and it may result in even more aggressive electoral malpractices. We cannot rule out this possibility in the light of our track record in past elections and the political culture in which these have operated. If not muscle power, it is also possible that even bigger amount of money might change hands to get intermediaries to bring block votes to the polling station. It is also likely that for the run-off election the voter response will be lower partly due to election fatigue and to the fact that one of the candidates might use muscle or money power to keep unfriendly voters away.

Notwithstanding these probable problems, this suggestion has to be valued primarily to uphold the spirit of representative democracy. To overcome the defects in the system, the best remedy could be to hold the elections on two consecutive days (the second day being for run-offs). If that is done, there will not be time enough to generate fresh violence or to indulge in other malpractices like horse trading and using money power to buy votes. As for the voter turn out, battle lines being more sharply drawn between only two contestants, it is equally likely that the turn out may be better.

If the two-day election plan is difficult or not acceptable, attempt should be made to reduce the gap between the main election and the run-off election. In any case, there should not be a long gap. No further campaigning should be permitted. The less the time available between the two polls, the less are the chances for the candidates to create hurdles in the way of the system. Secondly, and more importantly, any electoral offence in the run-off should carry a higher penalty for the candidate than the original election. The possibility of disqualification and perhaps a mandatory hefty imprisonment and a hefty fine, should loom large on the horizon for both the finalists.

We hope that if implemented properly, this suggestion has the potential of forcing political parties and candidates to think of strategies to obtain over 50 per cent votes in the first election itself. This will discourage the non-serious candidates and fringe players from jumping in the fray and it will encourage making of pre-election agreements between parties and if viewed together with the suggestions on defection, this should lead to moderation and stability. The proposal of run-off elections may push up the cost of elections marginally only. The mobilization is one time and when EVMs are used, there are no ballot papers to print either. Also, while on the first occasion, there may be many run offs, with each successive election the number may be reduced to only a few.

REFERENCES

Abrahamsen, Rita (2000): *Disciplining Democracy: Development Discourse and Good Governance in Africa*, Zed Books, London.

Chandhoke, Neera (2003): 'Governance and the Pluralisation of the State: Implications for Democratic Citizenship,' *Economic and Political Weekly*, 38(28): 2957-68.

Duverger, M. (1963): *Political Parties: Their Organization and Activity in the Modern State*, New York: Wiley Science Ed.

Government of India (2002): Tenth Five Year Plan (2002-07): Dimensions and Strategies, Vol. I., Planning Commission, New Delhi.

Joseph, T.M. (2000): 'Proportional Representation as a Means of Increasing Women's Role in Legislatures: A Case for Electoral Reform in India', *Journal of Asian Women's Studies*, 9:44-52.

Joseph, T.M. (1999): 'Proportional Representation is the Answer to the Quota Problem', *The Hindu*, February 9.

Lijphart, Arend (1994): *Electoral Systems and Party Systems: A Study of Twenty-Seven Democracies 1947-1990*. Oxford: Oxford University Press.

Moncrief, Gary F., and Joel A. Thompson. (1992): 'Electoral Structure and State Legislative Representation: A Research Note', *Journal of Politics* 54: 246-56.

NCRWC (2001): http//lawmin.nic.in/ncrwc

OECD (1995): *Participatory Development and Good Governance*, Development Co-operation Guidelines Series, Paris.

Oommen T. K. (2003): 'Civil Society and the Goal of Good Governance' in Rajesh Tandon and Ranjita Mohanty ed. *Does Civil Society Matter?* Sage, New Delhi, pp. 125-144.

Rae, D.W. (1967). *The Political Consequences of Electoral Laws*, New Haven: Yale University Press.

Riker, W.H. and Ordeshook, P.C. (1968). 'A Theory of the Calculus of Voting', *American Political Science Review*, 62: 25-42.

Shylendra, H.S. (2004): 'The Emerging Governance Paradigm and its Implications for Poverty Alleviation and Equity', Working Paper 182, Institute of Rural Management, Anand.

UNDP (1997), *Governance for Sustainable Development*, A UNDP Policy Document, New York.

World Bank (1992): *Governance and Development*, Washington DC.

World Bank (1994): *Governance: The World Banks's Experience*, World Bank, Washington DC.

World Bank (1997): *World Development Report*, Washington DC.

Index